PCI Express[†] Electrical Interconnect Design

Practical Solutions for Board-level Integration and Validation

Dave Coleman
Scott Gardiner
Mohammad Kolbehdari
Stephen Peters

INTEL
PRESS

ISBN 0-9743649-9-1

Publisher: Richard Bowles
Content Architect: Matt Wangler
Managing Editor: David B. Spencer
Program Manager: Stuart Goldstein
Editor: Jack Falk
Text Design & Composition: Wasser Studios, Inc.
Graphic Art: Wasser Studios, Inc. (illustrations), Ted Cyrek (cover)

Library of Congress Cataloging in Publication Data:

Printed in the United States of America

    10 9 8 7 6 5 4 3 2

First printing, November 2004

Contents

Acknowledgments

The PCI Express[†] specifications bring many new and exciting challenges in system design, board layout, and validation. While we realize that this book does not offer a perfect or exhaustive guide to all the nuances of such tasks, we hope that this book will aid the many engineers who are attempting to implement new designs based on PCI Express.

As with any great effort, this book represents collaboration among many people and organizations. As authors, we are privileged to have the opportunity to act as the voice for many of the great ideas and efforts of others. In particular, we'd like to thank the many engineers at Intel who collaborated with the authors on the original design guidelines and research that gave life to this book, including Marco Beltman, Pelle Fornberg, Bryce Horine, Lilly Huang, Rich Mellitz, Jeff Morriss, Scott Noble, Henry Peng, Zale Schoenborn, Tudor Secasiu, Weimin Shi, Harry Skinner, Michael Smith, Mark Trautman, and Dan Willis, among many others. Special thanks go to our primary technical reviewer, Cliff Lee.

Additional thanks go out to the many individuals who reviewed the book and provided us with invaluable feedback: Eric Duchesne from Avnet Design Services; Clair Alan Hardesty from Alereon, Inc.; Dean McCoy from NCR Teradata; Norihiro Andou from JAE, Ltd.; Ashish P. Kuvelkar from C-DAC; Allen C. O'Neil; Ademir Piazza; Carlos Santiago from AMD; Alan Simmonds from Quantum3D Inc.; Chuck Stancil from HP Corporation; Gord Caruk, ATI Technologies, Inc.; and others.

We'd also like to acknowledge the encouragement and help of our managers at Intel, particularly Ajay Bhatt, Randy Bonella, Bala Cadambi, Roger Rees, and Jeff Watters.

Many thanks also go to the folks at Intel Press who helped guide us through the process of developing the book. In particular, we wish to thank Jack Falk for his excellent editing support, and Stuart Goldstein and David Spencer for their invaluable assistance and overall coordination during review, validation, editing, and production. The Wasser Studios staff deserves thanks for assistance in preparing the book's artwork, index, and text layout.

Of course we'd also like to acknowledge the PCI-SIG and PCMCIA consortium, not only for their help and cooperation, but also for their efforts to bring forth some very cool specifications which have "energized" the PC industry and which form the backbone of this book.

Finally, as authors, we could not attempt to complete such a book without the cooperation of our families. We'd especially like to thank Epiphany Coleman, Sarah Gardiner, Maryam Kolbehdari, and Margaret Peters for their support.

Chapter 1

PCI Express† Electrical Architecture

The best way to predict the future is to invent it.

— Alan Kay

The Peripheral Component Interconnect (PCI) architecture is well-established and widely implemented in the industry. Initially defined as a parallel 32-bit, 33-MHz interface, PCI—as the specification extension PCI-X†—has developed to include a 64-bit wide parallel bus at transfer rates of 133 MHz, with specification extensions to allow for higher parallel data rates. While the specifications allow higher data rates, a single-ended, parallel bus has a limited technological capacity.

PCI Express†, the high-speed signaling extension to the Conventional PCI† and PCI-X architectures, provides a signaling architecture that supports the higher data rates. Initially defined at 2.5 billion transfers per second (2.5 GT/s), the PCI Express signaling architecture will be extended to sustain the higher data rates needed to satisfy future performance needs.

PCI Express preserves the Conventional PCI load/store programming model, but incorporates three significant changes:

■ *PCI Express has an embedded clock.* Unlike Conventional PCI and PCI-X, PCI Express data signal timing doesn't utilize an external clock or strobe signal to qualify the data. The PCI Express clock is embedded in the data signal itself. This eliminates the data-to-clock setup and hold time constraints and the data path-to-clock path timing skew.

1

■ *PCI Express signaling is differential, not single-ended* as are Conventional PCI and PCI-X. With differential signaling, the "difference" in the D+ and D– signals of each signal differential pair constitutes the signal amplitude, not the signal to external ground voltage. Some key advantages to differential signaling are significantly lower crosstalk, improved electromagnetic compatibility (EMC), and a matched signal return path.

■ *PCI Express independent transmit and receive signal paths* allowing data to be sent and received simultaneously. This is also called *dual simplex* transmission.

With these changes, the timing and voltage requirements for PCI Express have changed as well. Conventional PCI and PCI-X timing require the data and control signals to have a fixed timing relationship to the external clock or data strobe. PCI Express, with the clock embedded in each data signal, has a different set of specifications to adhere to—loss, jitter, and common mode voltage.

With a completely different set of electrical requirements, the board design approach needs to be different as well. However, board design is not necessarily harder for PCI Express than it was for PCI/PCI-X. In fact, you will find that board design becomes easier for PCI Express than PCI-X133, and even more so than PCI-X 2.0. You only need to be aware that some board design targets and matching requirements are different for the serial signaling than the parallel bus.

As a general note for guidance, the PCI Express Specification is a living organism and continues to grow and adapt. This book comprehends the existing specifications and errata, including the 1.0a and the 1.1 releases of the specification, and presents the most up-to-date information at the time this book was written. Some methods and interpretations are sure to evolve as the PCI Express specifications evolve. Information that relies on a specific release is called out where applicable. As a designer, however, you should always verify specific numbers and information against the most recent version of the specifications.

Electrical Advantages and Built-in Capabilities

PCI Express electrical signaling has been defined specifically to extend frequency data transfer rates far beyond the rates made possible by the parallel single-ended signaling of Conventional PCI and PCI-X. Critical areas of performance improvement include:

- Signal performance
- Clocking
- Electromagnetic compatibility (EMC)
- AC coupling

In addition to these signaling improvements, PCI Express provides built-in architectural features that further enhance signal performance and board design flexibility: 8b/10b encoding, data scrambling, de-emphasis, and training sequences to invert signal polarity, reverse lane orientation, and de-skew lanes. This section discusses these signaling improvements and architectural features in turn.

Signal Performance

PCI Express minimizes the signal degradation effects, such as crosstalk and inter-symbol interference (ISI), that limit Conventional PCI and PCI-X. In addition to the change in signaling from a single-ended parallel bus to serial differential signaling, PCI Express has some architectural features that provide significant advantages for high-speed signaling.

Differential Signaling

The transmit and receive signals of PCI Express are differential pairs. Each differential pair has a positive (+) and negative (–) complementing signal of opposite polarity. An ideal differential signal consists of equal and opposite signals—each having the same rise and fall ramp time and signal duration, with no timing skew between the signals. Figure 1.1 illustrates an ideal differential signal waveform.

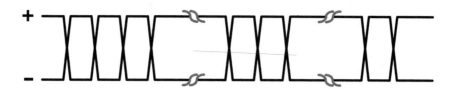

Figure 1.1   Ideal Differential Signals

With differential signaling, signal-to-signal coupling, or *crosstalk*, is greatly reduced since the primary coupling in system designs is common-mode coupling. Also, EMC is improved for both radiation and interference, because the equal and opposite signal coupling within each transmit and receive pair cancels out the far field differences.

Inter-symbol interference (ISI) is the signal degradation effect on a signal state, called a symbol, from previous data signal transitions. This interference is commonly due to impedance mismatch reflections and signal transitions starting at different voltage points. ISI is significantly reduced due to the 50 Ω matched-end termination on each signal. Any reflections back to the transmitter have minimal reflection from the transmitter, due to its matched termination to the signal line.

Even though PCI Express has the built-in advantage of differential signaling, a successful board design must preserve the differential signaling. Through careful control of the PCB layout and component placement, the designer should minimize common mode conversion, which results from introducing mismatches between the differential pair signals. For example, if the transmit (+) signal trace is routed longer than the transmit (−) signal, the differential signal has a common mode component that contributes to crosstalk, electromagnetic radiation, and susceptibility and signal degradation.

De-emphasis

Another benefit of PCI Express architecture is *de-emphasis*. When multiple bits of the same polarity, such as 111, are transmitted sequentially, the first bit of the sequence is fully emphasized employing the maximum voltage swing. The first bit is also known as the transition bit, since it is transitioning from the opposite polarity bit. All following bits of the same polarity are then de-emphasized in voltage to a lower voltage swing, as compared to the fully emphasized bit. Figure 1.2 provides an illustration of de-emphasis. PCI Express supports single-bit de-emphasis, which means that the same level of de-emphasis is shared by all of the bits of the same polarity following the transition bit.

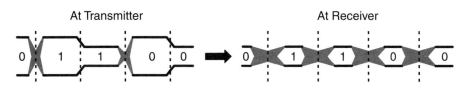

Figure 1.2   PCI Express† De-emphasis

De-emphasis provides the signal conditioning to further reduce frequency-dependent loss and jitter. In a high-loss channel, the de-emphasis increases the valid signal strength at the receiver by reducing the impact of previous signal patterns. This effectively matches the loss and jitter across the frequency band, or range of data patterns transmitted. Figure 1.3 presents an example of a high-loss channel with and without de-emphasis.

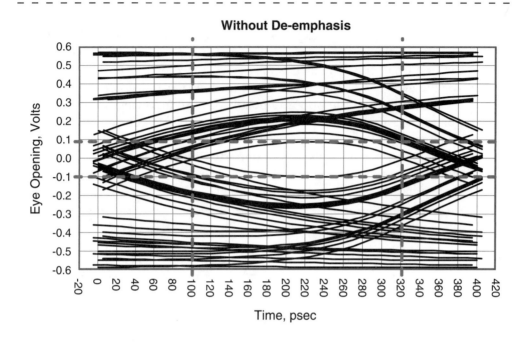

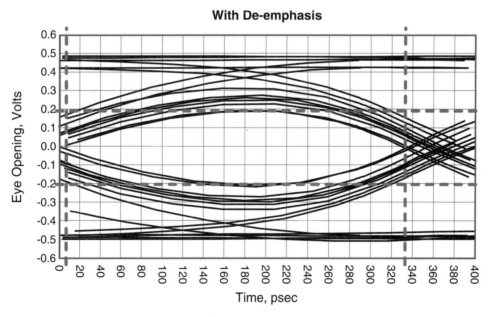

Figure 1.3   High-Loss Channel With and Without De-emphasis

Clocking

With an embedded clock, PCI Express is designed to transfer data at much higher rates than Conventional PCI and PCI-X.

■ Conventional PCI employs a common clock, which is an independent but in-phase clock provided to the transmitting and receiving components.

■ Conventional PCI-X uses a common clock for control signals and a higher frequency source synchronous data strobe for the data signals. The common clock scheme is the lowest performing scheme, requiring a setup and hold time to the clock, including not only a skew and jitter between clock and data paths, but also a transmit and receive device clock skew. Source synchronous timing only limits the clocking frequency to the setup and hold time requirement of the unidirectional data strobe, and is thus a better choice than common clock.

■ PCI Express signals have an embedded clock, which allows the clock to be extracted directly from the data signal. This design allows for the highest frequency data transfer rate among the common clock, source synchronous clock and embedded clocking architectures. The data signal need not meet any setup or hold specification to an external clock, only a voltage and jitter specification to an internally derived clock within the receiver.

Figure 1.4 shows these three approaches to clocking.

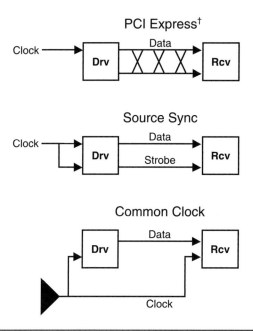

Figure 1.4 PCI Express† versus Conventional PCI†/PCI-X† Clocking

Electromagnetic Compatibility

The PCI Express architecture has built-in features to minimize EMC problems. Differential signaling limits the electromagnetic radiation emitted and susceptibility to incoming interference by limiting common mode signal transmission. PCI Express also employs data scrambling and 8b/10b encoding, which further reduce the EMI transmission.

Data Scrambling and 8b/10b Encoding

The PCI Express architecture employs two data modification schemes, data scrambling and 8b/10b encoding that significantly improve EMC and electrical signal performance. Neither of these schemes is employed with PCI and PCI-X; both are introduced with PCI Express.

Data scrambling is a default option—that is, it can be disabled—that does just what it says: it scrambles the data. With a polynomial equation defined in the PCI Express Base specification, each 8-bit data byte is converted to a different data byte value, which reduces the EMI radiation emitted by "spreading" the data patterns over a wide range of values to limit repeat occurrences of specific data values. For example, if three consecutive byte values of 0xAA (10101010 10101010 10101010) were transmitted, this pattern of alternating ones and zeros without data scrambling would emphasize a high-frequency clock at 1.25 GHz. With data scrambling, no single frequency in the sequence would be emphasized; for example, the scrambling of the three consecutive 0xAA bytes may generate the byte sequences 01001101 10110010 01011100, which are more randomized. Figure 1.5 shows how data scrambling may be applied to a repeating sequence of 0x00 bytes. Each 0X00 byte is changed to a byte sequence to randomize the data and thus spread out the pattern-based signal frequencies.

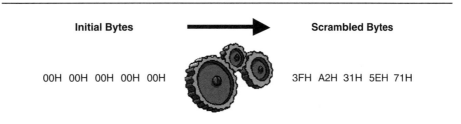

Figure 1.5   Effect of Data Scrambling on Data Patterns

The 8b/10b encoding scheme has a number of important benefits for PCI Express. One of the features, frequency band range limit, directly benefits the signal transmission performance. Two other features, disparity and limited "dead" cycles, benefit the DC balance and clock recovery.

With 8b/10b encoding, each 8-bit byte of data is encoded as one of two defined 10-bit codes. Figure 1.6 presents an example of this encoding method. The 10-bit code selected is based on running disparity, which is the difference of the total running count of zeros and ones within a given bit-block. The code also limits the maximum number of sequential ones or zeros to minimize "dead" time.

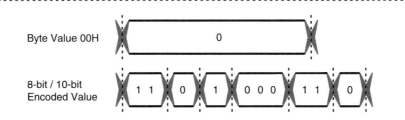

Figure 1.6   8b/10b Encoding Example

By limiting the dead time, the defined 10-bit codes effectively limit the minimum transfer frequency (11111000001) to 250 MHz. The upper frequency of 1.25 GHz is already limited by the maximum defined 2.5 GT/s data rate. The frequency band transmitted is limited to this smaller frequency range, which has the effect of limiting the frequency-dependent loss and jitter. Figure 1.7 shows this effect.

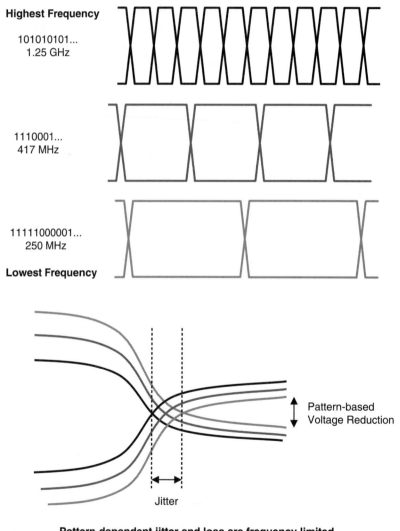

Pattern-dependent jitter and loss are frequency limited.

Figure 1.7   Frequency Band Limit on Loss and Jitter

The running disparity is continuously updated for each symbol, maintaining the maximum difference between the number of zeros and ones transmitted across multiple symbols at a delta of 2. This difference limit keeps a DC balance at both the transmitter and the receiver. It is important to limit the DC voltage drift on either side to meet the PCI Express common mode voltage specifications.

The other benefit of the 8b/10b encoding and the frequency band limit is that a minimum number of data signal transitions always occurs, which ensures that the clock can be recovered from the data stream. With the encoding, no more than five consecutive zeros or ones are transmitted, allowing the receiving component phase-lock loop to retain its frequency lock.

AC Coupling

PCI Express utilizes AC coupling on each signal to electrically isolate each transmitter and receiver. This isolation allows for easy hot-plug capability, as well as decoupling the transmitter and receiver common mode voltages. The receiver must be at 0V within a specified tolerance for common mode voltage, but the transmitter can be at a non-zero voltage.

Ports, Links, and Lanes

Unlike the PCI and PCI-X parallel interfaces, PCI Express is a point-to-point serial interface between two components. Each point-to-point connection is unidirectional, which simplifies the signal routing since only one receiver is connected to each transmitter and stubs are eliminated. This interface makes use of three concepts that are important to understand for board design: ports, links, and lanes.

A *port* is a grouping of transmitters and receivers on a component that constitute a *link* when connected to another component. A component may have multiple ports, but a given port can only support a single link. Figure 1.8 shows the relationship between ports and links.

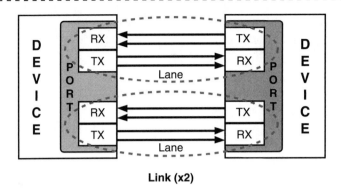

Figure 1.8   PCI Express† Ports, Links, and Lanes

A *lane* is one set of transmit and receive differential pairs. Each lane includes a single transmit signal pair and a single receive signal pair—four signals in all. Similarly, a x4 (pronounced "by four") link consists of four lanes and includes four transmit signal pairs and four receive signal pairs—16 signals in all.

The link between the transmit and receive ports can contain a single lane or multiple lanes. For example, a x1 link includes one transmit and receive port on each component and one lane. A x4 link includes four transmit and receive ports on each component and four lanes.

Link Training

PCI Express employs an intelligent training sequence to detect and establish deterministic communication between component ports. This *link training sequence* is initiated upon the downstream device being detected by the upstream device in the hierarchy. For details about the PCI Express hierarchy, refer to "Topology and Interconnect Overview," later in this chapter. Link configurations that depend upon correct board design include data rate, polarity, lane width, ordering, and de-skew.

Detect

The upstream device—that is, the root complex or component hierarchically closest to the I/O control hub or chipset—polls each transmit lane to detect an RC time constant which indicates that a load, instead of

an open line, is present. Once the upstream device detects a load that satisfies the RC time constant, it initiates a polling process to determine, by
the response, whether the load is an active device or a test load. If the
device responds with recognizable response patterns, the training sequence is initiated. If not, the upstream device assumes that the load is a
test device and initiates compliance test patterns. Figure 1.9 illustrates
the RC time constant detection method.

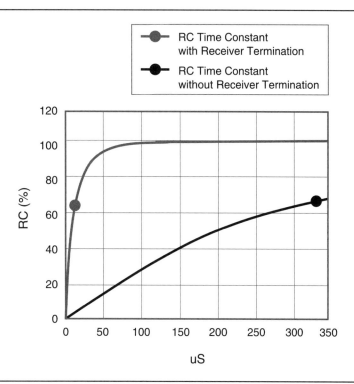

Figure 1.9   Detect RC Time Constant

Data Rate Negotiation

The PCI Express specification initially supports a 2.5 GT/s data rate,
which corresponds to a maximum frequency of 1.25 GHz. All PCI Express components are required to support this initial data rate. A training
sequence is defined to accommodate future data rates that are yet to be
defined in the specification.

Polarity Inversion

As mentioned previously, the transmit and receive differential pairs consist of a positive (+) and negative (–) polarity signal. The PCI Express specification requires each transmit and receive pair to be checked for correct polarity. That is, for each pair, the (+) polarity signal on the transmitter is checked to determine whether it is connected to the (+) polarity signal on the receiver. If any pairs are connected to the opposite polarity signal, the specification requires the receiver to invert its signal polarity. Figure 1.10 shows how polarity inversion operates. Keep in mind that polarity inversion is required on any individual pair that is inverted.

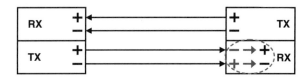

Figure 1.10   Polarity Inversion

Polarity inversion provides two clear benefits. First, if the board design signal routing has inadvertently inverted polarity on one or more transmit or receive pairs, the training sequence will detect and correct the polarity; no board re-design is needed. Second, individual transmit or receive pairs may be purposely routed "inverted" to optimize routing. For example, inverted routing can eliminate a trace crossover.

Lane-to-Lane De-skew

Whereas within-pair routing lengths need to be closely matched for each lane, lane-to-lane trace lengths have very loose matching requirements. This loose lane-to-lane skew requirement is 20 ns, and is allowed because the PCI Express training process includes a lane-to-lane de-skew sequence, which inserts *skip ordered sets* to de-skew the lanes. A skip ordered set consists of one COM symbol followed by three consecutive SKP symbols. Effectively, the 500 ps + 2 UI skew bucket frees the designer to focus only on meeting the individual transmit and receive pair requirements for loss, jitter, and common mode. Still, one should try to keep lane-to-lane skew low to minimize the number of skip ordered sets inserted. Adding skip ordered sets adds latency to the overall timing performance.

Clock Compensation and Skip Ordered Sets

In most desktop systems, the transmitter and receiver devices operate off the same clock source. In such systems, the transmitter's data rate—rate at which it sends data—exactly matches the receiver's absorption rate—rate at which it can accept data sent to it by a transmitter, and there is no need for clock tolerance compensation.

To accommodate systems in which a plug-in card operates from its own clock source, separate from the baseboard clock, the PCI Express specification allows up to a 600 parts per million (ppm) difference between the frequency of the clock at the transmitter and the frequency of the clock at the receiver. To compensate for the resulting mismatch between the transmitter's data rate and the receiver's absorption rate, the transmitter inserts a skip ordered set into the data stream at periodic intervals every 1,180 to 1,538 symbols. The following example illustrates the mechanism by which skip ordered sets are used to compensate for clock tolerance.

Assume that the transmitter is sending data at a slightly faster rate than the receiver can absorb it. Over time, this causes the receiver's input buffer to fill with data. With the receiver's input buffer near full, it now detects an incoming skip ordered set. Because the skip ordered set is not part of the data being transferred, the receiver is allowed to "throw away" the COM and three SKP symbols. The receiver continues to process the legitimate data that is already in its buffer. By the time the COM and three SKP symbols have been transferred and dropped, the legitimate data in the buffer has been removed and processed, thus making room for more legitimate data. Because the receiver is allowed to discard the skip ordered set and not absorb it, the transmitter data rate and receiver absorption rate are effectively equalized.

Skip ordered sets are also used when the receiver is operating at a faster clock rate than the transmitter. In this case, the transmitter cannot supply data fast enough to keep up with the receiver's data requirements, and the tendency is for the receiver input buffers to run out of data.

To prevent this, when the receiver buffer is near empty and it receives a skip ordered set, the receiver effectively "stalls"—that is, it does not accept any more data from its input buffer—until it sees more legitimate data arrive at its input. This approach effectively equalizes the difference between the transmitter and receiver data rates.

To aid lane de-skew, skip ordered sets must be inserted onto all lanes of a multi-lane link simultaneously, as described in Chapter 8, "Validating the Design."

Lane Number and Width Negotiation

The link lane width and lane numbering within the link are assigned during the training process. PCI Express requires that all links of width greater than x1 support training down to x1. Any widths less than the maximum supported are optional by design of the individual component. For example, if the upstream component supports x8, x2, and x1, but the downstream component supports x4 and x1, the width negotiation selects x1, since it is the only common link width supported by both components. As another example, if the upstream component supports x4 and x1, and the downstream component supports x8, x4, and x1, the width negotiation selects x4, which is the greatest common link width. Figure 1.11 illustrates how width negotiation works.

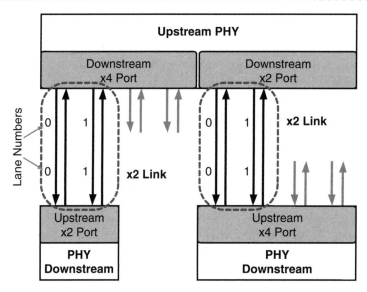

Figure 1.11   Lane Width Negotiation

The lanes within the link are assigned lane numbers. Therefore, a x4 link is assigned lanes 0, 1, 2, and 3.

The PCI Express specification supports optional link bifurcation. For example, if a component x8 link supports bifurcation into two x4 links, the lane numbering for some of the x8 lanes and x4 lanes will differ. As illustrated in Figure 1.12, if the link is configured as x8, the lane numbers are Lane [7:0]. If the link is bifurcated into two x4 links—we'll call them Link A and Link B—the lane numbers for both Link A and Link B are Lane [3:0]. So, the four lanes [7:4] of the x8 link are assigned to be Lane [3:0] when the link is bifurcated.

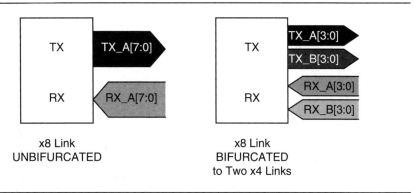

Figure 1.12   Link Bifurcation

Lane Reversal

Another optional configuration supported by the PCI Express specification is full lane reversal. As shown in Figure 1.13, if a component port supports lane reversal, then either all lanes or no lanes are reversed. Reversing a subset of the lanes within a link is *not* supported. As with polarity inversion, lane reversal allows trace routing flexibility to avoid crossovers and potentially reduces the number of trace vias required for signal routing. Either component may change the lane ordering—this is negotiated during the training process.

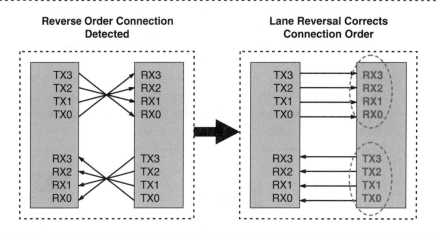

Figure 1.13   Lane Reversal

PCI Express† Electrical Specifications

Combining the embedded clock implementation with differential signaling and AC coupling, PCI Express offers a new means to measure signal timing and quality. The basis of the electrical specifications is derived from these interconnect and signaling features.

Topology and Interconnect Overview

The PCI Express signal topology consists of a transmitter (TX) located on one device and connected through a differential pair interconnect, consisting of a D+ and a D– signal, to a receiver (RX) on a second device.

Because the PCI Express interface is defined as dual-simplex, each connection consists of both a transmit pair and a receiver pair. In other words, data is always sent from a given device on one differential pair while a separate differential pair receives it on the same device. Each connection between PCI Express devices must be point-to-point. As mentioned earlier, each transmit and receive pair constitutes a lane. PCI Express links may consist of 1, 2, 4, 8, 12, 16, or 32 lanes in parallel, referred to as x1, x2, x4, x8, x12, x16, and x32 links respectively.

The *PCI Express Base Specification* (PCI-SIG 2004a) requires each lane of a link to be AC-coupled between its corresponding transmitter and receiver. The AC coupling capacitance is required either within the transmitter component or along the link on the printed circuit board (PCB). In most scenarios, it is expected that the AC coupling will be located external to the transmitter or receiver device components in the form of discrete capacitors. Each transmitting device's data sheet is required to inform the system designer whether or not the AC capacitors are required external to the TX component.

Each end of the link is terminated on-die into a nominal 100 Ω differential DC termination; no additional external termination is required for the differential pairs. Additionally, the PCI Express Base specification requires each TX component to utilize on-die equalization by means of de-emphasis for all PCI Express signals. The de-emphasis is required to be a typical value of 3.5 dB (±0.5 dB) down with respect to the nominal output voltage. No additional external equalization is required for the differential pairs on the PCB.

A PCI Express link is formed when the TX and RX differential pairs of an "upstream" device connect to the RX and TX differential pairs of a "downstream" device. The term *upstream device* refers to the PCI Express component that is on the end of the link that is hierarchically closer to the root of the PCI Express tree hierarchy. Similarly, the *downstream device* is on the end of the link that is hierarchically farther from the root of the PCI Express tree hierarchy. The upstream device contains a downstream port, which connects to the downstream device. Likewise the downstream device also contains an upstream port.

The device at the top of the hierarchy is called the *root complex*. One example of a root complex device is a "host or north bridge" type of chipset, while an example of a downstream device might be a switch or an *endpoint* device on a baseboard or add-in card. Figure 1.14 illustrates this hierarchy and the directional references.

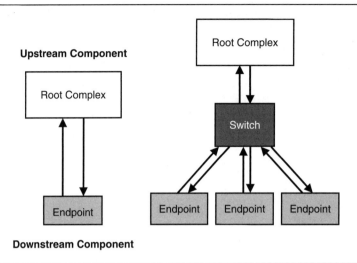

Figure 1.14 PCI Express† Hierarchy

Each lane on a PCI Express link is assigned a sequential numerical value and is identified as such in the component's pinout. As defined in the *PCI Express Card Electromechanical Specification* (PCI-SIG 2004b), the pin name includes the designation PET for TX originating signals or PER for RX destination signals, with respect to a system board device. The pin name also includes a "p" or "n" to represent the D+ or D– signals, respectively. For example, a link with a width of x2 has TX and RX pairs with respective labels that would be similar to the following: PETp0, PETn0, PERp0, PERn0, PETp1, PETn1, PERp1, PERn1.

A Paradigm Shift

Signal timing and quality measurements need to conform to the signaling basis. As illustrated in Table 1.1, the timing and quality measurements defined for PCI Express are different from those defined for Conventional PCI and PCI-X. The key differences are due to clocking, differential signaling, and AC coupling. You can think of the different measurement methods as a paradigm shift.

Table 1.1   PCI Express† versus Conventional PCI†/PCI-X† Signaling

	PCI Express†	Conventional PCI†	PCI-X†
Clocking	Embedded clock	External common synchronous	External common, source synchronous
Signal Reference	Differential	Single-ended	Single-ended
TX-RX Coupling	AC	DC	DC

With Conventional PCI and PCI-X, the data signal timing must be specified with respect to an external clock or strobe. Specifically, the clock has a data setup and hold time. Also, since the data and clock signals are routed on separate signal traces, there is skew and jitter timing uncertainty between the data and clock signals.

Because the PCI Express clock is within the data signal, the setup, hold, and skew specifications for PCI and PCI-X can't be used here. Instead, PCI Express specifies a signal data rate that includes a data rate timing tolerance. The PCI Express embedded clock offers much more flexibility. Each transmit pair doesn't need to be tightly matched in time to any other transmit pair. The lane-to-lane skew allowance at the transmitter is 500 ps + 2 UI; at the receiver, the skew allowance is 20 ns. This allows repeaters to be inserted between transmitters and receivers.

With Conventional PCI and PCI-X, quality measurements include voltage thresholds, overshoot, and monotonic edges, all referenced to DC voltages. Since PCI Express utilizes differential signaling, the voltage thresholds and tolerances are specified as voltage differences between the D+ and D– signals for each differential signal pair.

Signal Integrity Essentials

Even though PCI Express has a different signaling basis than PCI/PCI-X, it still needs to meet AC, DC, and timing performance requirements. For example, instead of DC ground-referenced voltage thresholds, PCI Express has peak-to-peak differential voltage thresholds. This allows the transmitter to operate at a flexible DC voltage range so long as it satisfies the differential voltage amplitude. Instead of data setup and hold time to clock, PCI Express has eye width and jitter specifications. Table 1.2 lists the differences between performance metrics for PCI Express and those for Conventional PCI/PCI-X. Bear in mind that that the metrics are defined to apply to the specific signaling context for each architecture.

Table 1.2   Comparison of Performance Metrics for PCI Express† and Conventional PCI†/PCI-X†

PCI Express†	Loss (dB) Vout/in P-P	Jitter (UI)	AC/DC Common Mode (V)
Conventional PCI† and PCI-X†	Voh, Vol	Tsetup	Overshoot
		Thold	Duty Cycle
	Vih, Vil	Data to Clock Skew	Monotonic Transition
			Ringback

Unit Interval and Eye Diagrams

A good place to begin understanding the PCI Express signal performance requirements is with the unit interval and eye concepts. As stated previously, the data transfer rate of PCI Express is 2.5 billion transfers per second (2.5 GT/s) per differential pair/direction. This data rate translates to a *unit interval* (UI) of 400 ps nominal. The UI is defined as the width—that is, the high or low time—of an individual one or zero bit.

The PCI Express specification states that the unit interval will be 400 picoseconds (ps) ±300 parts per million (ppm). This requirement translates to a UI range of 400 ps ±120 fs, or 399.88 ps to 400.12 ps. In the case of *spread spectrum clocking* (SSC), the absolute UI will change but the difference between the transmitter and receiver clocks must still meet the ±300-ppm specification.[1]

Note that a data pattern of alternating ones and zeros forms a repetitive signal with a period of 800 ps, so the maximum frequency of a data pattern is half the bit rate, or 1.25 GHz.

Figure 1.15 illustrates a differential signal UI.

---

[1] SSC is an EMI reduction technique in which the frequency of a clock signal is slowly varied around its center frequency, thus "spreading" the energy present in the clock signal across a wider band and reducing the peak energy at the fundamental. The PCI Express specification allows but does not require SSC. The important thing to remember is that under all conditions, the transmitter and receiver UIs must remain within ±300 ppm of each other.

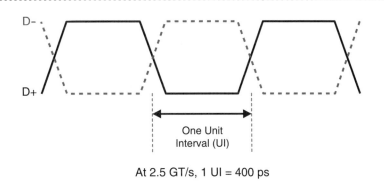

At 2.5 GT/s, 1 UI = 400 ps

Figure 1.15   Unit Interval

High-speed serial links are usually characterized by an "eye diagram." The *PCI Express Base Specification* (PCI-SIG 2004a) documents two related eye diagrams: one at the transmitter and one at the receiver. In addition, the *PCI Express Card Electromechanical Specification* (PCI-SIG 2004b) documents specific eye diagrams that apply to the interface between a connector and an add-in card. While these eyes are not discussed here, the concepts discussed in this section apply to those eye diagrams as well.

Figure 1.16 represents an eye diagram at the transmitter. If this eye diagram were placed over a scope display and centered in the UI, no part of the displayed waveform should be inside the triangle defined by $V_{TX\_DIFF\_PP}$ and T_{TX_EYE}. Transmitter specifications are measured at the pins of the device package into a 50 Ω reference load to ground.

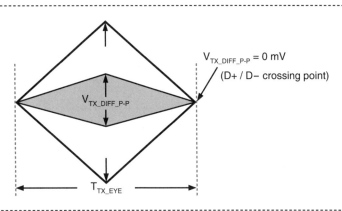

Figure 1.16   Eye Diagram at the Transmitter

Note that the eye signal performance specifies both the eye width (time) and eye height (voltage). The transmitter and receiver eye height are specified in terms of differential peak-to-peak volts and the eye width in terms of UI. The channel performance between the transmitter and receiver is specified in terms of jitter, loss (dB), and AC and DC common mode.

Jitter

Jitter is a measure of how accurately an edge or differential signal-crossing is placed with respect to its ideal placement. For example, for the PCI Express bus, transferring data at 2.5 GT/s, the differential signal-crossings should be at 400 ps (one UI) intervals from one another. Any deviation from this interval represents jitter. Excessive jitter closes the eye beyond the T_{TX_EYE} or T_{RX_EYE} specification. Figure 1.17 illustrates how jitter closes an eye diagram.

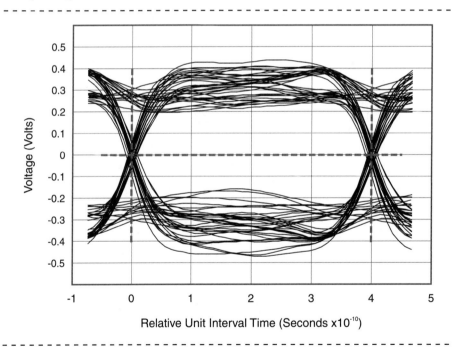

Figure 1.17   Eye Diagram Showing Jitter

Total jitter is composed of two distinct types of jitter: random and deterministic. Random jitter is the result of the random noise and thermal effects present in any semiconductor device affecting the transmitter's edge rate and propagation time from one cycle to the next. Random jitter is assumed to have a Gaussian or bell-shaped distribution that can be characterized by a mean and a standard deviation. Note also that random jitter is *unbounded*; the tails of the distribution asymptotically approach the x-axis. See Figure 1.18.

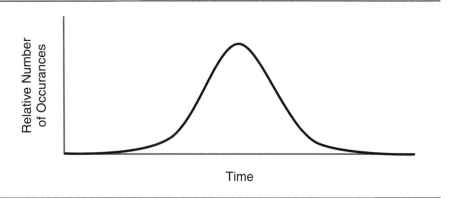

Figure 1.18   Random Jitter Distribution

On the other hand, deterministic jitter is data dependent, the result from system and transmission line effects. Inter-symbol interference (ISI), crosstalk, impedance discontinuities, and power supply fluctuations are all examples of phenomena that cause deterministic jitter. Unlike random jitter, deterministic jitter distribution is non-Gaussian and its amplitude is *bounded.* In other words, given a particular set of design rules and a physical implementation, it is possible to determine the maximum amount of jitter due to ISI, crosstalk, and other phenomena.

Random and deterministic jitter combine to form a total jitter distribution profile similar to that shown in Figure 1.19.

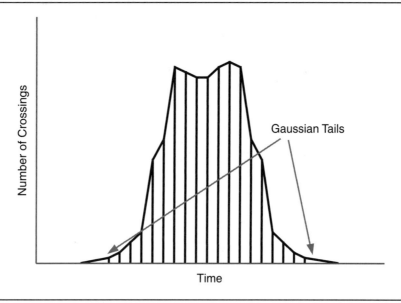

Figure 1.19   Total Jitter Distribution

In this example, the jitter distribution has two humps, and then tails off dramatically. Most of the jitter is concentrated around the center of the distribution—the bounded deterministic portion, with jitter towards the edges having a much lower likelihood of occurring—the random portion. Due to the random component of jitter, most high-speed serial busses specify jitter in terms of a mean and a maximum value. However, because of the low probability of capturing the maximum value, a jitter measurement must be made over an extended period of time.

The PCI Express specification addresses jitter performance in a slightly different manner. Due to the nature of most high-speed serial bus clock recovery methods, as explained below, PCI Express specifies jitter in terms of a median value and maximum outlier from that median value. The jitter median is the point in time at which there are as many differential signals crossing to the left of the point as there are to the right of it. Figure 1.20 illustrates this concept using a histogram of jitter crossing values.

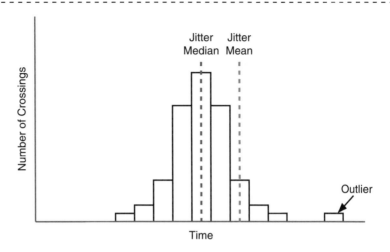

Figure 1.20   Jitter Histogram Showing Jitter Median and Mean Points

Note how a jitter outlier affects the value of the jitter median as opposed to the jitter mean. Because a mean is calculated using the magnitude of each value—that is, the time value of the jitter crossing point—an extreme outlier value will greatly affect the mean value. On the other hand, because the median value only looks at the number of crossing points to the left and right of a given point, the time magnitude of the jitter outlier is unimportant. In point of fact, many high-speed serial clock recovery circuits locate the edges of the data eye—which locates the proper place to capture the data—by finding the jitter median. Therefore, specifying jitter in terms of a median value and maximum deviation from that median is a closer match to the way a receiver reacts to jitter.

Chapter 9, "Measurement Techniques," examines implications of measurement due to the PCI Express method of specifying jitter.

Loss

Loss is signal amplitude degradation. In the forward signal direction, from the transmitter to the receiver, reduction of the signal strength is called *insertion loss*. The reflected loss of the signal in the opposite direction is called *return loss*. PCI Express specifications restrict the allowed insertion and return losses, to ensure that the transmitter and receiver package designs don't overly degrade the signal performance, and to make sure that the transmitted signal has adequate amplitude at the receiver signal pin. Figure 1.21 illustrates insertion and return losses.

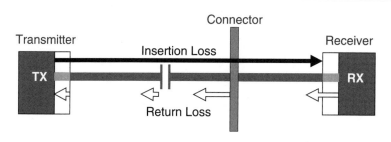

Figure 1.21   Insertion and Return Loss

Insertion loss is a physical property of the packages, circuit board traces, and other interconnect elements in the signal path. You need to consider loss variations due to signal conductor width, spacing, and roughness. Other sources are dielectric variations, interconnect features including vias, capacitor parasitics, and connectors. The material and component loss randomness comes from the manufacturing variations, and the fact that the interconnect components are combined from independent sources.

Pattern-dependent loss also occurs from the data signaling pattern. The signal bit pattern, consisting of a stream of ones and zeros, generates different signal transmission loss depending upon the pattern. A string of alternating ones and zeros, such as 10101010..., at PCI Express data transmission rates would exhibit more loss at the receiver than a slower transitioning data pattern, such as "111110000011111..." Figure 1.22 shows this *pattern-dependent loss* in terms of the min and max voltage range of the eye opening. The loss is predictable based on the data pattern, and is thus deterministic. PCI Express employs single-stage de-emphasis to reduce the loss variation across the allowed signal bit patterns.

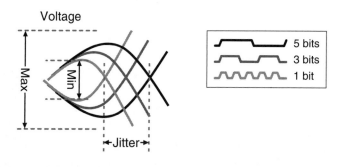

Figure 1.22   Pattern-dependent Loss

AC and DC Performance

In addition to the eye jitter and loss performance, you should be aware of some other AC and DC performance requirements. As shown in Figure 1.23, DC blocking capacitors on the transmitter end of the lane provide the PCI Express AC coupling on each signal trace. AC coupling means that any DC voltage at the output of the transmitter is blocked from the receiver, allowing the receiver and the driver to be biased at separate voltages. The capacitors are associated with the transmitting device. If the topology includes an add-in card, the capacitors are located on the substrate with the transmitter.

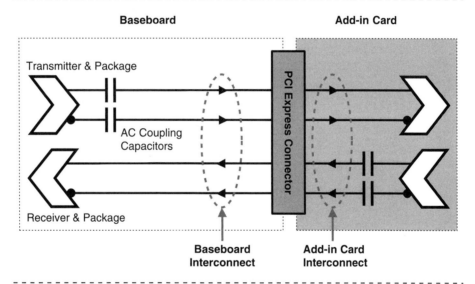

Figure 1.23 PCI Express† AC Coupling

The PCI Express specification allows the transmitter common mode voltage to be non-zero, but requires the receiver's DC common mode voltage to be 0V. The DC blocking capacitors provide another benefit: the transmitter can use RC time constants to detect the presence of a receiver at the end of a lane, and to detect an insertion or removal of a receiver.

Because of the AC coupling, the DC average of the data sent across each D+ or D– trace must be zero. If it is not, then the common mode voltage seen by the receiver will start to drift. If left unchecked, this drift may push the common mode voltage seen by the receiver beyond its compliance range. Rapidly changing shifts in common mode voltage also contribute to signal jitter. As a result, the PCI Express electrical specifications include parameters intended to control this drift, namely AC and DC common mode parameters.

DC Common Mode Voltage

Common mode voltage is defined as the voltage that is "common" to both the D+ and D– outputs. For purposes of the PCI Express specification, the DC common mode voltage is calculated as the average voltage on the D+ and D– outputs over a large number of unit intervals, with a minimum of 250 UI. Figure 1.24 illustrates a differential signal pair, both with a positive and different DC voltage range, in which the average voltage—that is, the DC common mode—is 0.2V. The DC blocking capacitors allow the transmitter and receiver DC common mode voltages to be different. In general, for lower power it is preferable to have the DC common mode voltage at 0V, but this level may be precluded by other circuit requirements.

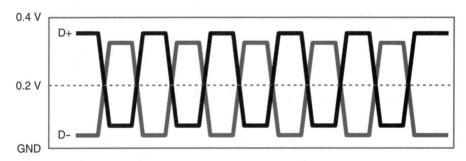

DC common mode voltage is the long-term average
of the D+ and D– signal voltage.

Figure 1.24 DC Common Mode Voltage

AC Common Mode Voltage

AC common mode voltage is the "short-term" voltage difference between the D+ and D– signals within each signal differential pair. This is in contrast to DC common mode voltage, which is the longer-term average voltage of the two signals. The two main causes of AC common mode variation are within-pair phase difference, causing the rise/fall signal-crossing voltage to deviate, and crosstalk, which can occur at any point that affects either the eye opening or rise/fall signal-crossing. Figure 1.25 illustrates a within-pair phase shift effect on AC common mode voltage. As shown in Figure 1.25, the AC common mode occurs during voltage transitions.

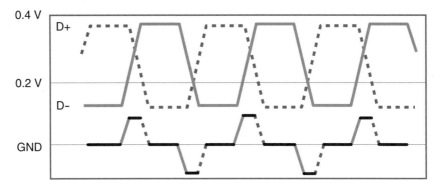

AC common mode voltage is the average
of the D+ and D– signals during voltage transitions.

Figure 1.25   AC Common Mode Voltage

Rise and Fall Times

The *PCI Express Base Specification* (PCI-SIG 2004a) also includes a rise and fall time requirement. The spec states that the minimum allowable signal rise and fall time, 20 percent to 80 percent, at the transmitter package pins into the standard test load of 50 Ω to ground is 0.125 UI, or 50 ps. For a complete discussion on the relationship between rise time and bandwidth and how they affect measurement, see Chapter 8, "Validating the Design."

Chapter 2

Signal Integrity Design Modeling

The PCI Express[†] electrical interconnect channel is a point-to-point, low-voltage swing differential (LVSD) bus, operating at 2.5 GT/s per differential pairs. An advantage of LVSD signaling is providing a great flexibility for high-speed design, including a greater bandwidth per pin. The PCI Express electrical interconnect channel needs careful modeling and validation methods to support a robust and reliable operation. This chapter presents detailed simulation models for all elements of the PCI Express interconnect channel, and discusses design challenges and ways to achieve the best performance.

Component Loss-based Method

The PCI Express interconnect design must specify the loss on each inter-connect element as well as the defined boundaries between segmented elements. From a platform viewpoint, the end-to-end loss must include and specify the package and interconnect characteristics. In the loss-based method, the package characteristics are defined at the package pins, including the driver and/or receiver on-die capacitance to include impact of the package on the interconnect loss budget.

In this method, you model the package and die as a single entity. For the package design, you can model the package by measuring the frequency domain data, S-parameters, and the time domain data—that is, the voltage eye measured at the package pins, where the interconnect system is terminated into an ideal 100 Ω differential test load. Most designers find it helpful to characterize the receiver in the same way when it is excited by a controllable differential source to obtain a minimum eye at the package pins.

In the loss-based method, you can analyze the PCI Express channel in either of two topologies:

- In single-segment topology, the PCI Express interconnect is analyzed from die-to-die on a typical one-substrate platform.

- In multi-segment topology, the PCI Express interconnects are routed on two or more separate substrates, such as a motherboard and an adaptor.

In the multi-segment topology, the overall loss must be partitioned between the various interconnect segments so that the total loss meets the specification. However, this PCI Express channel partitioning is not easy and depends on the interconnect loss profiles. In cases where all interconnects behave well—that is, those with no resonances or impedance mismatch at each segment—the end-to-end loss of a multi-segment interconnect is the product of its constituent losses. For the well-behaved interconnect segment, the product of loss is independent of the order in which the segments are assembled.

PCI Express† Interconnect Simulation Models

The recommended model for a PCI Express interconnect channel is a die-to-die model that includes a victim differential pair surrounded by one differential aggressor pair on each side, to capture effects of far-end crosstalk (FEXT) and of near-end crosstalk (NEXT) caused by neighboring differential pairs. Our initial visibility studies have shown that increasing the number of aggressor differential pairs by more than a single pair on each side of the victim differential pair cannot increase accuracy by more than 3 percent.

Package and Circuit Characterization

PCI Express differential busses operate at 2.5 GT/s and require a rigorous design method for the package and the driver characterizations as a single entity. The PCI Express interconnect channel, from the package pins to the silicon die-bump, consists of package mechanical stackups and material properties and the driver's on-die capacitance. In this analysis, the package and driver's on-die capacitance are considered as a single entity, and the simulation results are measured at the package-to-PCB pins that are loaded by an ideal 100 Ω differential test load.

You need to consider the package parasitics and on-die capacitance as a single entity for two key reasons. First, package performance is sensitive to the on-die capacitance value. Second, you have to understand the package's impact on the PCI Express interconnect channel loss.

For PCI Express differential busses that are routed on the package in conjunction with the silicon parasitics, the best method for accurate modeling is to measure the frequency and/or time domain data at the driver's and/or receiver's package pins that meet the specifications. From a specification viewpoint, the frequency domain data, S-parameters, should be sustained under a certain design target across the range of frequency operation as follows:

- Return loss remains below –10 dB for the frequency range from 300 MHz to 1.25 GHz.

- Insertion loss guidelines are described in Chapter 4, "Loss Budget Partitioning."

In addition, the time domain data—the voltage eye measured at the package pins—must meet voltage specifications.

FCBGA and WB-BGA Package Types

This section presents the detailed model extraction of S-parameters and simulation examples for two package types: flip-chip ball grid array (FCBGA) and wire-bond ball grid array (WB-BGA).

You can route PCI Express busses on a typical six-layer FCBGA flip-chip package stackup or a bond-wire package. A typical PCI Express differential bus on the package has a nominal differential impedance of 100 Ω ±10 percent by considering the acceptable manufacturing tolerance to be about ±10 percent. The recommended method for routing is to locate the differential traces on a top layer of package-like microstrip lines. A typical routing of the PCI Express differential pairs includes breakout sections and many transmission line sections with many different spacings and widths, so long as the impedance is kept at about 100 Ω ±10 percent. In the case of a bond-wire package, we recommend using the same routing method, except that the bond-wire section should be routed with optimal signal/ground ratio. That is, for every signal pair, two ground wires are needed at both sides to minimize the crosstalk noise.

Figures 2.1 and 2.2 show three-dimensional views of FCBGA and WB-BGA packages, respectively.

A. Breakout Section   B. Transmission Line Section   C. Via and Ball Section

Figure 2.1   FCBGA Package

A. Bond-wire Section   B. Transmission Line Section   C. Via and Ball Section

Figure 2.2   WB-BGA Package

Two-Dimensional and Combined Segment Modeling

A typical FCBGA package consists of the following electrical elements: die-bump attachment, microvias, traces, plating through-hole (PTH) vias, and solder balls attached to the substrate. In the 2-D modeling method called *combined segment modeling*, a typical package is decomposed into these constituent elements and each element is then modeled independently.

Since the traces for the differential pairs range from 10 mm to 25 mm in length, they must be modeled as distributed transmission lines (Bansal 2004). The other electrical elements are short enough to be modeled as lumped-equivalent models up to 10 GHz.

Traces are modeled in a variety of methods, such as extracting resistance, inductance, capacitance, and conductance RLCG frequency-dependent, per-unit length matrices, using Ansoft 2D or the XFX extraction tool, and either the multi-layer interconnect library of ADS or Ansoft Designer. Designers using both ADS and Ansoft need the mechanical dimensions and the material properties of the traces that can be routed as microstrip or stripline. After defining the traces' parameters using any of the simulators, you can perform time or frequency domain analyses.

HSPICE and SigXPlorer use methods called W-elements and N-elements, respectively. Both methods use RLCG frequency-dependent, per-unit length matrices to perform frequency or time domain analyses.

A comparison between the simulator tools shows a very good correlation up to 10 GHz. Crosstalk is one of the important factors in PCI Express interconnect design, particularly for microstrip package topology, so it is important to make sure that the trace modeling method takes crosstalk into account.

The remaining electrical elements in the package—die-bump attachment, microvias, vias, and solder balls—can be modeled as lumped-equivalent models. You can use a variety of methods to generate a lumped-equivalent model for these elements. The methods typically used involve Ansoft and Agilent products called Q3D static field solver, 3-D full wave solver HFSS, ADS multi-layer library, and Ansoft Designer field solver in demand. You can also use the measured base model as an alternative or as a complementary tool.

The WB-BGA package is similar to the FCBGA package except that the microvias and die-bump attachments are replaced with bond wires. The remaining signal path, including traces, vias, and solder ball sections, can be modeled in the same way as the FCBGA package. Bond-wire parasitics can be calculated using any of the 3-D field solvers mentioned previously.

In 2-D segment modeling, each section of the package is modeled with lumped-equivalent, or transmission lines, or both. All the modeled elements are brought together in an ADS schematic circuit display, Ansoft Designer circuit display, or HSPICE format. With any of the simulation tools, you can simulate time domain, frequency domain, or both.

In Figure 2.3, the 2-D model of the differential pair of the FCBGA package shown in Figure 2.1, is broken into six sections, and each section is modeled with proper lumped-equivalent or transmission lines approach. The model includes die parasitics, I/O on-die capacitance, breakout sections, transmission lines sections, micro-vias, plating through-hole (PTH) vias, and solder ball attachments. The 50 Ω probes or ports are placed on the ball terminations, representing an equivalent of the package's pin measurements.

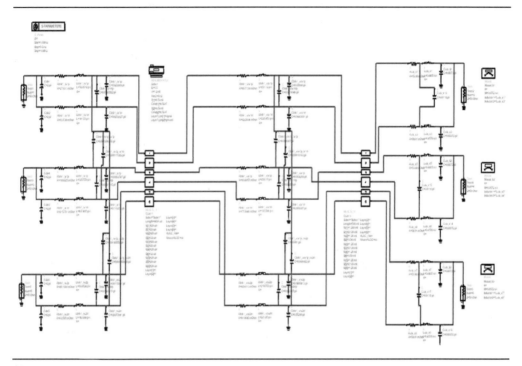

Figure 2.3   Lumped-Equivalent Modeling

Three-Dimensional Full Wave Modeling Method (HFSS)

In the 3-D full wave modeling method, you import the end-to-end PCI Express package into an HFSS Simulator. The end-to-end package includes all elements from die-bump attachment through the signal traces, and ending where the solder balls attach to the substrate. The import file can be obtained using the Ansoft link software program (Ansoft 2003). You can revise the model in the HFSS simulator by defining the material properties, boundary conditions, and port assignments so that they reflect the package's stackup, materials, and physical dimensions. To complete the solution process, you need to define the frequency of adaptive solution, sweep frequency, and the method of solution. For details, see the *HFSS Version 9.0 Manual* (Ansoft 2003).

The S-parameter results are computed and imported to an Ansoft Designer or ADS circuit display, then the on-die capacitances are included into the model on the die-bump attachment. The frequency domain simulation is performed at the solder ball attachments, which is equivalent to the package pins, calculating the return loss and insertion loss of the differential pairs. Figure 2.4 shows the sample simulation results of package characterization, including return loss and insertion loss of the package using HFSS 3-D field solver.

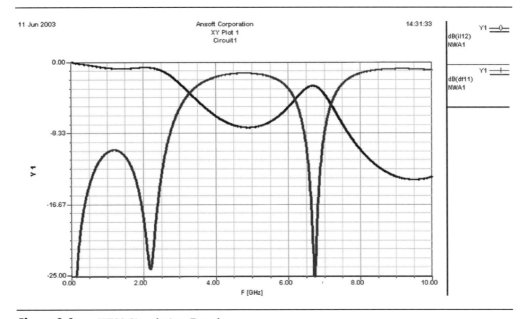

Figure 2.4   HFSS Simulation Results

Package and Die Validation Model

As discussed in previous sections, you can validate a typical PCI Express package and die by using the package model with the driver's parasitic. As shown in Figure 2.5, this model includes a one-victim differential pair and a two-aggressor differential pair that are terminated into an ideal 50 Ω single-ended test load. In this example, the PCI Express interconnect consists of transmission lines of package traces and package vias terminated into the 50 Ω test load terminations. For this example, the frequency domain data, S-parameters, and time domain data, voltage, and eye margins can be measured across 50 Ω terminations. The differential voltage is obtained by (D2+ - D2-), where D2 represents the victim signal, and D1 and D3 are two aggressors.

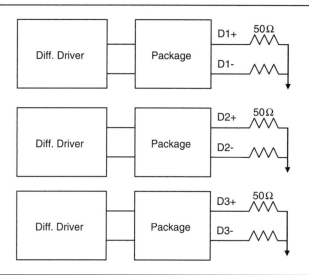

Figure 2.5   Package and Die Driver Validation Model

Driver Model

The most accurate driver model would derive a device model from the actual unit process files such as the BSIM3 model, which is compatible with HSPICE. Since making such a detailed model is so difficult, you might prefer the alternative choice—that is, the I/O Buffer Information Specification model (IBIS 2004). This modeling method extracts the device information and behavior and converts the data into a series of I/V and V/T curves. Typically, PCI Express designers simulate the PCI Express interconnect with fast, slow, and nominal device corners. You can assume an ideal Power Delivery Network (PDN) to specify the driver's output characteristics. In this case, the driver is modeled based on assumptions of process voltage and temperature variables.

IBIS Model

Unlike the traditional CMOS or GTL busses, the PCI Express buffers are not ideally suited to be modeled as IBIS models. In PCI Express, the IBIS models can be constructed by separating the strong and weak bits and developing separate IBIS models with de-emphasis capabilities. In this approach, a full differential pair requires four separate IBIS models.

After you have developed an appropriate 8b/10b data pattern, you must set up four separate buffer controls. The main portion of the positive half of the differential pair can be controlled by a signal that follows the data pattern exactly, toggling from 0 to 1 volt with a fast edge rate. The main portion of the negative buffer must be controlled with the inverse of the positive signal. For example, if the pattern driving the main portion of the positive buffer is 1001011101, the pattern to the main portion of the negative buffer must be 0110100010. See Figure 2.6 for a graphical representation of these bit patterns.

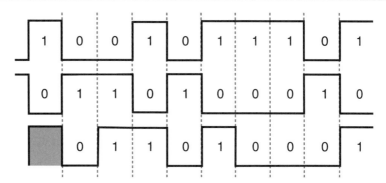

From top: Bit patterns for main positive buffer, main negative buffer, and de-emphasis

Figure 2.6   Bit Patterns in the IBIS Model

The controls for the de-emphasis portion of the buffers should be the main portions delayed by one UI, or 400 ps, and inverted. The de-emphasis portions also operate with fast edge rates. The positive buffer's de-emphasis control is the negative buffer's main control inverted and delayed 400 ps. As shown in Figure 2.6, the data pattern passed to the positive de-emphasis buffer would be X011010001, where X is uncertain. Figure 2.7 illustrates how this relationship results in a de-emphasized waveform.

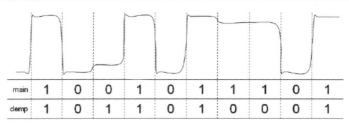

| main | 1 | 0 | 0 | 1 | 0 | 1 | 1 | 1 | 0 | 1 |
| demp | 1 | 0 | 1 | 1 | 0 | 1 | 0 | 0 | 0 | 1 |

The generation of a fully de-emphasized positive waveform through the simultaneous use of a 'main' and 'de-emphasis' buffer

Figure 2.7   De-emphasized Waveform

On-die Decoupling Capacitance

Typically, you use on-die decoupling capacitance to source a high-frequency current at the driver. The on-die decoupling capacitance usually is covered in power delivery network analysis. If we assume an ideal power delivery source, it is not necessary to include on-die decoupling capacitance in the signal integrity analysis. However, in some driver models, it is difficult to separate the on-die decoupling capacitance from the driver model because of the complexity of the special driver circuit implementation. You can add or remove on-die decoupling from the simulation model.

Receiver Model

The PCI Express receiver model consists of a termination, a receiver differential amplifier, and the receiver's parasitics based on the receiver's implementation. The receiver's voltage eye usually is measured at the receiver's pins. The differential voltage is computed by measuring the voltage difference (D+ – D–) at the receiver's pins.

PCB Modeling

For PCI Express interconnect analysis, performance is the key factor in enabling reliable system operation. The initial PCI Express interconnections visibility study demonstrated that the interconnect lengths are the major factor limiting PCI Express performance over distances greater than 10 inches. For interconnect lengths greater than 10 inches, the loss consists of frequency-dependent transmission loss, dispersion loss, dielectric loss, and skin effect loss (Bansal 2004)—all of which can significantly degrade PCI Express system performance and reliability. For interconnect models, the assumptions are a uniform cross-section model, and as much as possible, a straight segments model. Other cases, such as bends, vias, later changes, and connections to package and sockets, need to be modeled independently.

In modeling the PCB interconnect of PCI Express, take care to accurately capture crosstalk, reflection, and frequency-dependent transmission line loss. All simulator tools such as Advanced Design System (ADS), Ansoft Designer (Ansoft 2004), SigXplorer (Cadence 2003) and HSPICE (Synopsys 2004) have capabilities to model PCB interconnect with crosstalk, reflection, and frequency-dependent loss. You can use a lumped model for the interconnect segment if the interconnect propagation delay is much shorter than the rise time of the signal propagating through the interconnect.

PCB Interconnect Model

To accurately model the PCB interconnect, three differential pairs are required: one-victim pair and two aggressor pairs, one on each side of the victim pair. Figure 2.8 shows a typical stripline stackup consisting of three differential pairs, and shows the trace dimensions and material properties that must be defined in ADS.

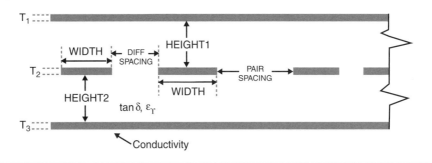

Figure 2.8   PCB Interconnect Mechanical Dimensions and Material Properties

The corresponding circuit, a schematic-level ADS library model, is shown in Figure 2.9. Notice the one-to-one correspondence between the parameters in Figure 2.8 and the ADS model. ADS transmission line models are defined in terms of a substrate, as shown on the left side of Figure 2.9, and trace dimensions, as shown on the right side.

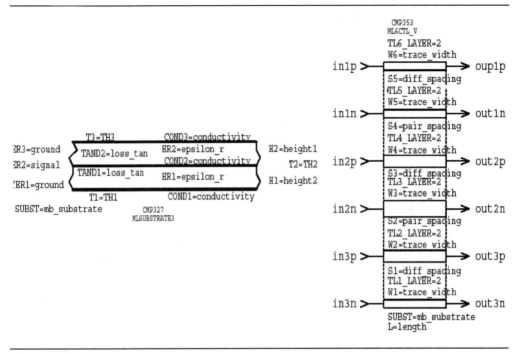

Figure 2.9   ADS Three Differential Pairs Transmission Lines Model

In Figure 2.9, name labels are included for each connection point. Each name label refers to a pin name on the symbol. The symbol references the dimensions and material properties from the schematic. For an example of the symbol model, see Figure 2.10.

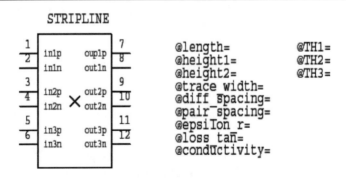

Figure 2.10   ADS Three Differential Pairs Transmission Lines Symbol Model

Including a PCB trace in a die-to-die model is as simple as adding the symbol and filling in numbers for its parameters. With the die-to-die model for stripline, the trace easily can be modified to represent a microstrip stackup.

An ADS converts the transmission line model into an equivalent N-port, S-parameter matrix. Each interconnect element is processed this way, and then an end-to-end impulse response is computed. When the user specifies a time domain analysis of an interconnect, the ADS tool performs a convolution of the impulse response with the excitation pattern at the driver side of the interconnect, and finally produces a time domain response at the receiver end.

W-element and N-element Models

The W-element (HSPICE) and N-element (SigXplorer) modeling methods allow you to include impedance mismatch, crosstalk, and frequency dependent loss in the modeling approach. A W-element model is generated through a field solver front end that generates an RLCG per-unit length matrix. In this model, your first step is to define an interconnect geometry, including trace dimensions and material properties, as shown in Figure 2.11.

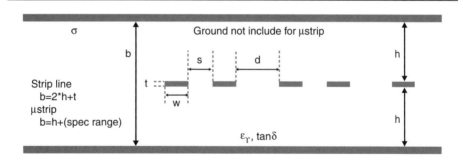

Figure 2.11 PCB Trace Parameters

The next step is to enter the parameters from Figure 2.11 into the tabular form required by XFX. To obtain the highest accuracy, you must specify the *integral* mode and the first X dimension, at least 10x the largest trace dimension. Figure 2.12 shows XFX input parameters.

A similar method is applied in the N-element method, except that all steps are automated in SigXplorer software.

############################## Strip Line ##############################						
MODE ENGLISH						
INTEGRAL						
CONFIG 3difflines	e: 1 mu: 1 rho: .667	x:	-106.000	106.000	y:	-0.600	11.200
CONDUCTOR A RECTANGLE		x:	-21.000	-26.000	y:	5.000	5.600
CONDUCTOR B RECTANGLE		x:	-14.000	-19.000	y:	5.000	5.600
CONDUCTOR C RECTANGLE		x:	-1.000	-6.000	y:	5.000	5.600
CONDUCTOR D RECTANGLE		x:	1.000	6.000	y:	5.000	5.600
CONDUCTOR E RECTANGLE		x:	14.000	19.000	y:	5.000	5.600
CONDUCTOR F RECTANGLE		x:	21.000	26.000	y:	5.000	5.600
DIELECTRIC	e: 3.4 tan: 0.016	HORIZ PLANE			y:	0.000	10.600
GROUND	HORIZ PLANE				y:	-0.600	0.000
GROUND	HORIZ PLANE				y:	10.600	11.200
;						

Figure 2.12   XFX Input Parameters

Example

In the following example, six conductor rectangles are defined, each one corresponding to one element of a differential pair. Running the XFX field solver yields a 6x6 matrix with parameters for capacitance, inductance, even and odd impedance, and loss, as shown in Figure 2.13.

```
    LOSS MATRICES
    i    j      Rsij         Gij          Rdcij        Gdcij
    from to  (ohm-nsec^.5)  (mS-ns)       (ohms)       (mS)        PER INCH
    ------------------------------------------------------------------------
    1    1     0.26706      0.040774      0.12429      0.00000
    1    2     0.00885      0.001366      0.00000      0.00000
    1    3     0.00022      4.57e-6       0.00000      0.00000
    1    4     8.62e-6      2.34e-8       0.00000      0.00000
    1    5     2.13e-7      5.13e-12      0.00000      0.00000
    1    6     3.62e-9      0.000000      0.00000      0.00000
    2    2     0.25786      0.041231      0.12412      0.00000
    2    3     0.00562      0.000888      0.00000      0.00000
    2    4     0.00022      4.66e-6       0.00000      0.00000
    2    5     5.39e-6      1.51e-8       0.00000      0.00000
    2    6     2.08e-7      0.000000      0.00000      0.00000
    3    3     0.26561      0.040792      0.12412      0.00000
    3    4     0.00888      0.001364      0.00000      0.00000
    3    5     0.00022      4.59e-6       0.00000      0.00000
    3    6     8.54e-6      2.39e-8       0.00000      0.00000
    4    4     0.26600      0.040806      0.12412      0.00000
    4    5     0.00571      0.000874      0.00000      0.00000
    4    6     0.00022      4.59e-6       0.00000      0.00000
    5    5     0.26588      0.040802      0.12412      0.00000
    5    6     0.00891      0.001365      0.00000      0.00000
    6    6     0.26600      0.040767      0.12412      0.00000
```

Figure 2.13   Loss Matrix

Symmetry rules permit you to define a matrix with significantly fewer than 36 elements. For example, the 36 matrix elements can be reduced to 21, as shown in Figure 2.14.

i from	j to	Lij (nh/in)	Cij (pf/in)	Ze (ohms)	Zo (ohms)	Se (ns/ft)	So (ns/ft)	Fwdx (s/s)	Rvsx (v/v)
1	1	10.363	2.912	59.69	-	2.08	-	-	-
1	2	0.344	0.098	61.68	57.70	2.08	2.08	-3.5e-4	0.033
1	3	8.65e-3	3.27e-4	59.68	59.62	2.09	2.08	7.2e-4	4.7e-4
1	4	3.35e-4	1.67e-6	59.65	59.65	2.08	2.08	3.2e-5	1.6e-5
1	5	8.28e-6	3.68e-10	59.65	59.65	2.08	2.08	8.0e-7	4.2e-7
1	6	1.40e-7	0.000	59.65	59.65	2.08	2.08	0.000	0.000
2	2	10.253	2.945	59.05	-	2.08	-	-	-
2	3	0.223	0.063	60.30	57.74	2.09	2.08	2.6e-4	0.022
2	4	8.65e-3	3.33e-4	59.03	58.98	2.09	2.08	7.3e-4	4.8e-4
2	5	2.14e-4	1.08e-6	59.00	59.00	2.09	2.09	2.0e-5	1.1e-5
2	6	8.27e-6	0.000	59.00	59.00	2.09	2.09	8.0e-7	4.2e-7
3	3	10.364	2.914	59.69	-	2.08	-	-	-
3	4	0.347	0.097	61.67	57.68	2.08	2.08	8.6e-6	0.033
3	5	8.61e-3	3.28e-4	59.67	59.61	2.09	2.08	7.2e-4	4.7e-4
3	6	3.33e-4	1.70e-6	59.64	59.64	2.09	2.09	3.2e-5	1.6e-5
4	4	10.360	2.915	59.67	-	2.08	-	-	-
4	5	0.222	0.062	60.91	58.35	2.08	2.08	3.4e-5	0.021
4	6	8.61e-3	3.28e-4	59.65	59.59	2.09	2.08	7.2e-4	4.7e-4
5	5	10.361	2.914	59.67	-	2.08	-	-	-
5	6	0.347	0.098	61.66	57.66	2.08	2.08	3.1e-5	0.033
6	6	10.365	2.912	59.70	-	2.08	-	-	-

Figure 2.14   RLCG Matrix

XFX also calculates even and odd Z, S, forward, and reverse crosstalk parameters, but these are not used in generating W-elements. However, you use a custom script to convert the XFX files into an HSPICE-compatible format, as shown in Figure 2.15.

```
* Number of Conductors = 6 *
*********************************
6

***************
*** Lo (H/in) *
***************
 8.771000e-09
 3.300000e-10  8.763000e-09
 5.060000e-12  1.240000e-10  8.776000e-09
 2.080000e-13  5.090000e-12  3.320000e-10  8.846000e-09
 3.130000e-15  7.690000e-14  5.020000e-12  1.230000e-10  8.778000e-09
 2.150000e-16  3.170000e-15  2.060000e-13  5.070000e-12  3.330000e-10  8.847000e-09
***************

*** Co (F/in) *
***************
 3.606000e-12
-1.360000e-13  3.610000e-12
-1.580000e-16 -5.100000e-14  3.605000e-12
-5.280000e-19 -1.580000e-16 -1.350000e-13  3.576000e-12
-0.000000e+00 -2.250000e-19 -1.580000e-16 -5.000000e-14  3.604000e-12
-3.510000e-20 -5.800000e-23 -5.480000e-19 -1.560000e-16 -1.360000e-13  3.575000e-12
********************

*** Ro (ohms/in) *
********************
 2.750900e-01
 0.000000e+00  2.750900e-01
 0.000000e+00  0.000000e+00  2.750900e-01
 0.000000e+00  0.000000e+00  0.000000e+00  2.750900e-01
 0.000000e+00  0.000000e+00  0.000000e+00  0.000000e+00  2.750900e-01
 0.000000e+00  0.000000e+00  0.000000e+00  0.000000e+00  0.000000e+00  2.750900e-01
**********************

*** Go (Siemens/in) *
**********************
 0.000000e+00
 0.000000e+00  0.000000e+00
 0.000000e+00  0.000000e+00  0.000000e+00
 0.000000e+00  0.000000e+00  0.000000e+00  0.000000e+00
 0.000000e+00  0.000000e+00  0.000000e+00  0.000000e+00  0.000000e+00
 0.000000e+00  0.000000e+00  0.000000e+00  0.000000e+00  0.000000e+00  0.000000e+00
**************************

*** Rs (ohms/(in*Hz^.5)) *
**************************
 3.890175e-05
 0.000000e+00  3.892078e-05
 0.000000e+00  0.000000e+00  3.880980e-05
 0.000000e+00  0.000000e+00  0.000000e+00  4.024459e-05
 0.000000e+00  0.000000e+00  0.000000e+00  0.000000e+00  3.877492e-05
 0.000000e+00  0.000000e+00  0.000000e+00  0.000000e+00  0.000000e+00  4.029373e-05
********************

*** Gd (S/(in*Hz)) *
********************
 3.851667e-13
-1.450116e-14  3.855814e-13
-1.683844e-17 -5.447361e-15  3.850348e-13
-5.642134e-20 -1.683844e-17 -1.446975e-14  3.819750e-13
 0.000000e+00 -2.406389e-20 -1.690127e-17 -5.353116e-15  3.849594e-13
-3.750951e-21 -6.113359e-24 -5.849473e-20 -1.664995e-17 -1.450116e-14  3.818682e-13
```

Figure 2.15   HSPICE RLCG File

Finally, you must create a netlist file as shown in Figure 2.16. The W-element can then be included in the HSPICE model along with other elements.

```
.lib          'tlib.lib'       b1 s25.11 d29.4 w9.3 h15.81 z059 zd118
. Xbrd1 pos_brd1ac1            pos_brd1ac2       pos_brd1ac3
+       neg_brd1ac1            neg_brd1ac2       neg_brd1ac3
+       pos_con1_a1            pos_con1_a2       pos_con1_a3
+       neg_con1_a1            neg_con1_a2       neg_con1_a3
+       Vssbrd1   BRD1

********************************-----------------------------------
********************************
.LIB          b1_s25.11_d29.4_w9.3_h15.81_z059_zd118
.subckt       BRD1
+             pos_in1    pos_in2    pos_in3
+             neg_in1    neg_in2    neg_in3
+             pos_out1   pos_out2   pos_out3
+             neg_out1   neg_out2   neg_out3
+             Vssbrd
RVssbrd       Vssbrd     0          1G
Wline
+             pos_in1   neg_in1   pos_in2       neg_in2   pos_in3   neg_in3   Vssbrd
+             pos_out1  neg_out1  pos_out2      neg_out2  pos_out3  neg_out3  Vssbrd
+ RLGCFILE=              './rlc/s25.11_d29.4_w9.3_h15.81_z059_zd118.rlc   ' N=6 L=len_brd1
.ENDS
.ENDL
```

Figure 2.16   HSPICE Netlist

Signal Integrity Phenomena

Signal integrity issues can significantly degrade PCI Express system performance and reliability. Phenomena such as reflection, losses, crosstalk, dispersion, mismatched impedance, return path discontinuities, Inter-Symbol Interference (ISI), and simultaneous switching output (SSO) can limit reliable PCI Express system operation. To simulate and accurately predict the effect of these phenomena, you must be able to obtain accurate interconnect models for each part of the interconnect—from the driver chip, through the package into the PCB, and the receiver chip.

■ Deterministic jitter and eye diagram degradation are caused by frequency-dependent losses and crosstalk in interconnects.

■ Signal distortion and digital switching errors result from crosstalk, reflections, and ringing in interconnections.

- Understanding reflection demands increased impedance measurement accuracy and transmission line modeling.

- Signal ringing requires an understanding of interaction between the lumped (RLCG) and distributed transmission line elements in the system.

The best method for improving PCI Express bus performance is to calculate and optimize the losses, crosstalk, reflection, dispersion, mismatched impedance, return path discontinuities, ISI, and delay on a PCI Express bus using frequency domain analysis. For more details, see Chapter 4, "Frequency Domain Analysis."

Loss

Frequency-dependent transmission line losses can significantly degrade the robustness of PCI Express bus performance and limit PCI Express bit rates. The transmission line losses, which include dielectric loss and skin effect loss, can significantly reduce the eye voltage at the receiver's pins by affecting both the rise time and amplitude degradation. The rise time degradation can cause a significant difference in delay between the driver and receiver, and amplitude degradation can cause a function failure at the receiver. Both of these effects, combined with crosstalk-related pattern-dependent jitter, can result in significant degradation of the eye diagram. Skin effect loss is more common below 1.0 GHz, while dielectric loss dominates above 1.0 GHz.

At the receiver, the losses manifest as inter-symbol interference (ISI). ISI effectively limits the dV/dt rate at the receiver such that the voltage level at which a transition occurs is dependent on previous data states. Figure 2.17 shows an example of ISI.

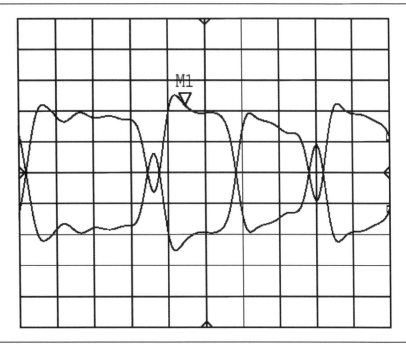

Figure 2.17   ISI Example

Loss in a transmission line is a strong function of frequency, contributing both skin effect loss and dielectric loss. Figure 2.18 illustrates the magnitude of the typical PCB interconnect forward loss as a function of frequency. As shown in the figure, the relationship between the frequency and loss is almost linear when plotted logarithmically against frequency. Transmission lines exhibit both AC loss and, to a lesser extent, DC loss. The presence of DC loss explains why the curve does not intercept the Y-axis at precisely 0 dB.

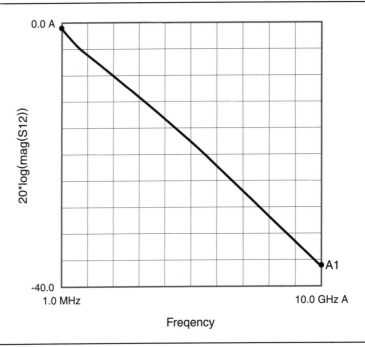

Figure 2.18   Typical PCB Interconnect Loss

Crosstalk

Crosstalk is caused by a transformation of energy from one signal trace to another, resulting in a change in the voltage measured at the receiver's pins.

Backward crosstalk appears at the driver, and can affect signal integrity by forcing the driver out of its normal I/V operating area. Backward crosstalk is more important when impedance discontinuities occur near the driver end of the interconnect.

Forward crosstalk appears at the receiver and is manifested as a change in the effective ε_R of the dielectric. Consider the case of a multi-conductor microstrip interconnect. The **E** field lines align themselves in accordance with the direction of current flow in the traces. Since a microstrip topology is open on one side, some **E** field lines pass through the dielectric, and the remainder pass through the air. Figure 2.19 (Ansoft 2003) shows a field distribution on the wave port of odd mode excitation of differential microstrip. Depending on whether the currents are opposed or in the same direction, a differing proportion of field lines pass through the PCB dielectric or through the air. The more lines that pass through the dielectric, the higher effective ε_R and the lower the effective signal propagation velocity. Thus, a signal on a victim line experiences a variation in velocity as a function of the direction of current flow in it and in neighboring lines.

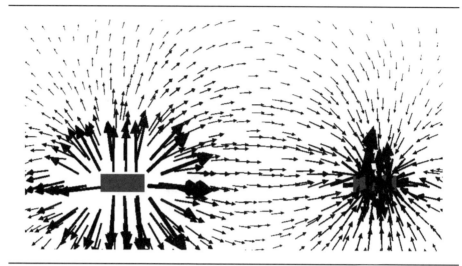

Figure 2.19   Field Distribution of Microstrip Differential Odd Mode

Forward crosstalk in stripline is very small. For a stripline geometry, all of the field lines are constrained within the dielectric between the upper and lower return planes shown in Figure 2.20 (Ansoft 2003). If the dielectric is uniform, there is no change to ε_R as a function of current distribution or to velocity sensitivity to data patterns. However, impedance discontinuities such as vias and sockets cause stripline to experience a small, and usually negligible, amount of forward crosstalk.

Forward crosstalk in microstrip is the limiting phenomenon. The magnitude of forward crosstalk in microstrip varies linearly with the interconnect length. For example, an 8-inch microstrip trace has been shown through simulation to exhibit worse signal integrity than a 24-inch stripline. Forward crosstalk is the primary reason that a microstrip length greater than 16 inches is a limiting factor for the PCI Express bus.

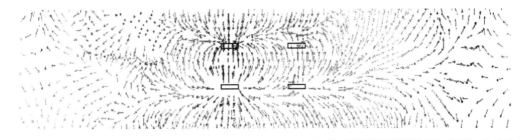

Figure 2.20   Field Distribution of Stripline Differential Field

Reflections

An ideal PCI Express interconnection would consist of perfectly matched transmission line segments, with 100-percent signal transmission efficiency across each segment-to-segment interface. In a real PCI Express interconnection system, the mismatches between transmission line segments are caused by manufacturing tolerances, connectors, vias, and other factors. Reflections adversely affect signal integrity in two ways:

■ Wave reflections cause less energy to propagate forward to the receiver. This is the most common effect, especially for long PCI Express interconnects.

■ Wave reflections can cause the equivalent of multi-path distortion, whereby the reflected signal arrives at the receiver some time later than the main signal.

The best way to control wave reflections is to minimize impedance discontinuities between the driver and receiver. Impedance discontinuities are usually caused by vias, layer changes, connectors, and sockets.

Wave reflections can also affect the driver if the magnitude of the voltage reflected back into the driver is sufficient to force it outside its normal operating conditions. Normally, the maximum impedance mismatch is small enough that this phenomenon should not be of concern. In fact, the stipulation that all die-to-die elements be impedance-matched to within some tolerance is driven by the need to constrain loss as well as the need to limit reflected energy to the driver.

AC Coupling Capacitance

AC coupling isolates the driver and receiver's grounds from each other. AC coupling capacitance is important for chassis-to-chassis connectivity, and it must be implemented between the PCI Express driver and receiver. In the role of DC isolation devices, the coupling capacitors must pass the complete spectrum of signaling from its low-pass cutoff point to approximately 3x its highest fundamental. For 2.5 GT/s, the 3x frequency is approximately 5.0 GHz. The PCI Express Base Specification stipulates a capacitance of 200 nF to ensure that the low-frequency components of the 8b/10b signaling can pass through the capacitor undistorted.

At the frequencies encountered in PCI Express signaling, a capacitor exhibits significant parasitics—in particular, an inductance and resistance in series with the capacitance. The effective Equivalent Series Inductance (ESL) of the capacitor is a strong function of the loop area formed by the capacitor and its mounting lands on the substrate. An alternative option is to characterize the capacitor using a vector network analyzer (VNA). The output of the VNA is an S-parameter representation, which can be converted to an RLC series model or used as an S-parameter model if an ADS simulation environment is available.

PCB Vias Model

A via connecting a differential pair of transmission line segments can be modeled as a capacitance to ground in series with a resistance and an inductance. For differential signaling, vias should be modeled as pairs, as shown in Figure 2.21.

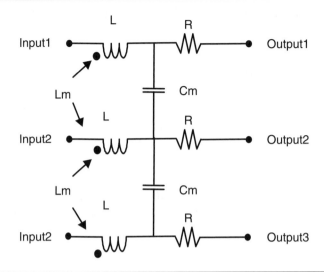

Figure 2.21   PCB Via Modeling

Table 2.1 lists parameters for common via dimensions for through-via connectivity. The drill diameter is the hole size in the PCB before plating is done. The parameters assume that the signal connections to the via are from the outermost external layers on the PC board. If the via connects between internal layers, the inductance and resistance can be scaled, but the capacitance remains the same. The values in Table 2.1 assume that the anti-pad diameter is equal to twice the drill diameter, and that the dielectric constant for the PCB is 4.2. The via center conductor is assumed to be a solid cylinder of metal.

Table 2.1   PCB Via Parameters

Drill Diameter	PCB Thickness	L_{SELF} (per via)	L_{MUTUAL} (.05" spacing)	R	C
9 mils	63 mils	1.05 nH	0.18 nH	0.87 mΩ	0.60 pF
14 mils	63 mils	0.91 nH	0.18 nH	0.36 mΩ	0.60 pF
17 mils	63 mils	0.84 nH	0.18 nH	0.24 mΩ	0.60 pF
20 mils	63 mils	0.74 nH	0.18 nH	0.18 mΩ	0.60 pF

Connectors

The usual method of simulating connectors is with a lumped element equivalent model. Most connector manufacturers can furnish a SPICE model. Typically, these models represent each mated pair of connector contacts as an inductor with mutual-inductance and capacitive coupling to its neighbors. You must verify that the manufacturer's connector model is valid at the frequencies of interest for PCI Express.

Properly modeling a connector requires that you model the connector's intrinsic characteristics as well as its particular connections to signals and return paths. The ratio between self- and mutual- inductance can be substantial, and proper inter-digitation of signals and returns can offer a significant reduction in effective connector inductance. At present, most connector models are HSPICE representations utilizing large numbers of current sources and lumped element equivalents. The accuracy of such models above ~10.0 GHz is questionable, but the most connectors have been characterized at the frequencies encountered in PCI Express signaling.

Die-to-Die Simulation Model

A desktop platform example of the PCI Express interconnect channel consists of the driver package, the receiver package, the PCB, the connectors, and the vias. This model can be implemented in both frequency and time domain simulation.

Time Domain Simulation Model

The time domain simulation model includes the PCI Express interconnect channel for the desktop platform with PCB traces, connectors, vias, and adaptors. The model contains a single victim pair and a two-aggressor pair, as shown in Figure 2.22.

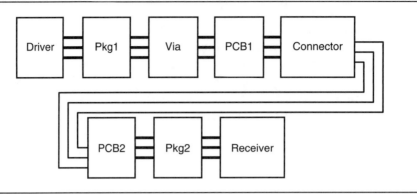

Figure 2.22   Top-level Time Domain Model

Frequency Domain Simulation Model

The frequency domain simulation model, shown in Figure 2.23, includes the PCI Express interconnect channel for a desktop platform with the same elements used in the time domain model.

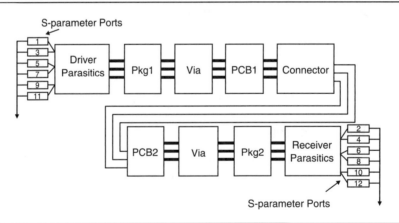

Figure 2.23   Top-level Frequency Domain Model

Power Delivery Network

The Power Delivery Network (PDN) model includes the components that are interposed between the I/O buffer (driver and receiver) and voltage regulator. These components include the package, PCB interconnect, vias, connectors, traces, decoupling capacitors, and on-die capacitance. For PCI Express differential busses, the signal return path is coincident with the signal path; that is, D– is the return path for D+. In other words, for a proper design, there is not any sharing current on the ground/power plane. As a result, the differential signal integrity and I/O power delivery must be modeled orthogonally. However, PCI Express differential busses involve some mode conversion that converts common mode to differential mode. Mode conversion is also required because the frequency of operation is in multi-gigahertz speeds. To reduce the risk of possible signal degradation, you must include the power delivery network effects in the system simulation model.

Power Delivery Analysis

The primary goal of PDN analysis is to determine the required on-die capacitance, the package, and PCB decoupling capacitors to produce a robust and reliable design. Studying the power delivery network involves a combination of frequency and time domain analysis.

Frequency domain analysis lets you identify the resonance frequency of the PDN and determine the worst-case parameter values. Validation steps include a combination of vector network analyzer (VNA) measurements, time domain and step response tests, and pattern sensitivity testing.

Time domain analysis cannot predict accurately the test patterns and parameters that yield worst-case timing and voltage margins, but it is useful for system interconnect analysis. Time domain analysis cannot successfully predict resonance frequency of PDN even by running many sweeps and simulations.

PDN Drivers

The PDN of differential drivers depends on the driver configuration and its characteristics. An ideal differential driver with perfectly balanced rise and fall times, matched P and N devices, and balanced load would draw only a DC current. In such a situation, the PDN must meet a DC PDN requirement. However, a "real" driver design has various imbalances that are inherent in the nature of drivers. Typically, the two driver types are voltage mode and current mode.

PDN Time Domain Design Parameters

PDN time domain requirements usually are set by the tolerance of the $(V_{DD} - V_{-ss})$ supply voltage at the driver's rails. This number usually is identified as V_{-DD} (nominal) ±10 percent and includes both DC tolerance and AC modulation. The 10 percent includes a 5-percent DC component that allows for voltage regulator tolerance plus IR drop and a 5-percent allocation for high-frequency AC noise that is caused by multiple outputs switching simultaneously.

PDN Frequency Domain Design Parameters

PDN design is best characterized in terms of frequency domain data, which makes for easier validation and measurement. You can also specify the PDN's impedance characteristics in terms of the frequency data, as follows:

$$Z(f) <= (V_{DD} - V_{SS})/SF * I(f)$$

where $Z(f)$ is the PDN impedance, $I(f)$ is the maximum current drawn by the drivers at a given frequency, and SF is scale factor to reflect the AC variation. For example, with a 5-percent AC variation, the scale factor is 20. This relationship must be maintained at frequencies from an 8b/10b lower cutoff to the highest spectral component.

PDN Modeling

This section discusses how to develop a PDN simulation model and convert the power delivery network components from the driver outward to
the voltage regulator. The process requires conversion of the physical
structures and components of the drivers, package parasitics, package
decoupling, PCB, PCB decoupling, and voltage regulator module VRM
parasitic to the appropriate model. Figure 2.24 shows the power delivery
component blocks.

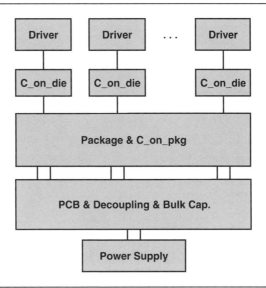

Figure 2.24   Power Delivery Block Diagram

Driver and On-die Capacitance

The on-die decoupling can be modeled as a capacitance with a series resistance between the driver's V_{DD} and V_{ss} rails. The on-die capacitance model needs to reflect the effect of the maximum number of I/O drivers switching simultaneously and their associated decoupling. On-die resistance is a function of the layout of metallization. It has strong impact on resonance frequency of the PDN. On-die capacitance is the first energy storage component and supplies high-frequency current to the drivers. You must design on-die decoupling correctly since the on-die capacitance varies with the driver configuration. We recommend an on-die decoupling capacitance of 50 pF per driver.

Package and PCB Models

You can model package power planes and vias by partitioning the package and PCB into many mesh elements with connection to the die through micro-vias and to the PCB at the location of V_{CC} and V_{ss} balls. The mesh size is determined by requiring the time of flight for a distance across an element to be less than the rise time of the disturbance. You can model the PCB in the same fashion, except that the mesh elements can be larger.

Decoupling Capacitor Model

At the frequencies encountered in PCI Express power delivery, a capacitor exhibits parasitics inductance and resistance in series with the capacitor. You can obtain the capacitor parasitics from the developer.

Vias and Socket Model

Vias and sockets can be modeled as lumped-RLC elements or S-parameters obtained by HFSS. Typically, the lumped model includes a series inductance and resistance with a capacitor to ground corresponding to each pin. Since the package and PCB planes are meshed, each mesh element can contain a number of V_{DD} and V_{ss} pins, and an equivalent LRC element is modeled for multiple V_{ss} and V_{DD} pins.

Power Supply Model

The VRM can be modeled by using a large zero-ohm inductance, typically 500 nH or larger. This model represents low impedance at low frequencies and provides decoupling at higher frequencies.

PDN Simulation Method

In a PDN model, the impedance sweep versus frequency typically is measured at the die outward to the VRM. The result is a plot to detect the resonance frequency of PDN. See Figure 2.25 for an example.

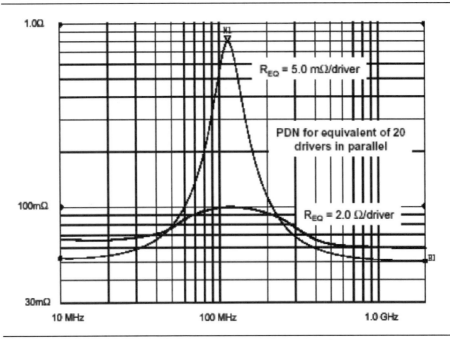

Figure 2.25   Typical PDN Impedance versus Frequency Plot

The next step is to reduce the resonance's peaks below the threshold level defined by the design goal. You can perform frequency domain simulation with ADS, Ansoft Designer, or HSPICE, as shown in Figure 2.26.

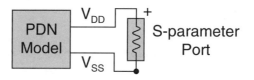

Figure 2.26   Typical Circuit for Impedance Computation

Simplified PDN Model

For an intuitive understanding of PDN, it is possible to reduce a complex PDN to simplified lumped-RLC elements, where each set of elements represents a different structure. Figure 2.27 shows a simplified model of a typical PDN circuit. The model has elements for each of the PDN network components including on-die capacitance, package and package decoupling, PCB and PCB decoupling, and bulk capacitance. ADS optimization or other tools can be used to adapt the simplified model to a complex structured extraction.

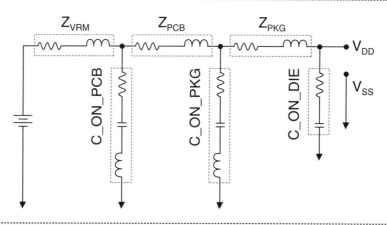

Figure 2.27   Simplified PDN Model

Chapter 3

Time Domain Analysis

This chapter describes a system-level time domain simulation, including a model of a PCI Express[†] interconnect channel constructed using the signal integrity modeling method discussed in Chapter 2. Performing time domain simulation requires that you know the following parameters:

- Driver model with corner cases
- Receiver load model
- Package model
- Connector and via models
- Printed circuit board (PCB) model with parametric variations
- Minimum acceptable voltage and time levels at the receiver pins
- Worst-case data pattern
- Mode conversions

This chapter covers the following topics:

- Excitation patterns of a PCI Express channel to measure the following terms: inter-symbol interference (ISI), crosstalk, and simultaneous switching outputs (SSO)
- Design of Experiment (DOE) analyses, focusing on finding the solution space based on the sensitivity of the sweep parameters
- Eye voltage margin and jitter modeling methods

Voltage Modes

For PCI Express differential busses, time domain data typically are measured in terms of three voltage modes:

■ Differential mode voltage, defined as $(V_{D+} - V_{D-})$

■ Common mode voltage, defined as $|(V_{D+} + V_{D-})| / (2 - V_{CM\_avg})$

■ Single-ended mode voltage, defined as V_{D+} or V_{D-}

The most important of the three modes is differential mode voltage. However, both single-ended mode voltage and common mode voltage are also significant, so you should know how to measure all three voltages.

Mode Conversion

Another phenomenon plays a significant role in the PCI Express differential busses. *Mode conversion* is defined as a transformation of the differential mode voltage to common mode voltage and vice versa. Mode conversion can result from imperfections in the driver and the PCI Express interconnect channel. The term *driver-to-receiver differential insertion loss* applies to driver differential mode excitation effect at the differential receiver, which is a limiting factor in PCI Express differential system performance. The term *driver-to-receiver common mode noise* applies to driver common mode excitation effect at the differential receiver, which reduces the margins and increases crosstalk and EMI effects.

Differential-to-common mode conversion can result from the following conditions:

■ Propagation delay that occurs within a differential pair due to length mismatch (Bansal 2004)

■ Uneven loading on a differential pair with respect to ground

■ Edge mismatch between D+ and D– on a driver's output

Differential-to-common mode conversion causes EMI noise (Bansal 2004). A small mismatch of a few picoseconds in either driver or interconnect balance can increase EMI by 10 to 100 times. Table 3.1 presents a list of mode conversion methods that can happen in PCI Express differential busses.

Table 3.1 Mode Conversions

Driver Mode Excitation	Conversion Method	Receiver Model
Driver Differential Mode	Diff → Diff	Receiver Differential Mode
Driver Common Mode	CM → CM	Receiver Common Mode
Driver Differential Mode	Diff → CM	Receiver Common Mode
Driver Common Mode	CM → Diff	Receiver Differential Mode

Transmitter Parameters

Typically, the transmitter output is characterized by an eye diagram, as shown in Figure 3.1. Table 3.2 lists the parameters that are represented in the eye diagram, along with other transmitter parameters that are defined in the *PCI Express Specification, Rev 1.1* (PCI-SIG 2004a).

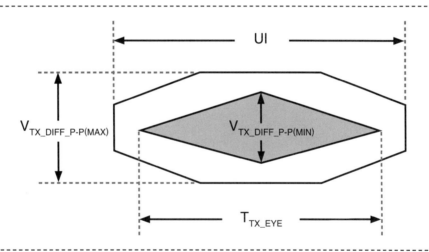

Figure 3.1 PCI Express[†] Transmitter Eye Diagram

In some cases, the transmitter output can be characterized by driver corners—RFFF, TTTT, and RSSS—rather than an eye diagram.

Table 3.2   PCI Express† Transmitter Parameters

TX Spec	Parameter	Min	Nom	Max	Units	Comments
UI	Unit Interval	399.88	400	400.12	ps	Each UI is 400ps ±300 PPM. UI does not account for SSC dictated variations.
$V_{TX\text{-}DIFF\,p\text{-}p}$	Differential Peak-to-Peak Output Voltage	0.800		1.2	V	$V_{TX\text{-}DIFFp\text{-}p} = 2^*\|V_{TX\text{-}D+} - V_{TX\text{-}D\text{-}}\|$ Measured at the package pins of the Transmitter.
$V_{TX\text{-}DE\text{-}Ratio}$	De-Emphasized Differential Output Voltage (Ratio)	−3.0	−3.5	−4.0	dB	This is the ratio of the $V_{tx\text{-}Diffp\text{-}p}$ of the second and following bits after a transition divided by the $V_{tx\text{-}Diffp\text{-}p}$ of the first bit after a transition.
$T_{TX\text{-}EYE}$	Minimum TX Eye Width	0.75			UI	The maximum transmitter jitter can be derived as $T_{TX\text{-}MAX\text{-}JITTER} = 1 - T_{TX\text{-}EYE} = 0.25\ UI$
$T_{TX\text{-}EYE\text{-}MEDIAN\text{-}to\text{-}MAX\text{-}JITTER}$	Maximum time between the jitter median and maximum deviation from the median			0.125	UI	Jitter is defined as the measurement variation of the crossing points ($T_{TX\text{-}DIFFp\text{-}p} = 0\ V$) in relation to recovered TX UI.
$T_{TX\text{-}RISE},\ T_{TX\text{-}FALL}$	D+/D− TX Output Rise/Fall Time	0.125			UI	Measured between 20%–80% at Transmitter package pins into a test load.
$V_{TX\text{-}CM\text{-}Acp}$	RMS AC Peak Common Mode Output Voltage			20	mV	$V_{TX\text{-}CM\text{-}AC} = RMS\ (\|V_{TX\text{-}D+} + V_{TX\text{-}D\text{-}}\|/2 - V_{TX\text{-}CM\text{-}DC})$ $V_{TX\text{-}CM\text{-}DC} = DC_{(avg)}$ of $\|V_{TX\text{-}D+} + V_{TX\text{-}D\text{-}}\|/2$

Table 3.2   PCI Express† Transmitter Parameters *(continued)*

TX Spec	Parameter	Min	Nom	Max	Units	Comments
$RL_{TX\text{-}DIFF}$	Differential Return Loss	10			dB	Measured over 50 MHz to 1.25 GHz
$RL_{TX\text{-}CM}$	Common Mode Return Loss	6			dB	Measured over 50 MHz to 1.25 GHz
$Z_{TX\text{-}DIFF\text{-}DC}$	DC Differential TX Impedance	80	100	120	Ω	TX DC Differential Mode Low impedance
$L_{TX\text{-}SKEW}$	Lane-to-Lane Output Skew			500 + 2 UI	ps	Static skew between any two Transmitter Lanes within a single Link
C_{TX}	AC Coupling Capacitor	75		200	nF	All transmitters shall be AC-coupled to the media.

Receiver Parameters

Table 3.3 lists the PCI Express receiver time and voltage parameters that are defined in the *PCI Express Specification, Rev 1.1* (PCI-SIG 2004a). The receiver eye parameters are measured at the pins of the receiver package as shown in Figure 3.2.

Table 3.3   PCI Express† Receiver Parameters

RX Spec	Parameter	Min	Nom	Max	Units	Comments
$V_{RX\text{-}DIFF\ p\text{-}p}$	Differential Input Peak-to-Peak Voltage	0.175		1.200	V	$V_{RX\text{-}DIFF\ p\text{-}p} = 2*$ $|V_{RX\text{-}D+} - V_{RX\text{-}D\text{-}}|$ Measured at the package pins of the Receiver.
$T_{RX\text{-}EYE}$	Minimum Receiver Eye Width	0.4			UI	The maximum interconnect media and Transmitter jitter that can be tolerated by the Receiver can be derived as $T_{RX\text{-}MAX\text{-}JITTER} = 1\text{-}T_{RX\text{-}EYE} = 0.6UI$

Table 3.3   PCI Express† Receiver Parameters *(continued)*

RX Spec	Parameter	Min	Nom	Max	Units	Comments
$T_{RX\text{-}EYE\text{-}MEDIAN\text{-}to\text{-}MAX\text{-}JITTER}$	Maximum time between the jitter median and maximum deviation from the median			0.3	UI	Jitter is defined as the measurement variation of the crossing points ($T_{RX\text{-}DIFF\ p\text{-}p}$ = 0 V) in relation to recovered TX UI.
$V_{RX\text{-}CM\text{-}ACp}$	AC Peak Common Mode Input Voltage			150	mV	$V_{RX\text{-}CM\text{-}AC} = \|V_{RX\text{-}D+} + V_{RX\text{-}D\text{-}}\| /2 - V_{RX\text{-}CM\text{-}DC})$ $V_{RX\text{-}CM\text{-}DC} = DC_{(avg)}$ of $\|V_{RX\text{-}D+} + V_{RX\text{-}D\text{-}}\| /2$
$RL_{RX\text{-}DIFF}$	Differential Return Loss	10			dB	Measured over 50 MHz to 1.25 GHz
$RL_{RX\text{-}CM}$	Common Mode Return Loss	6			dB	Measured over 50 MHz to 1.25 GHz
$Z_{RX\text{-}DIFF\text{-}DC}$	DC Differential Input Impedance	80	100	120	Ω	RX DC Differential Mode impedance
$V_{RX\text{-}IDLE\text{-}DET\text{-}DIFF\ p\text{-}p}$	Electrical Idle Detect Threshold	65		175	mV	$V_{RX\text{-}IDLE\text{-}DET\text{-}DIFF\ p\text{-}p} = 2*\|V_{RX\text{-}D+} - V_{RX\text{-}D\text{-}}\|$ Measured at the package pins of the Receiver.
$L_{RX\text{-}SKEW}$	Total Skew			20	ns	Skew across all Lanes on a Link. This includes variation in the length of a SKP ordered set (e.g. COM and one to five SKP Symbols) at the RX as well as any delay differences arising from the interconnect itself.

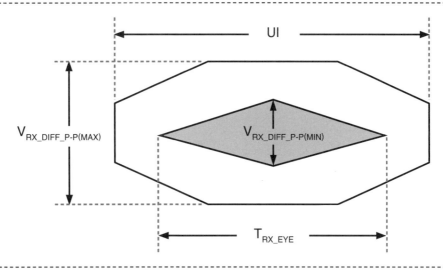

Figure 3.2 PCI Express[†] Receiver Eye Diagram

Excitation Pattern

PCI Express differential busses use the 8b/10b coding scheme, which limits data patterns to a maximum of five consecutive ones or zeros, and controls the ones and zeros disparities between 10-bit characters. Several data patterns can be used to excite the PCI Express differential busses to measure the effects of inter-symbol interference (ISI), crosstalk, and simultaneous switching output (SSO) on the PCI Express interconnect channel and power delivery network.

Alternating Comma Pattern

```
101000011, 0101111100, ...
```

CJT Pattern

```
COMMA, x95, xb5, xb5, COMMA, X95, xb6, ...
COMMA, xb6, x36, x36, x7e, x7e, x7e, ...
```

TS1 Pattern

```
1010000011, 0010111001, 0010101110, 0010111001,
0010101110, 0010111001, 1010101010, ...
1010101010, 1010101010, 1010101010, ...
1010101010, 0101111001, 1101000110, ...
```

ISI Pattern

The alternating Comma pattern can excite the worst-case inter-symbol interference (ISI). This ISI can take place in two forms in PCI Express signaling: driver-to-receiver frequency-dependent loss and reflection loss. In both cases, ISI is defined by a voltage shift due to the presence of the previous values of the symbol driven onto the channel. The worst-case loss dependent ISI occurs when a one is embedded in a block of zeros, or vice versa.

Crosstalk Pattern

A PCI Express interconnect channel can be routed using either of two methods: a non-interleaved transmitter pair, which is recommended for stripline layout, and an interleaved transmitter-receiver pair, which typically is used for microstrip line layout. The worst-case crosstalk requires the driver and receiver to excite with an appropriate even and odd mode excitation pattern.

Figure 3.3 and Figure 3.4 show the worst-case crosstalk data pattern applied to non-interleaved and interleaved routing methods, respectively. The maximum time of flight difference between D+ and D− of the victim pair occurs when the D+ of the victim pair generates odd coupling to D− of the aggressor #1 pair, while the D− of the victim pair generates even coupling with the D− of the aggressor #2 pair.

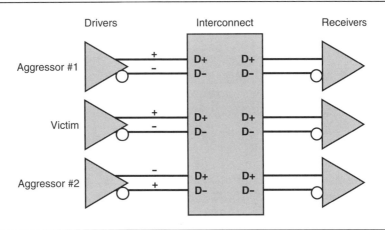

Figure 3.3   Non-interleaved Transmit and Receiver Pairs Layout Model

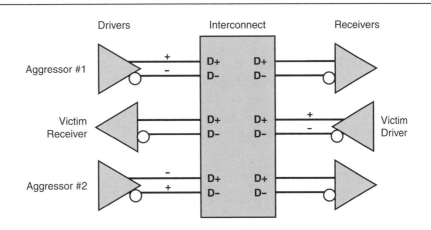

Figure 3.4   Interleaved Transmit and Receiver Pairs Layout Model

For this design, you also must skew the aggressor's phase with respect to the victim pair, especially in the case of the interleaved layout method, as shown in Figure 3.4. Typically, the worst-case crosstalk excitation occurs when the two aggressors are in phase with each other but 90 degrees out of phase behind the victim pair.

SSO Pattern

To perform SSO worst-case data pattern excitation of PCI Express differential busses, you need to know the resonance frequency of the PDN and the peaks of the PDN impedance versus frequency profile. An SSO data pattern must be chosen close to those frequency peaks of PDN impedance, because the maximum spectral energy is generated at those frequencies. PCI Express differential busses use the 8b/10b coding scheme, which limits the full amplitude peak to a frequency corresponding to five consecutive bit times. At a 2.5 GT/s data rate, this frequency is 250 MHz. However, the 8b/10b coding scheme exhibits lower amplitude spectral components below 250 MHz due to zeros and ones disparity that can span multiple characters.

For more about PDN analysis and PDN impedance peaks, see the "Power Delivery Analysis" section in Chapter 2.

Data Bit-Stream Length

The type of analysis determines the length of the data bit-stream. For example, a worst-case ISI can be determined by a single one or zero embedded in long data bit-stream of zeros or ones. Similarly, crosstalk can be captured by generating and exciting worst-case even and odd mode coupling to the victim pair. For PDN or SSO and PLL tracking, you might need a longer data pattern in combination with longer simulation time.

DOE Analysis

Design of Experiment (DOE) is a mathematical method that determines interrelations between variables and predicts outcomes from experiments using those variables. In the most common context, the experiments represent a stochastic set of outcomes from a given set of input. For the simulation paradigm, the outcomes are deterministic and used to create a predictive equation for new values of input variables without actually simulating those cases. Using this predictive capability, it becomes possible to determine the limits of the predictive equation and thus define a solution space for variables that correspond to those limits.

DOE computes the n-dimensional surface response where n is the number of input parameters. The output surface response can determine the performance of the system simulation model for any set of input parameter values that are defined initially within a minimum and maximum range. After computing the surface response, DOE tools find the output values by mapping parameters into the surface response. DOE minimizes the number of simulation runs, and allows you to understand the effect of the input parameters on the output simulation results.

To run the DOE method, you perform the following steps:

- Define a system time domain model, using any simulation tool such as ADS, HSPICE, or Ansoft Designer/Nexxim.

- Define input parameters with a given minimum and maximum range.

- Define fixed parameters such as process corners.

- Define input worst-case data patterns.

- Define a DOE curve fitting order.

Figure 3.5 is a flowchart of the DOE method.

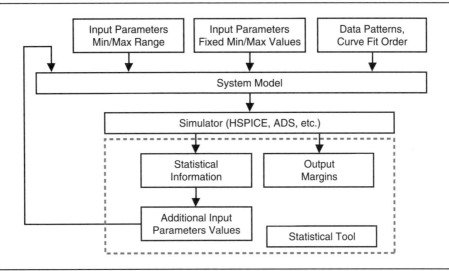

Figure 3.5   DOE Flowchart

DOE Input Parameters

Table 3.4 lists typical input parameters for DOE time domain analysis. The primary input parameters are the driver and receiver parameters, and each of the interconnect components that are subject to variations with an impact on the signal integrity at the receiver pins.

Table 3.4 Typical DOE Input Parameters

	MAX	MIN	Units
Slew	0.04	0.125	UI
Tx Term R	53	47	Ohms
Tx Term C	1.30	1.00	pF
Tx Swing	1.2	0.8	Volts
dB demp	4	3	dB
Rx Term R	53	47	Ohms
Rx Term C	0.9	1.3	pF
Z Mb	Max	Min	Ohms
Mb Length	0.25	15	Inches
Z Cd	Max	Min	Ohms
Cd Length	0.25	4.5	Inches
VIA Count	6	2	N/A

You need to define the input parameters with minimum and maximum ranges. The limits define the boundaries for the n-dimensional surface response. The outside of the boundary surface response cannot use by extrapolating method. The outside of these boundary limits for the surface response is not accurate by using any extrapolating method.

Order of Curve Fitting

You must define the order of the curve fitting to map the curve into the surface response. Typically, a quadratic order is fine for computational efficiency and accuracy. If a quadratic does not fit well, then an expect phenomena is likely and should be investigated.

Drive Inputs

Three different corners can characterize the driver: fast (RFFF), typical (TTTT), and slow (RSSS). The parasitic parameters of the driver mounted in a package must be defined for DOE time domain analysis.

Interconnect Inputs

Interconnect parameters are usually defined by the interconnect manu-facturer. For example, PCB traces usually are defined in terms of imped-ance variations as well as the trace thickness. Similarly, vias, sockets, and connectors can be defined in terms of a maximum and minimum lumped capacitance and inductance.

Receiver Parameters

Receiver parameters—the receiver package and silicon parasitics—include package traces, vias, package ball and pins, and so forth.

DOE Example

Figure 3.6 presents an abstracted sample platform that includes the die-to-die simulation model. After you have built the model, you perform the following steps to run DOE time domain analysis.

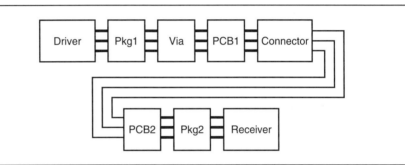

Figure 3.6   Sample Platform model

Define the Input Parameters within their Minimum and Maximum Ranges

This sample test specifies 11 input parameters, including segment differ-ential impedance, segment length, transmitter and receiver impedance and capacitance.

Table 3.5 lists these input parameters and their minimum and maximum ranges. Figure 3.7 shows the driver and receiver model with these input parameters highlighted.

Table 3.5   DOE Input Parameters with Minimum and Maximum Ranges

Tx Parameters	Min	Max	Unit
R_term_tx	45	55	Ohm
C_term_tx	0.4	1.3	pF
dB_demph.	3	6	dB
Rx Parameters			
R_term_rx	40	55	Ohm
C_term_rx	0.4	1.5	pF
Package Parameters			
Len_pkg1	1.2	2.2	Inch
Z0d_pkg1	87	104	Ohm
PCB Parameters			
Len_pcb1	10	15	Inch
Z0d_pcb1	70	105	Ohm
Package2 parameters			
Len_pkg2	1.2	3	Inch
Z0d_pkg2	80	104	Ohm

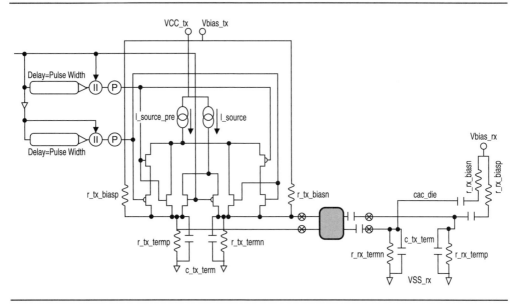

Figure 3.7   Driver and Receiver Parameters

Run the Statistical Software Program to Determine the Degree of Fit

The statistical software program allows you to fit the surface response to any degree of freedom.

Figure 3.8 shows the degree of fit and statistical software program results. If the number of simulation runs had been insufficient, the variance plot would show the points that are scattered around the diagonal axis.

Choose Aggressor and Victim Data Patterns to Excite Worst-case System Simulation Including ISI and Crosstalk

For example:

```
Victim data pattern     Aggressor data pattern
0010110110              1010110010
1010001011              0101100101
1101000100              1110001011
1011001101              1010001011
```

Figure 3.9 presents sample output results. In Figure 3.9, each sub-graph plots the variation of an output parameter as a function of one of the input parameters. The vertical lines present the current value of parameter. The horizontal lines present value of parameter at the current settings. The slope of the line indicates the sensitivity of the parameter.

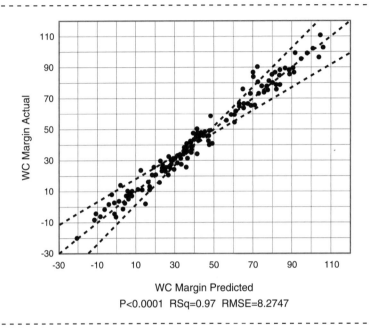

Figure 3.8 Curve Fitting Output Results

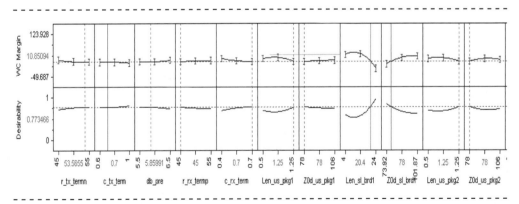

Figure 3.9 Typical Output Results

Determine the Worst-case Corners

The worst-case corners are determined by optimizing for maximum values for each of the major output parameters. By comparing the maximum and minimum output values against the PCI Express specification, you can determine the worst-case input parameters within the simulation.

Choose the Worst-case Input Parameters

The final step is to choose the worst-case input parameters by loading those inputs into a time domain simulator and measuring the output eye diagram. As shown in Figure 3.10, the eye opening is almost closed, and the diagram represents the worst-case corners.

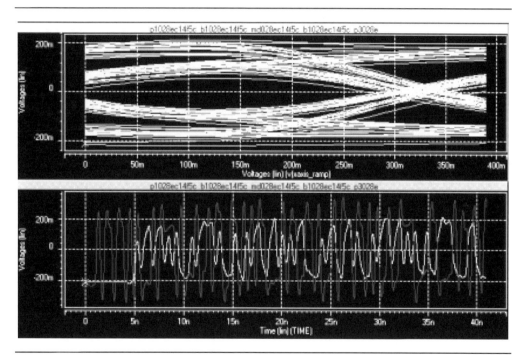

Figure 3.10 Worst-case Eye Opening

Margin Mode Computation

In determining the magnitude of the output parameters for PCI Express time domain analysis, you will rely on these margin mode computations:

- Differential mode margin, including eye voltage and time margins
- Common mode voltage margin at the receiver
- Common mode voltage margin at the driver

For example, to determine the differential mode eye voltage and time margins, you compare the simulated voltage and time margins against the specification. As shown in Figure 3.11, V_{RX_DIFF} – $V_{RX\_DIFF\_SPEC}$ represents the voltage margin between a typical simulation run and the PCI Express receiver specification. Similarly, T_{RX_EYE} – T_{SPEC_EYE} is the time margin between a typical simulation run and the specification. Both eye voltage and time margins must be positive.

In addition to the differential mode eye voltage and time margins, you must measure the common mode voltage at the driver and receiver pins.

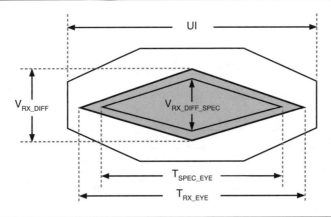

Figure 3.11   Sample Receiver Eye Voltage and Time Margins

Eye Measuring

In performing eye measurement for a PCI Express interconnect channel, you must define a die-to-die model platform in combination with the system board and possible add-in card. This methodology includes the measurement techniques, the data extraction, and the jitter calculation for the end-to-end system platform using the simulation model given in Chapter 2.

The jitter margin is determined with respect to the driver and receiver compliance eye as shown in Figure 3.1 and Figure 3.2, respectively.

Unless otherwise specified, the differential mode voltage between D+ and D– signal pairs is the specification eye value. You must consider the driver uncertainties at the simulated receiver eye. These unaccounted quantities, or uncertainties, are called jitter and must be added to the receiver eye. Figure 3.12 illustrates the minimum receiver eye requirement, showing the receiver compliance eye with driver uncertainties.

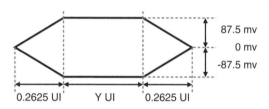

Figure 3.12   Receiver Compliance Eye Diagram with Driver Uncertainties

In Figure 3.12, YUI represents the amount of driver jitter, which is unaccounted for in the system simulation. For example, the simulation data can subtract the resultant simulated data from the driver test load. This effectively removes all driver jitter from the simulation. In this case, YUI represents the entire allowable driver jitter as 0.25 UI. The receiver jitter shown in Figure 3.12 is actually combination of the two jitters: receiver jitter, which is 0.4 UI, and clock jitter, which is 0.125 UI. For more detail in the clock jitter refer to *PCI Express Card Electromechanical Specification* (PCI-SIG 2004b).

To capture the system margin, perform the following steps:

1. From the differential waveform at the receiver package ball, measure the time that the waveform crosses the 0 mV point.

2. Repeat step 1 for the test load simulation with the simulated data pattern used in step 1.

3. Subtract the time obtained from the test load simulation from the time domain obtained from the system simulation. Figure 3.13 shows this subtraction method. Tf1 and Tf2 are the flight times of the data signal through the system interconnects.

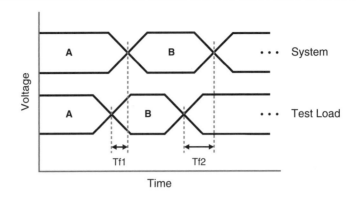

Figure 3.13   Flight Time Calculation

The difference between the maximum flight time and minimum flight time is the overall jitter. You also need to determine the jitter median across 250 UI. The number of transitions seen within the 250 UI may vary, depending on the data pattern used in the simulation.

Figure 3.14 shows the calculation of the jitter margin. The maximum flight time and the minimum flight time must be within 0.1125 UI of the jitter median. You use the jitter median to find the worst-case voltage margin. In Figure 3.14, the receiver compliance eye diagram is centered in the simulation eye diagram at jitter median +0.5 UI. The worst-case voltage margin is the minimum difference between the voltage on the eye mask and the simulated eye.

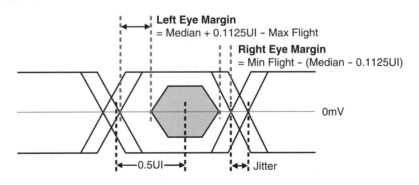

Figure 3.14   Jitter Median Calculation

System Model and Add-in Card Topologies

You should define the system sweep parameters based on your specific design. To cover all modes of operation on the end-to-end PCI Express simulation, you must consider four topologies. Each simulation model needs to include at least the three differential pairs to accurately simulate coupling crosstalk. Figure 3.15 shows the non-interleaved topologies for add-in card RX, add-in card TX, system board RX, and system board TX topologies.

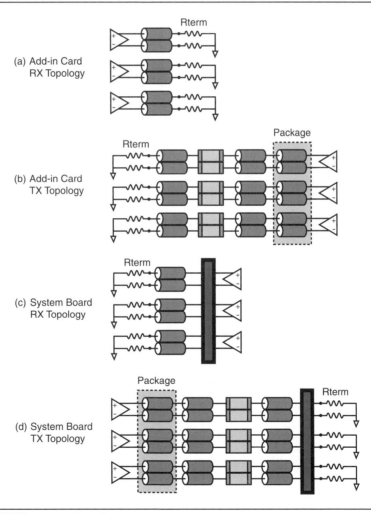

Figure 3.15   Four Topologies

Eye Diagram and Compliance Jitter

Jitter compliance should include some amount of simulation guard band for un-simulated effects. Figure 3.16 shows a methodology to account for jitter compliance in the eye diagram. The compliance jitter values can be accounted for during the post-processing of the simulation results. The jitter numbers shown in Figure 3.16 show an example of the compliance eye jitter.

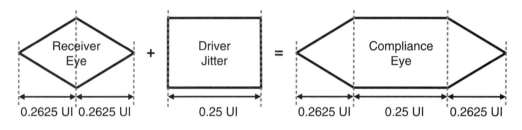

Figure 3.16 Compliance Jitter Calculation

Driver and Receiver Eye Requirements

In applying the proper stimulus and using the PCI Express driver with determined de-emphasis level, the transmit TX topologies must follow the *PCI Express Base Specification* (PC-SIG 2004a). On the other hand, the receiver RX topologies require custom driver interfaces that emulate the appropriate voltage magnitudes.

Table 3.6 lists the driver and receiver eye requirements for each of the four topologies. Keep in mind that the compliance jitter calculation and diagrams are different for each of these four topologies. You should pay attention to the fact that the driver and receiver eye requirements for the four topologies are more than the driver and receiver specification given in Table 3.3. The extra budgets are considered for both the driver and receiver compliance eyes to cover two things: the extra interconnect for add-in card or system interconnects, and the clock-recovery jitter. For detailed information about these numbers, refer to the *PCI Express Card Electromechanical Specification* (PCI-SIG 2004b).

Table 3.6 Driver and Receiver Eye Requirements

Topology	Receiver Eye	Driver Jitter	Compliance Eye
Add-in Card RX	0.2625 UI	0.4175 UI	0.2625+0.4175+0.2625 UI
Add-in Card TX	0.3425 UI	0.25 UI	0.3425+0.25+0.3425 UI
System Board RX	0.2625 UI	0.315 UI	0.2625+0.315+0.2625 UI
System Board TX	0.2912 UI	0.25 UI	0.2912+0.25+0.2912 UI

Table 3.7 lists the required compliance eye heights, which are need to drive into the card or the system board for four topologies. Keep in mind that the required compliance eye heights that drive into the card or system board are different for each of these four topologies.

Table 3.7 Receiver Eye Height Requirements

Topology	Minimum Receiver Eye	Minimum Receiver Eye with De-emphasis
Add-in Card RX	238 mv	219 mv
Add-in Card TX	514 mv	360 mv
System Board RX	445 mv	312 mv
System Board TX	274 mv	253 mv

Driver and Receiver Simulation Topology

For a unique PCI Express simulation model that includes both driver and receiver package combinations, the R-terms are replaced by the receiver package and dies model. As shown in Figure 3.17, eye measurements must be taken at the receiver die pad. Since the measurement is done at the die pad, the receiver compliance eye, or pad eye, must be adjusted to allow budget for the receiver package. By and large, this adjustment involves reducing the height and width of the compliance eye, as determined by the receiver input sensitivity.

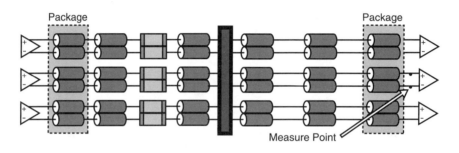

Figure 3.17 Driver and Receiver Topology

Chapter 4

Frequency Domain Analysis

Frequency domain analysis is well-suited for simulating and validating a PCI Express interconnect channel at either the system platform or package level. Compared to time domain analysis, frequency domain analysis offers the following advantages:

- Easier simulation and validation processes using vector network analyzer VNA data

- A solid and robust method of finding the worst-case pattern of the crosstalk coupling and power delivery

- Shorter simulation process time, compared with the number of time domain simulation runs

- Calculation of the desired output S-parameter data such as loss and reflection over the frequency range of operation

- Testing S-parameter outputs against the frequency data specifications

Frequency domain analysis provides an easy method for combining the cascaded electrical segment components, yielding the end-to-end characteristics of the system platform. The output data of the frequency domain analysis is an S-parameter matrix that is measured for passive electrical structure. S-parameter data can characterize the passive electrical structures with such quantities as reflection coefficient (Bansal 2004), insertion loss, and input impedance. S-parameter data can also characterize the interaction coupling between the signal pairs at both near and far ends of the interconnect platform, known as near-end crosstalk (NEXT) and far-end crosstalk (FEXT), respectively.

Single-ended and Differential S-parameters

Figure 4.1 presents a single-ended four-port interconnect system that can be characterized by a 4X4 S-parameter data matrix, as follows.

Equation 4.1   4X4 S-parameter Data Matrix

$$\begin{pmatrix} b_1 \\ b_2 \\ b_3 \\ b_4 \end{pmatrix} = \begin{pmatrix} S_{11} & S_{12} & S_{13} & S_{14} \\ S_{21} & S_{22} & S_{23} & S_{24} \\ S_{31} & S_{32} & S_{33} & S_{34} \\ S_{41} & S_{42} & S_{43} & S_{44} \end{pmatrix} \begin{pmatrix} a_1 \\ a_2 \\ a_3 \\ a_4 \end{pmatrix}$$

As shown in Figure 4.1, S-parameter matrix data define the transmitted power and the reflected voltage at each end of the circuit model. Vectors [b1, b2, b3, b4] represent the reflected excitation signals, and vectors [a1, a2, a3, a4] represent incident excitation signals. Each element of vectors a and b is the voltage or current of a signal moving *toward* or *away from* the device, respectively.

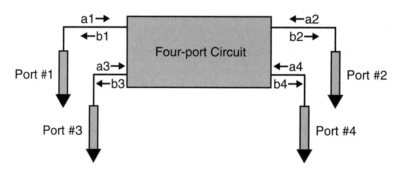

Figure 4.1   Four-port Interconnect System

The practical advantage of using S-parameter data over other frequency-dependent parameters such as Z-parameters and Y-parameters is the ease of measurement that is gained using VNA equipment. Measurements for Z-parameters and Y-parameters require open and short circuits that are very difficult to obtain. More complex single-ended circuit topologies, including many coupled pairs, can be formulated in a similar fashion; of course, the number of matrix elements increases according to the number of ports.

For the single-ended mode method shown in Figure 4.1, all ports are referenced to the ground. In contrast, in the differential mode method, the signal on one line of the coupled pair is referenced to the other line, or a signal propagates between the coupled pair—as opposed to propagating between one line and ground. However, practical implementation of the differential pair requires a ground plane or other global reference plane. This reference plane allows another mode to propagate, called common mode propagation. The differential mode voltage and current can be defined as follows:

$$V_{dm} = v_1 - v_2$$

In differential voltage mode, a current that is equal in both magnitude and phase enters into the positive terminal and leaves the negative terminal. The differential current mode is defined as:

$$I_{dm} = (i_1 - i_2)/2$$

The common mode voltage and current can be defined by the following equations:

$$V_{cm} = (v_1 + v_2)/2$$

$$I_{cm} = i_1 + i_2$$

Figure 4.2 shows a four-port network that includes both differential mode and common mode.

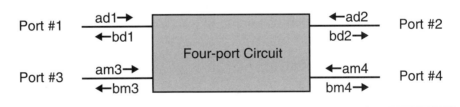

Figure 4.2   Four-port Circuit with Both Differential and Common Mode

The following equation defines generalized S-parameter matrix data for a four-port network such as that shown in Figure 4.2.

Equation 4.2   S-parameter Matrix Data for Four-port Network

$$
\begin{pmatrix} bd1 \\ bd2 \\ \hline bc1 \\ bc2 \end{pmatrix} = \begin{pmatrix} Sdd & Sdc \\ Scd & Scc \end{pmatrix} \begin{pmatrix} ad1 \\ ad2 \\ \hline ac1 \\ ac2 \end{pmatrix}
$$

Sdd represents the differential S-parameter matrix data, and *Scc* is the common mode S-parameter matrix data. *Sdc* and *Scd* are the mode-conversion or cross-mode S-parameter matrix data. Vector [*bd1*, *bd2*] is the differential mode reflected wave, and vector [*bc1*, *bc2*] is the common mode reflected wave. Vector [*ad1*, *ad2*] is the differential mode incident wave, and vector [*ac1*, *ac2*] is the common mode incident wave.

For the differential mode signal, you can reformulate Equation 4.1—the original equation—so that the signal at port 3 is the negative of that at port 1:

Equation 4.3   S-parameter Matrix for Differential Mode Signal

$$
\begin{pmatrix} b1 \\ b2 \\ b3 \\ b4 \end{pmatrix} = \begin{pmatrix} S11 & S12 & S13 & S14 \\ S21 & S22 & S23 & S24 \\ S31 & S32 & S33 & S34 \\ S41 & S42 & S43 & S44 \end{pmatrix} \begin{pmatrix} a1 \\ a2 \\ -a1 \\ a4 \end{pmatrix}
$$

By terminating the far ends with 50 Ω, you have the relationship $a_2 = a_4 = 0$. Solving the equation for the differential mode reflection coefficient, DS_{11}, and differential mode insertion loss, DS_{12}, gives the following results:

$DS_{11} = (S_{11} + S_{33} - S_{13} - S_{31}) / 2$

$DS_{12} = (S_{12} - S_{32} - S_{41} + S_{34}) / 2$

Frequency Domain Interconnect Model

PCI Express differential interconnect busses can be characterized using S-parameter data measured at the driver package and receiver package pins. In time domain analysis, you measure the time and voltage openings of the eye at each of the points that are at the same points that are defined in the specification. In frequency domain analysis, S-parameter data also must be measured at the same points.

Parameters of Measurement and Simulation

In both frequency domain and time domain analysis, three major parameters are required to measure or simulate for PCI Express differential busses:

∎ Differential mode voltage at the receiver

∎ Common mode voltage at the receiver

∎ Reflected common mode voltage at driver

In most cases, the measured data are same for both time domain and the frequency domain analyses. In the time domain method, eye openings are measured at the receiver and driver package pins to verify the three measured parameters against the specifications. In the frequency domain method, the magnitude and phase of the S-parameter data are measured at the same locations.

Multi-pair Aggressor-Victim Model

In frequency domain analysis, you must consider a tradeoff among accuracy, model complexity, and computation efficiency. In the time domain analysis, too, tradeoffs are required in the simulation model, including the two-aggressor signal pairs and one-victim signal pair. Frequency domain analysis requires the same topology that was used in time domain for correlation study. A topology with one-victim signal pair and a two-aggressor signal pair should capture over 96 percent of the crosstalk coupling. Figure 4.3 shows a PCI Express interconnect topology with a two-aggressor pair and single victim pair. This model has a 12-port network circuit and results in a 12x12 S-parameter data matrix.

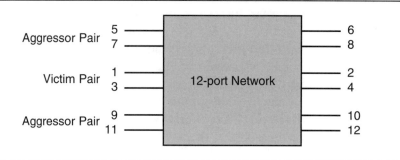

Figure 4.3   12-Port Network

This topology can be simplified as shown in Figure 4.4. In the simplified topology, the 12-port circuit, including two aggressor pairs, is scaled to an 8-port circuit with a single aggressor pair.

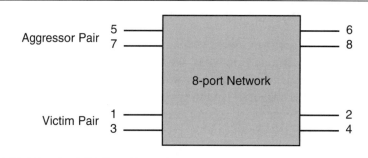

Figure 4.4   8-Port Network

You can use this simplified method in PCI Express differential interconnect busses, when you have more aggressor pairs. For example, if a connector model includes the four neighboring aggressors, you can scale down into two aggressors by doubling the aggressor-victim crosstalk coefficients. The simplified relationship between the two instances of matrix data can be shown as follows:

$S'_{ij} = 2 * S_{ij}$

S'_{ij} refers to the scaled crosstalk coefficients between the two differential pairs; for example, you would have the S15 and S38 pair and so on.

Excitation Matrix

The following 8x8 S-parameter data matrix represents the simplified model shown in Figure 4.4.

Equation 4.4   8X8 S-parameter data matrix

$$
\begin{pmatrix} b1 \\ b2 \\ b3 \\ b4 \\ b5 \\ b6 \\ b7 \\ b8 \end{pmatrix} =
\begin{pmatrix}
S11 & S12 & S13 & S14 & S15 & S16 & S17 & S17 \\
S21 & S22 & S23 & S24 & S25 & S26 & S27 & S28 \\
S31 & S32 & S33 & S34 & S35 & S36 & S37 & S38 \\
S41 & S42 & S43 & S44 & S45 & S46 & S47 & S48 \\
S51 & S52 & S53 & S54 & S55 & S56 & S57 & S58 \\
S61 & S62 & S63 & S64 & S65 & S66 & S67 & S68 \\
S71 & S72 & S73 & S74 & S75 & S76 & S77 & S78 \\
S81 & S82 & S83 & S84 & S85 & S86 & S87 & s88
\end{pmatrix}
\begin{pmatrix}
ad + ac \\ 0 \\ -ad + ac \\ 0 \\ \pm ad + ac \\ 0 \\ \mp ad + ac \\ 0
\end{pmatrix}
$$

In this equation, *ad* is the differential mode signal measured at the driver with respect to the ground. *ac* is the common mode signal at the driver's output as measured with respect to ground (Bansal 2004). The application of +/– to input #5 indicates that the aggressor could be either in or out of phase with respect to the victim line. Similarly, the –/+ on input #7 indicates that inputs #5 and #7 are always complementary to one another.

Assumptions for all driver outputs are that the magnitudes and phases of the aggressor and victim input signals and the common mode signal are equal. The input values of a2, a4, a6 and a8 are zero, indicating that the system is driven from the inputs and all signals are terminated at their ends with 50 Ω.

Solving this equation for the *b2* and *b4* transmitted signals and for the *b1* and *b3* reflected signals yields the following values:

$$b2 = (ad + ac)S21 + (-ad + ac)S23 + 2(\pm ad + ac)S25 - 2(\pm ad - ac)S27$$

$$b4 = (ad + ac)S41 + (-ad + ac)S43 + 2(\pm ad + ac)S45 - 2(\pm ad - ac)S47$$

$$b1 = (ad + ac)S11 + (-ad + ac)S13 + 2(\pm ad + ac)S15 - 2(\pm ad - ac)S17$$

$$b3 = (ad + ac)S31 + (-ad + ac)S33 + 2(\pm ad + ac)S35 - 2(\pm ad - ac)S37$$

These equations are based on the single-ended S-parameter data matrix. The factor of two on the last pairs shows the impact of two aggressors by approximating the scale factor by 2x of intra-pair coupling coefficients.

Differential Mode Voltage

As stated previously, the three key measurement parameters for frequency domain analysis are differential mode voltage at the receiver and common mode voltage at both the driver and receiver.

The differential mode voltage ($b2 - b4$) can be written as follows:

$$b2 - b4 = m \mid ad(S21 + S43 - S23 - S41) \pm 2ad(S25 - S27 - S45 + S47)$$
$$+ ac(S21 - S43 + S23 - S41) + 2ac(S25 - S45 + S27 - S47) \mid$$

This equation leads to the following observations.

- ■ (S21 + S43) represents the sum of differential forward insertion loss through the interconnect. For matched differential pairs, S21 and S43 are equal in phase and magnitude. By having any length mismatch, S21 + S43 shows a sharp dip at a frequency that corresponds to the length difference between the two differential traces. The sharp dip could be caused by the phase differences.

- ■ (-S23 - S41) defines the coupling within a differential pair, an intra-pair coupling. A tightly coupled microstrip differential pair has much lower loss than two isolated differential traces, because the intra-pair crosstalk decreases the effective insertion loss. This term is negligible for stripline, and it is important in microstrip line.

- ■ The other four terms, S25, S45, S27, and S47, represent pair-to-pair crosstalk, an inter-pair crosstalk. The factor of two shows the scaling of the two aggressors to one aggressor on either side of the victim.

- ■ The *m* element is a mismatch factor that accounts for any impedance mismatch between the channel and the driver or receiver impedance.

Phase Components of S-parameter Data

In frequency domain analysis, you can measure phase difference to verify the impacts of crosstalk in the PCI Express differential busses. The crosstalk impacts can be measured with two parameters: a phase versus frequency or, more usefully, a delay delta versus frequency profile. The impact of the delta delay or phase delay on the eye margin is independent of the channel loss.

The phase difference can be expressed by the following equation:

$$\Delta \Phi = T * 0.0055 * phase(b2 - b4)$$

where T is the bit-cell period, and the constant 0.0055 converts the phase (in degrees) into a time quantity.

Common Mode Voltages

The following equations give the common mode voltages at the receiver and driver, respectively:

$$b2 + b4 = m \mid ad(S21 - S43 - S23 + S41) \pm 2ad(S25 - S27 + S45 - S47)$$
$$+ ac(S21 + S43 + S23 + S41) + 2ac(S25 + S27 + S45 + S47) \mid$$

$$b1 + b3 = m \mid ad(S11 - S33 + S31 - S13) \pm 2ad(S51 - S17 + S35 - S37)$$
$$+ ac(S11 + S33 + S31 + S13) + 2ac(S15 + S17 + S35 + S37) \mid$$

For common mode voltages, the terms are summed, rather than differenced as in differential mode voltage.

The terms ($S11$ – $S33$) represent the return loss that is introduced in the driver common mode voltage. The other terms are defined in previous equations.

Theoretically, since the magnitudes and phases of $S21$ and $S43$, $S23$, and $S41$ are equal, any common mode voltage driven on the inputs must be cancelled by the differential input subtraction at the input of the receiver. By having any length mismatch or nonsymmetric rise and fall times, the impacts of length mismatch or nonsymmetric waveforms appear on the $S21$, $S43$, $S23$ and $S41$ terms, and consequently, on the common mode voltage transformed into differential voltage. Thus, the mismatch affects signal integrity.

You should minimize the length mismatch and input mismatch as much as possible. The mismatch factor *m* accounts for the lack of an ideal impedance-match between the driver and the interconnect, or between the interconnect and the receiver. The +/- sign reflects the aggressor polarity excitation.

Keep in mind that magnitudes must be obtained by adding complex components. Adding a sum of magnitudes does not work suitably. This distinction is particularly important if any mismatches cause the phase not to be equal.

Impedance Mismatch

In Equations 4.1 and 4.2, *m* represents mismatch impedance between the driver and interconnect, and between the interconnect and receiver. If you have any mismatches, you can account for the coefficient *m* of those mismatches in the equations. The following two equations define m_{MIN} and m_{MAX} as follows:

Equation 4.5   Minimum Impedance Mismatch

$$m_{MIN} = 1 + \frac{Z_{min\_load} - Z_{max\_trace}}{Z_{min\_load} + Z_{max\_trace}}$$

Equation 4.6   Maximum Impedance Mismatch

$$m_{MAX} = 1 + \frac{Z_{max\_load} - Z_{min\_trace}}{Z_{max\_load} + Z_{min\_trace}}$$

In these equations, Z_{min_load} is the minimum load impedance 35 Ω, Z_{min_trace} is the minimum interconnect impedance 42.5 Ω, Z_{max_load} is the maximum load impedance 70 Ω, and Z_{max_trace} is the maximum interconnect impedance 57 Ω.

The m_{MIN} mismatch coefficient is applied as a scale factor into (b2–b4) term to obtain the worst-case mismatch differential insertion loss. m_{MAX} is applied in (b2+b4) term to obtain the largest common mode voltage at the receiver. Using a channel tolerance of 50 Ω ±15 percent and a receiver impedance of 50 Ω ±30 percent, we calculate m_{MIN} and m_{MAX} to be –2.5 dB and +1.9 dB, respectively.

Multi-segment Topology and the ABCD Method

The PCI Express electrical interconnect channel includes many electrical interconnect elements, such as driver parasitic and impedance, package, socket, connector, printed circuit board, and receiver parasitic. In a well-behaved system such as those presented earlier in this chapter, the crosstalk terms are doubled, based on the simple assumption that the models are behaved linearly. However, for a general interconnect with multi-segment elements that have different impedances, simply doing the multiplication or addition of the individual S-parameters matrices is not correct and the results can be misleading. For such interconnects, the ABCD method is particularly well-suited for combining the S-parameters of the PCI Express channel.

Chain or ABCD Matrix Method

The chain or ABCD matrix method represents a two-port network in terms of input and output voltages and currents, as shown in Figure 4.5.

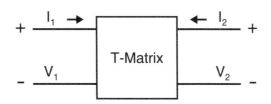

Figure 4.5   Chain Matrix

This method can be extended to an N-port network. The main advantages of the ABCD method (Ramo 1993) are computational accuracy and efficiency for the cascaded multi-segment interconnection networks.

This method is suitable for computing S-parameter data in a multi-segment topology. To compute the ABCD matrix of a cascaded multi-segment model, you simply multiply the ABCD matrices of each individual segments together. Equation 4.7 gives the relationship between input and output voltages and currents. In Equation 4.7, T is the ABCD matrix.

Equation 4.7   ABCD Matrix

$$\begin{pmatrix} V_1 \\ I_1 \end{pmatrix} = \begin{pmatrix} A & B \\ C & D \end{pmatrix} \begin{pmatrix} V_2 \\ -I_2 \end{pmatrix} = T \begin{pmatrix} V_2 \\ -I_2 \end{pmatrix}$$

The ABCD matrix of a cascaded multi-segment model is equal to the product of the ABCD matrices of the each segment, as shown in Figure 4.6.

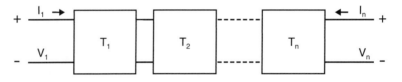

Figure 4.6   Multi-Segment Interconnect

Equation 4.8 gives the relationship between the input and output of a multi-segment interconnect.

Equation 4.8   Relationship between Input and Output of Multi-segment Interconnect

$$\begin{pmatrix} V_1 \\ I_1 \end{pmatrix} = T_1 T_2 ... T_n \begin{pmatrix} V_n \\ -I_n \end{pmatrix} = T \begin{pmatrix} V_n \\ -I_n \end{pmatrix}$$

S-parameters Versus ABCD Matrix

Using the scattering parameter matrix, and applying the relationship between the voltage and current and incident wave and reflected wave, Equation 4.9 transforms the normalized chain matrix to S-parameters.

Equation 4.9   Normalized Chain Matrix Transformed to S-parameters

$$\begin{pmatrix} S_{11} & S_{12} \\ S_{21} & S_{22} \end{pmatrix} = \frac{1}{A_n + B_n + C_n + D_n} \begin{pmatrix} A_n + B_n + C_n + D_n & 2(A_n D_n - B_n C_n) \\ 2 & -A_n + B_n - C_n + D_n \end{pmatrix}$$

In Equation 4.9, A_n, B_n, C_n, and D_n are the normalized chain matrix entities given by $T_n = N\,T\,N^{-1}$. T_n is the normalized ABCD matrix and N is the normalized matrix given by Equation 4.10, in which R_{ci} is the termination impedance.

Equation 4.10   Normalized Matrix

$$N_i = \begin{pmatrix} \dfrac{1}{\sqrt{R_{ci}}} & 0 \\ 0 & \sqrt{R_{ci}} \end{pmatrix}$$

S-parameters of the Cascaded Multi-segment

Figure 4.7 illustrates the energy flow of a two-port network (Adam 1991). In Port 1 and Port 2, the incident wave is denoted by node a and the reflected wave is denoted by node b.

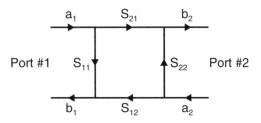

Figure 4.7   Flow Graph

Equation 4.11 presents a scattering matrix that defines the relationship between the reflected and incident waves in Figure 4.7. The scattering matrix consists of complex numbers and both nodes have magnitude and phase information. The signal flow between nodes is identified with the corresponding S-parameters. For example, the signal loss between the input and output ports correlates to S12.

Equation 4.11   Scattering Matrix

$$\begin{pmatrix} b_1 \\ b_2 \end{pmatrix} = \begin{pmatrix} S_{11} & S_{12} \\ S_{21} & S_{22} \end{pmatrix} \begin{pmatrix} a_1 \\ a_2 \end{pmatrix}$$

S-parameters with Load and Source

The flow graph in Figure 4.8 represents a network with three components including driver package, interconnect, and receiver.

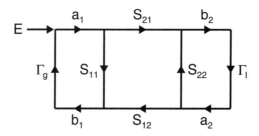

Figure 4.8   Signal Flow Graph for Three Elements

The PCI Express specification defines the interconnect from driver package pins to receiver package pins. As a result, you can replace the driver and receiver with a block that assigns them an impedance value and defines an impedance mismatch coefficient between the respective package and the interconnect.

The ratio between the output reflected wave and input incident wave is defined to be the reflection coefficient. When there is no impedance mismatch, the output reflection coefficient is zero.

In this case, the reflection coefficient b_1/a_1 and transmission coefficient b_2/E can be formulated using Mason's rule or "non-touching-loop" method. Applying Mason's rule, the reflection coefficient and transmission coefficients of Figure 4.8 with load and source coefficients can be written as shown in Equations 4.12 and 4.13, respectively.

Equation 4.12   Reflection Coefficient

$$\frac{b_1}{a_1} = \frac{S_{11}(1 - S_{22}\Gamma_l) + S_{21}\Gamma_l S_{12}}{1 - S_{22}\Gamma_l}$$

Equation 4.13   Transmission Coefficient

$$\frac{b_2}{E} = \frac{S_{21}}{1 - \Gamma_g S_{11} - S_{22}\Gamma_l - \Gamma_g S_{21}\Gamma_l S_{12} + \Gamma_g S_{11} S_{22}\Gamma_l}$$

If the impedances are matched at the source and load, Equations 4.12 and 4.13 can be simplified to S11 and S21 terms, respectively. For PCI Express interconnect, Γ_g and Γ_l are typically less than 10 percent so their quadratic terms are less than 1 percent and thus can be ignored.

Mason's Rule

Mason's rule is an analytical method for analyzing a flow graph model in microwave design and analysis. Mason's rule allows us to accurately compute the S-parameters of a cascaded multi-segment interconnect. Mason's rule consists of following rules:

- ∎ A "path" is a series of branches that follow in sequence and in the same direction such that no node is touched more than once, and the value of the path is the product of the coefficients of the branch. For example, in Figure 4.8 one path is from E to b2 with the value of S21. Also, two paths from E to b1 have the values of S11 and S21Γ_lS12, respectively.

- ∎ A "loop" is a path that starts and finishes in the same node.

  A "first-order loop" is a loop with no node passed more than once. The value of the loop is the product of the value of all branches in the route.

A "second-order loop" is defined as two first-order loops that do not touch each other. The value of the second-order loop is the product of the values of the two first-order loops.

Third- and higher-order loops are three or more first-order loops that do not touch each other. The value of the higher-order loop is the product of the values of all component first-order loops. For example, in Figure 4.8 there are three first-order loops with values of $S11\Gamma_g$, $S22\Gamma_l$, and $\Gamma_l S21 S22 \Gamma_g$, respectively, and one second-order loop $\Gamma_l S11 S22 \Gamma_g$. The non-touching-loop rule can be applied to any flow graph. Equation 4.14 gives the non-touching-loop equation.

Equation 4.14 Mason's Rule

$$T = \frac{\displaystyle\sum_k T_k \Delta_k}{\Delta}$$

where:

T_k = path gain of kth forward path

Δ_k = The value of Δ not touching the kth forward path

Δ = 1 − Σ (loop gain products of all possible combinations of 1 non-touching-loop)

  +   Σ (loop gain products of all possible combinations of 2 non-touching-loop)

  −   Σ (loop gain products of all possible combinations of 3 non-touching-loop)

  +   ...

Loss Budget Partitioning

In frequency domain analysis, one of the most important phenomena is the partitioning of the loss budget between the interconnect segments in the cascaded multi-segment model. As stated earlier, the m_{MIN} coefficient accounts for driver/receiver impedance mismatches. A minimum of −2.5 dB must be deducted from the loss budget to account for m_{MIN}.

The remaining loss can be partitioned between the interconnect segments in proportion to the length of interconnect segment as a first-order approximation. For a desktop platform, it is fair to assign 80 percent of the loss budget for the PCB and 20 percent to the adaptor. Using the 13.2 dB maximum package-to-package loss and deducting the 2.5 dB for mismatch impedance yields a budget of 10.7 dB for a single-segment topology and 8.6 dB for dual segment topologies.

Correlation Between Frequency and Time Domains

Examine the relationship between time domain data—the eye width and height openings at the receiver and driver pads—and frequency domain S-parameter data at the same locations. A close correlation can be quite helpful in developing a robust solution for the end-to-end PCI Express interconnect system.

Differential Insertion Loss

It is easy to compute the loss over the PCI Express interconnect channel, using the ratio of the minimum voltage at the driver to the minimum allowable voltage at the receiver. The PCI Express specification defines this ratio as 175 mv/800 mv = –13.2 dB (PCI-SIG 2004). This ratio number can be mapped in the frequency domain analysis, in which the end-to-end differential insertion loss (b2 – b4) term meets the –13.2 dB loss at the fundamental frequency 1.25 GHz. This equation is equivalent to the time domain requirement at the package pins.

In addition, with frequency domain analysis, you must also define the range at which the loss profile must be met. Since PCI Express uses the 8b/10b coding scheme, this signaling method is band-limited; that is, the frequency range is between one-half and one-tenth of the bit rates, or between 250 MHz and 1.25 GHz. Outside of this range, the frequency characteristics of the PCI Express interconnect are less important.

The loss curve S12, frequency domain data, can be added some additional information to account for the mode conversion and other effects. The differential insertion loss curve is shown in Figure 4.9. It is bounded between 250 MHz and 1.25 GHz. The flatness of curve represents the mode conversion.

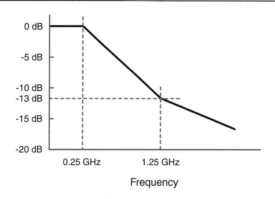

Figure 4.9   Differential Mode Insertion Loss

Common Mode Losses

Figure 4.10 reflects the worst-case condition for common mode return loss at the driver and at the receiver. This is the common mode amplitude versus frequency profile over the pass-band from 0.25 GHz to 1.25 GHZ.

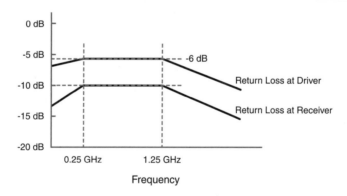

Figure 4.10   Common Mode Return Loss

Chapter 5

Successful System Layout Design— Getting Started

The secret of success is knowing something nobody else knows.

—Aristotle Onassis

As the system designer, you must be able to make informed tradeoffs that help you to meet the signal integrity requirements of the specification while also achieving the design targets of your particular system. The practical guidelines included in this and in subsequent chapters contain the information that you need in order to make those informed tradeoffs.

The examples and topologies examined in the next few chapters focus largely on standard desktop system implementations of PCI Express[†]. However, the general guidelines and suggestions presented here are applicable to a variety of designs. The range of implementations includes server backplanes, mobile systems, or even custom applications.

In addition to presenting general guidelines, this chapter addresses system design details with respect to add-in card and ExpressCard[†]-based systems. For details on the actual designs for the add-in cards and the ExpressCard modules themselves, see Chapter 7, "Add-in Cards and ExpressCard Modules."

To serve the needs of diverse applications, several variations of the *PCI Express Base Specification* (PCI-SIG 2004a) are available, with more on the horizon. For example, mobile systems might follow the *Mobile Graphics Low-Power Addendum to the PCI Express Base Specification* (PCI-SIG 2003b) which allows for reduced signal output swings in low loss interconnect systems. Desktop, mobile, and server systems that interact with PCI Express add-in cards and ExpressCard modules must follow the requirements set forth in the *PCI Express Card Electromechanical (CEM) Specification* (PCI-SIG 2004b) and the *ExpressCard Standard* (PCMCIA 2003a). It is beyond the scope of this chapter and this book to cover all the specification variations and their impacts on system designs.

System Topology Overviews

One of the great things about PCI Express interconnects is their flexibility and versatility. By taking advantage of the inherent features of PCI Express architecture and signaling, a system designer can easily incorporate PCI Express links into a variety of different topologies. This section presents some of the more common topologies or uses of PCI Express interconnects in a system environment.

Chip-to-Chip Interconnects

As PCI Express becomes more prevalent in the marketplace, it is likely to be used more and more to connect the various components on a system board together. Figure 5.1 presents an example of connections between two I/O hubs on a desktop system board. In server systems, however, backplane connections become prevalent and the chip-to-chip interconnect is made through connector interfaces as well as across the system board.

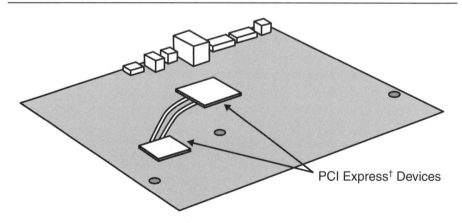

Figure 5.1   Chip-to-Chip Topology on a Desktop System Board

Video or Graphics Ports

As a high-bandwidth replacement for AGP graphics cards, PCI Express interconnects are likely to be implemented with a x16 link width and connector size. In ATX or micro-ATX form factors, for example, a PCI Express graphics port is likely to interface with Slot 7, shown with the x16 connector in Figure 5.2. For specific guidelines on add-in card design, see Chapter 7, "Add-in Cards and ExpressCard Modules."

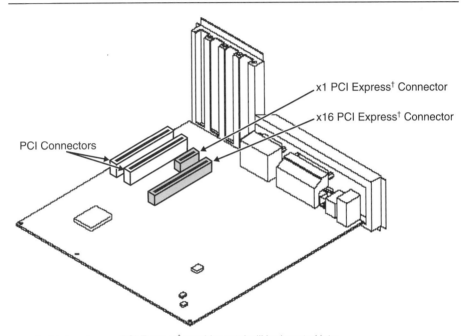

x1 PCI Express† Connector

x16 PCI Express† Connector

PCI Connectors

In this topology, a PCI Express† graphics card will be inserted into the x16 Connector and PCI Express† general purpose I/O card will be inserted into the x1 Connector.

Figure 5.2   Typical PCI Express† Micro-ATX Form Factor Topology

General Purpose I/O Interconnects

As the name suggests, PCI Express is the high-speed, high-bandwidth successor to the ubiquitous Conventional PCI[†] interface found in most system designs today. Whether the systems are desktop, server, or mobile, PCI Express is positioned to become a prevalent interconnect on any system board. Most general purpose I/O interfaces interface with a x1 connector, as shown in Figure 5.2. However, a system designer might choose to offer other link width interfaces as well, for example, x4 or x8.

The PCMCIA organization has crafted a specific form factor adaptation of PCI Express for general purpose I/O, resulting in the *ExpressCard†* *Standard* (PCMCIA 2003a). By definition, ExpressCard modules are a x1 width and are seen as the evolution of the current PCMCIA PC Card standard. Depending on whether the design is for a mobile or a desktop system, the ExpressCard topology is implemented differently. For example, on a desktop system, you might implement an interface to an ExpressCard slot by using a riser card mated with a x1 PCI Express connector. The ExpressCard module would plug into the riser card, while getting the PCI Express signals through the x1 PCI Express connector. Alternatively, you might mount the ExpressCard interface in an open drive bay to connect the PCI Express signals through a cable. Since there are many possible adaptations, you are free to innovate your own implementation as well. For details about ExpressCard module design, see Chapter 7, "Add-in Cards and ExpressCard Modules."

Figure 5.3 presents an example of an ExpressCard topology using a riser card in a desktop system.

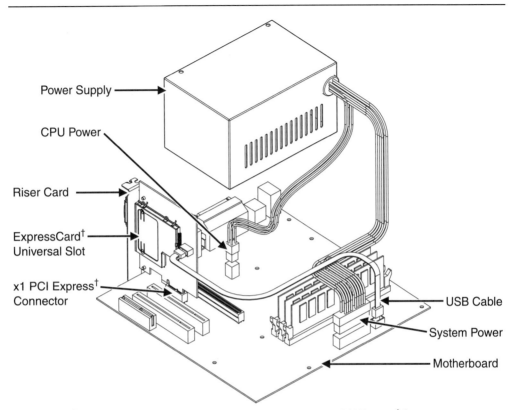

ExpressCard[†] riser card and attached USB cable are plugged into a x1 PCI Express[†] Connector.

NOTE: PCI Express[†] link, power, clock, and auxiliary signals are delivered through the x1 PCI Express[†] Connector.

Courtesy PCMCIA

Figure 5.3   Example Topology Using a Riser Card in a Desktop System

Taking Advantage of the PCI Express† Specification

By understanding the topology-related aspects of the PCI Express specification, you can plan effectively and implement your design with greater confidence. As discussed in Chapter 1, certain connectivity rules and conventions apply to PCI Express signals just as with any other interface. However, some inherent features that are built into the specification make your life as the system designer somewhat easier.

Connectivity Rules

As you learn to apply the PCI Express specification's connectivity rules to your designs, you can take full advantage of the allowances for PCI Express topologies and layouts. The following requirements and guidelines apply specifically to connectivity:

■ Each connection between PCI Express devices must be point-to-point. In other words, a connection can only exist between one driver and one receiver. Daisy-chaining, or connections of multiple transmitters and receivers on one wire or interconnect, is not allowed. You should make sure that all components in your designs are routed such that they directly connect with just one other PCI Express component.

Do not confuse this rule with link bifurcation and link width negotiation, in which point-to-point lanes are grouped together to form up to X32 links between two separate devices. For more on link width negotiation and bifurcation, see Chapter 1.

■ The PCI Express specification dictates that each lane of a link be AC-coupled between its corresponding transmitter and receiver. The AC coupling capacitance is required either within the transmitter component/package or along the interconnect link on the Printed Circuit Board (PCB). In most scenarios, the AC coupling must be located external to the transmitter or receiver device components in the form of discrete capacitors on your system PCB. It is your responsibility to verify the AC coupling capacitor requirements of each PCI Express Transmit (TX) component in your design. For more about this, see "AC Coupling Capacitors," later in this chapter.

■ Each end of a PCI Express link is terminated on-die into a nominal 100 Ω differential DC termination. This is often done by using 50 Ω terminations on each signal of the differential pair. Because each component contains this on-die termination, you do not need to worry about any external on-board terminations for the PCI Express high-speed differential pairs in your system.

■ The PCI Express specification also requires each TX component to utilize on-die equalization by means of de-emphasis for all PCI Express signals. The de-emphasis is required to be a typical value of 3.5 dB (±0.5 dB) down with respect to the nominal output voltage. You are not required to include any additional external equalization for the differential pairs in your design.

■ As discussed in Chapter 1, each lane on a PCI Express link is assigned a sequential numerical value and is identified as such in the component's pinout. Each TX pair on a transmitting device must connect with the identically numbered Receive (RX) pair on the receiving device. For example, two devices that constitute a link with a width of x1 might be identified as device A and device B. To represent the D+ or D− signals, respectively, a "p" or "n" is usually appended to the pin name. Each device's respective TX and RX labels would then be similar to the following:

A_PETp0, A_PETn0, A_PERp0, A_PERn0

B_PETp0, B_PETn0, B_PERp0, B_PERn0

To properly connect device A to device B, device A's TX pairs (A_PETp0, A_PETn0) should connect to device B's RX pairs (B_PERp0, B_PERn0) and vice versa. The same connectivity rules apply regardless of link size, including x16 or x32 links. For possible exceptions to this guideline, see the following section, "Bowtie Topology Considerations."

Note | Both the *PCI Express CEM Specification* and the *ExpressCard Standard* use the respective standard designations of PET and PER to signify TX originating signals and RX destination signals, each with respect to a system board device. The RX input on a component located on an add-in card or ExpressCard module connects with the PET pin of the connector. In these specifications, a "p" or "n" is also always appended to the pin name in order to represent the D+ or D− signals, respectively.

Bowtie Topology Considerations

When physically routing or interconnecting PCI Express devices, whether across a connector or on the same PCB, you might encounter one of the following "bowtie" or signal-crossing scenarios:

■ *D+, D– crisscrossing within a pair.* This scenario occurs when the D+ and D– signals of a differential pair from a transmitter device must crisscross in order to connect to the respective D+ and D– signals of the receiving device.

■ *Crossing of lanes.* This scenario occurs on a x2 or greater link, when lane 0 of the transmitting device must cross the other lanes in order to connect with lane 0 on the receiving device.

■ *Crossing of transmit and receive pairs within a lane.* This scenario occurs when the transmit and receive differential signal pairs that constitute an individual lane must crisscross each other in order to properly connect from one device to another.

To help you overcome the first two scenarios, the *PCI Express Base Specification* includes provisions for two features: polarity inversion and lane reversal. The specification does not provide a provision to overcome the third scenario.

Scenario 1: Crisscrossing Within a Pair—Making Use of Polarity Inversion

The PCI Express specification requires support for polarity inversion. This feature allows for the TX and RX devices to fix any connections automatically within a lane where the D+ and D– connections are reversed. Figure 5.4 illustrates polarity inversion.

Polarity inversion can make your life as a designer a lot easier. First, the inversion process is completely transparent and automatically happens on-die, within the component, becoming enabled only when necessary. As the system designer, you don't need to do anything to make it work! Second, you no longer have to scrutinize your CAD layout, double-checking all the differential pairs; polarity inversion effectively neutralizes the differential pair, and the D+ and D– designations may in fact become unnecessary during layout. You can simply tell your CAD layout engineer to "connect TX pair A to RX pair B and don't worry about the + and – signs." For debug purposes, it still makes sense to keep track of which signals are D+ and which are D–, but polarity inversion makes them irrelevant for layout purposes.

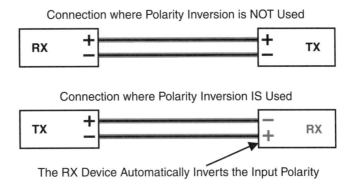

Figure 5.4   Polarity Inversion on an RX to TX Interconnect

Making use of polarity inversion allows you to reduce the number of via transitions for your differential signals, have a more uniform differential route on the PCB, and subsequently reduce the amount of PCB real estate used for differential pair routing. For more about PCI Express polarity inversion, refer to Chapter 1.

Scenario 2: Crossing of Lanes—Making Use of Lane Reversal

The *PCI Express Base Specification* does not require support for this optional feature. Where supported, lane reversal allows you to reassign the TX and RX lane 0 pairs on a given device to connect respectively to the highest ordered lane RX and TX pairs on a second device, and so on for the entire link.

Only one component forming part of a link needs to support lane reversal in order to make it operational. Consider an example design with a x8 component, located on the system PCB, that supports lane reversal and is routed to a connector interface. In such a scenario, if the x8 component pinout is "reversed"—forcing you to crisscross lanes in order to properly route and connect lane 0 through lane 7 with the connector— you could simply rearrange the link so that lane 0 of the x8 PCB component is now connected with lane 7 of the connector. The remaining lanes would be similarly connected such that lane 1 of the PCB component would now connect with lane 6 of the connector, and so on. Figure 5.5 illustrates this scenario.

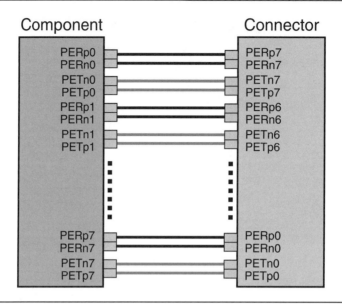

Figure 5.5   Example of Lane Reversal on a x8 Link

Unless you are certain that lane reversal is supported and guaranteed by at least one of the devices in question, do not rely upon this feature. Instead, follow the basic connectivity rules, which dictate that the lane 0 differential pairs on the first device must connect to the lane 0 pairs on the second device or connector. For more about lane reversal, refer to Chapter 1.

Scenario 3: Crossing of Transmit and Receive Pairs Within a Lane—Making Use of Vias and Layer Transitions

While polarity inversion and lane reversal help to overcome the first two bowtie scenarios, the *PCI Express Base Specification* does not include any provisions to alleviate the third bowtie scenario. Simply put, an RX input on a device always remains an RX input and cannot switch roles to become a TX output. If you find that your particular design forces you to crisscross RX and TX pairs within a lane, you must untangle them during layout by means of bowtie routing—using vias to transition layers in order to alleviate RX and TX pair crisscrossing. Figure 5.6 depicts this scenario.

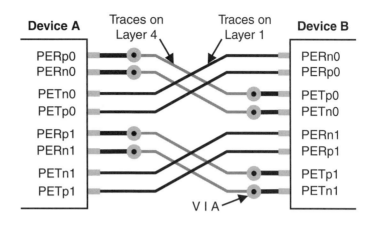

Figure 5.6   Bowtie Routing to Alleviate Crisscrossing RX/TX Pairs

System-level Floor-planning

Proper floor-planning for PCI Express interfaces allows you to position your system for success before any actual CAD time is spent routing—or *re*-routing—the interface. A simple approach to floor-planning might involve these basic steps:

1. *Create a block diagram connectivity plan for devices and/or connectors and placement studies.* In addition to the actual PCI Express components, your initial diagram should include the necessary peripheral components interacting with your PCI Express components: clock sources, power supply connectors, and the like. As you apply this diagram to initial placement studies with your CAD tools, you can size up the general location on the system board of each component and assess the routing distances and areas that apply to each component or connector. The location and placement of your components is also influenced by the type of system board form factor you follow, such as ATX, micro-ATX, BTX, etc.

2. *Verify connectivity rules, as explained in this chapter.* Making sure that you comply with all of the specification requirements can save you from design changes down the road. Note general locations of AC capacitors and verify whether the pinouts of the PCI Express devices and components require any bowtie routing to achieve proper connectivity. Also follow the EMI and Power

Delivery guidelines later in this chapter, and determine the ability to maintain good reference planes for your signals and place high power consuming devices close to their power sources.

3. *Assignment of routing restrictions.* You should revisit this step several times throughout your design. For four-layer desktop designs, begin by using the routing length guidelines in this chapter. After applying the initial trace length recommendations, refine your initial floor-planning in Step 1 so that all devices and components conform to the maximum routing length limits for your design. Then conduct your own simulations, adhering to the recommendations in the previous chapters. By following this approach, you can properly customize the layout guidelines for your own particular situation.

Of course, proper system floor-planning should also include consideration of all the guidelines presented in Chapter 6, "PCB Design." And, as mentioned earlier in this chapter, your floor-planning also hinges on the type of design you are undertaking—whether it be a desktop, server, mobile, communications, or even a customized design lying somewhere in between—and the associated variations of the PCI Express specifications that you plan to follow.

Routing Length Recommendations and Restrictions

As mentioned in Step 3 above, successful floor-planning involves an early consideration of the routing length restrictions and requirements for the PCI Express differential signals. While each design dictates its own requirements, it is possible to state some general guidelines, based on a common implementation.

Table 5.1 presents a summary of PCB-related PCI Express *microstrip routing criteria for a common four-layer board.* Designs that are not four-layer microstrip implementation will of course have slightly different guidelines. The recommendations in the table are based on system-level simulations and test board implementations. While the details of these guidelines are more fully explained in subsequent chapters, you can use the length recommendations in the table to ensure that as you do the floor-planning for a four-layer microstrip design, you also meet the timing/jitter and loss/attenuation budgets across the entire PCI Express interconnect path. Routing guidelines for add-in cards and ExpressCard module designs are provided in Chapter 7.

Table 5.1   Example PCB Routing Guidelines for a Common Microstrip-Routed, 2116 Dielectric-Based, Four-Layer PCB

Parameter	System Board: Main Routes	Special "Breakout-Area" Rules
Diff. Impedance Target	~100 Ω ±20% (~60 Ω SE ±15%)	N/A
Trace Width	5 mils	7 mils if un-coupled length ≥ 100 mils
Diff Pair (within-pair) Air Gap	7 mils	5-mil air gap OK
Pair-to-Pair Air Gap Spacing	≥ 20 mils	7-mil air gap OK
Trace Length Restrictions	≤ 15" chip-to-chip ≤ 12" chip-to-add-in card and ExpressCard[†] connectors	"Breakout Area" limited to ≤ 250 mils (included in the overall trace length recommendations in the left column)
Length Matching Within a Pair	Max 5 mil delta per segment	N/A
Length Matching Pair-to-Pair	No strict requirement[1] (keep moderate for latency)	N/A
Reference Plane	GND plane best Pwr plane OK with stitching caps Stitching vias when changing layers	GND islands on VCC layer must be tied to GND here
Splits/Voids	No routing over splits No routing over voids	No more than half of the trace width should be over via anti-pad
Via Usage (maximum) (6 total, entire path)	4 vias per TX trace 2 vias per RX trace	OK to include one via in breakout area
Bends	Match left and right turn bends where possible No 90-degree or "tight" bends	Avoid "tight bends" when routing in breakout areas

[1] While the PCI Express[†] Base Specification allows for a wide skew tolerance of 20 ns between lanes or differential pairs, the PCI Express CEM Specification does call out a maximum allowable lane-to-lane skew value of 1.25ns for system board traces that route to an add-in card connector. This value is roughly equivalent to a maximum of 7–8 inches of trace length mismatch across all lanes or differential pairs (PCI-SIG 2004). As the system designer, you should determine the necessity of this requirement for your particular design.

While the general physical guidelines and suggestions in Table 5.1 help to ensure good high-speed signal design practices, they might not necessarily guarantee adequate performance of the interconnect for all layout variations and implementations. In fact, these guidelines should only be applied to designs where a four-layer, 2116-based dielectric is used for the PCB stackup. For more details, see Chapter 6, "PCB Design."

As system designer, you should simulate and model each of your interconnect designs based on the techniques in the preceding chapters. This practice ensures that your system achieves optimum margins and performance, in addition to compliance with all the applicable specifications.

System Reference Clock Considerations

The clocking requirements for PCI Express topologies differ from those of most other interconnects. As explained in Chapter 1, unlike most common clock designs, PCI Express interconnects no longer require a clock-to-data timing relationship to be enforced. As the system designer, having no clock-to-data timing relationship to worry about means your life just got a whole lot easier! By understanding the implications of the embedded clocking nature of PCI Express components, you can improve the performance and simplify the layout of your PCI Express interconnects.

The "embedded clock" feature of the specification essentially means that components in a PCI Express link can extract the data timing and phase information directly from the data stream, rather than having to rely on strict setup and hold times between the data bits and a clock provided by the system. Most of your PCI Express components only require that you provide them with a differential seed or reference clock of the same frequency supplied to other PCI Express components on the same link. The components can use this frequency reference, along with the phase information they extract from the data stream, to adequately sample the data bits they receive.

As mentioned previously, you no longer need to worry about clock-to-data signal phase and skew relationships; the only thing that matters is the relative frequency of the clocks themselves. On the system board, this narrowed focus translates into the removal of any cumbersome serpentine trace routes that you might be accustomed to placing on clock and data signals for non-PCI Express busses. Refer to the "Proper Routing and Termination" section that follows for additional details.

Although the CEM specification introduces certain requirements for reference clocks, the *PCI Express Base Specification* itself does not explicitly require components to use a seed clock, nor does it call out a specific reference clock frequency that all components must use. If a component can extract all the frequency and phase information it needs directly from the data stream, the component might not even require a reference clock. Due to the difficulty, however, of extracting all the timing and frequency information directly from the data stream, almost all components are likely to require you to provide them with a reference clock at the same frequency that is being supplied to the other PCI Express component that connects to the link. This need is especially true if Spread Spectrum Clocking is used, as described later in this section. As the system designer, you should make sure that you understand the reference clock requirements, if any, for each of the components in your system.

However, eliminating the clock-to-data skew requirement does not mean that the frequency reference clocks for PCI Express can be treated lightly. On the contrary; if you want to have a robust design, you must know in explicit detail the clocking requirements of the individual components, as well as the nature of the clock sources that you are going to use. The following paragraphs discuss key elements that you must consider when choosing and implementing reference clocks for PCI Express topologies.

Frequency, PPM Performance, and Jitter

While the *PCI Express Base Specification* does not dictate a specific reference clock frequency, both the *PCI Express CEM Specification* and the *ExpressCard Standard* require that the target frequency of clocks supplied to add-in card connectors and ExpressCard module connectors be 100-MHz differential clocks. While the PCI Express components on the add-in card are not required to use this differential reference clock, most do. The implication of this to your design is that most other components, especially those designed to potentially interface with an edgefinger connector or ExpressCard module, will also likely demand that the same 100-MHz frequency reference clock be supplied to them. You must plan ahead and choose a clock source that has an adequate number of 100-MHz differential outputs.

Additionally, the *PCI Express Base Specification* requires that the data rate transmitted by the components at either end of a link be within 600 parts per million (ppm) of each other at all times. This means that each clocking device is limited to no more than a ±300-ppm variation on the reference clock frequency it provides. As the system designer, you must ensure that the clock sources you select meet both the 100-MHz target frequency and the ±300-ppm requirement.

In addition to frequency and ppm performance, you must also ensure adequate jitter performance on the clock outputs. Any jitter variations that are present on the clock source have the potential to manifest themselves as jitter on the data link, depending on the characteristics of the PLLs used on-die for the TX and RX signals. Be sure to verify your clock source for cycle-to-cycle and potential phase noise jitter performance. Many clock sources offer a two-chip solution as well: a main clock source and a companion buffer chip to provide additional outputs. When using a two-chip clocking solution, make sure that the companion buffer doesn't impact the integrity of the clock signals in any way.

Spread Spectrum Clocking (SSC)

Spread spectrum clock sources have become somewhat ubiquitous in recent years. Their ability to effectively mitigate electromagnetic interference (EMI) issues in a system is well-known and appreciated. For PCI Express topologies, however, SSC poses a bit of an issue. To make PCI Express systems work properly and meet the ±300-ppm tolerance, all PCI Express devices must receive or replicate the same SSC profile. Since most components find it difficult to extract the SSC information solely from the data stream, they must gather it from an external source. In other words, for almost all designs, you are required to distribute the same spread spectrum modulated clock to all devices within a given system. If a certain PCI Express component is provided with some other clock source, the link will most likely fail. For each SSC modulated clock device you use, ensure that it only modulates that data rate "from +0% to –0.5% of the nominal data rate frequency, at a modulation rate in the range not exceeding 30 kHz–33 kHz" in order to fully comply with the *PCI Express Base Specification* (PCI-SIG 2004a).

For system debugging efforts, you might find it helpful to select a clock source that allows you to turn the SSC modulation on PCI Express on and off.

Appropriate Number of Clock Outputs

When doing the floor-plan for your system, you need to identify how many discrete components as well as connectors that must be supplied with a reference clock. Since clock signals can not be daisy-chained between devices, each of the components must be allocated an individual clock. Keep in mind that based on the SSC requirement in the previous section, along with the explicit 100-MHz *PCI Express CEM Specification* and *ExpressCard Standard* requirement, you must supply a commonly sourced reference clock to each connector or component. In other words, your clock chip or buffer must be able to provide enough copies of the same differential clock signal to all of the system components and connectors.

Proper Routing and Termination

The four-layer microstrip routing guidelines for PCI Express traces in Table 5.1 can also be used when routing the differential reference clock traces. The maximum trace length recommendations found through simulations for the reference clock, however, are a bit longer than those listed in Table 5.1: up to approximately 14 inches when routing to an add-in card or ExpressCard module or a maximum of about 16 inches when routing chip-to-chip. Keep in mind that the references clocks must be routed point-to-point—no daisy-chain routing is allowed. Additionally, even with no clock-to-data skew requirement, the *PCI Express CEM Specification* does place an upper limit on the trace length skew that can exist from one clock to another when the clocks are routed to PCI Express connectors. In fact, the 1.1 CEM specification states that the "reference clock distribution to all devices must be matched to within 15 inches on the system board" (PCI-SIG 2004b). While this requirement should be relatively easy to achieve by simply following the maximum length restrictions as previously stated, you should consider it during the initial layout of your system design.

It is important to properly terminate the reference clock signals. The termination schemes can vary based on the supplier of the clock source, but some general guidelines are useful. To minimize unwanted reflections that may impact performance, use proper series and parallel termination, and limit overall trace lengths on the clock signals. Always terminate your clock outputs at the clock source component. This is especially true when routing clocks to add-in card connectors or ExpressCard modules. Do not rely on either the add-in card or ExpressCard module to provide termination for clocks. For the best system performance, terminate the clock outputs at the clock source, so that even when a module or add-in card is not plugged into a connector, the clock is still terminated. Figure 5.7 provides an example of a commonly used termination scheme, as well as trace length recommendations for microstrip routing on a four-layer PCB and add-in card. These guidelines are derived from system-level simulations and test board implementation.

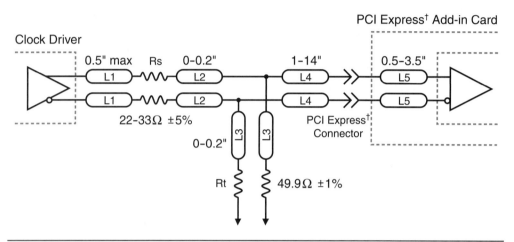

Figure 5.7   Example of Proper Termination and Routing for a PCI Express[†] Reference Clock Supplied to an Add-in Card

AC Coupling Capacitors

The *PCI Express Base Specification* requires that each lane of a PCI Express link be AC-coupled between the driver and receiver. The actual AC coupling capacitors can be located either on or off the die/component. In most cases, the AC coupling is separate from the component, and you must use discrete capacitors on the PCB board itself to satisfy the AC coupling requirement of the specification. The following guidelines apply to AC coupling capacitors.

■   For add-in cards and ExpressCard modules, the AC coupling capacitors are located on the card for each of the TX pairs originating from the add-in card PCI Express device. You do not need to place any AC capacitors on the system or host board for these signals.

■ For the system board, the AC coupling capacitors are required on the TX pairs originating from the system board PCI Express device and traveling to the respective connector interface.

■ For chip-to-chip connections, all PCI Express differential pairs should have AC caps located on them somewhere along the interconnect.

■ Because most four-layer system boards allow only single-sided, top layer component placement, all TX pairs originating on the system board are likely to be routed on the top layer. Knowing this, you should plan to route all the RX pairs on the bottom layer of your board. This separation of the RX and TX pairs also helps to reduce near-end crosstalk (NEXT), which can severely limit the performance of PCI Express signals. If necessary, TX signals routed on the bottom layer may transition through a via pair in order to place the capacitors on the top layer.

■ Capacitors for the coupled traces should be located at the same place within the differential pair. The capacitors should not be staggered in distance from one trace of the differential pair to the other.

— Capacitors should be placed as close to each other as possible per Design for Manufacturing (DFM) rules to avoid creating large uncoupled sections within the differential pair traces.

— The relative location of AC capacitors from one differential pair to another differential pair is not important.

■ While it appears that size 603 capacitors are acceptable, size 402 capacitors are strongly encouraged. The smaller the package size, the less Equivalent Series Inductance (ESL) is introduced into the topology.

■ The same package and capacitor size should be used for each signal in a differential pair.

Note | Do not use capacitor packs (C-Packs) for PCI Express AC coupling capacitor purposes. At the high frequencies and data rates of PCI Express signals, C-Packs can have undesirable effects.

■ To minimize any parasitic impacts, pad sizes for each capacitor should be the minimum allowed per DFM.

- ■ The spec requires a value between a minimum of 75 nF and a maximum of 200 nF for each of the capacitors.

  Specific tolerance values of the capacitors are not required, so long as the overall range of tolerances falls within the specified minimum and maximum values. Consider the effects of temperature and voltage on capacitor tolerance values.

- ■ Dielectric properties are not a major consideration for PCI Express AC coupling capacitors. Any type of capacitor—including X7R, Y5V, NPO, COG, and others—is acceptable so long as it meets all other requirements.

- ■ The "breakout" into and out of the capacitors should be symmetrical for both signal lines in a differential pair. To maximize the amount of coupling within the differential pair, you should minimize the breakout area. Figure 5.8 presents an example of how you might implement this.

AC Cap Pads

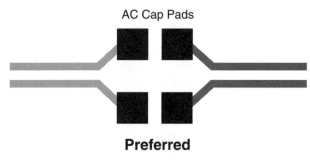

Preferred

(Cap placement is in same location & symmetric)

Avoid

(Cap placement is not in same location/symmetric!)

Figure 5.8   Symmetrical Routing into AC Caps

In general, for connector-based topologies, the AC capacitors tend to reside near the connector. Although you could theoretically place them anywhere along the interconnect, you should not locate them at the midpoint of a trace route, so as to minimize discontinuity effects. For example, you could place them next to the connector or one-third the distance between the connector and the chipset, but not halfway between the connector and the chipset. Figure 5.9 provides examples of capacitor placement.

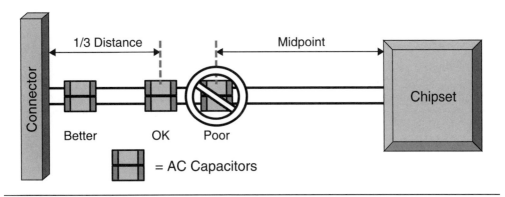

Figure 5.9   AC Capacitor Placement Examples

Similar guidelines also apply when routing chip-to-chip. For example, you should not place the capacitors in the center of the link but closer to one of the ends. As always, you should simulate the actual location of the capacitors because their exact placement can introduce potential discontinuity or resonance issues within the system.

Table 5.2 summarizes guidelines and requirements for AC capacitor use and placement.

Table 5.2   AC Coupling Capacitor Guidelines

Parameter *(For AC Coupling Capacitors)*	Requirement
Cap Size	603 acceptable (402 preferred) C-Packs NOT recommended
Cap Value	75 nF min 200 nF max
Cap Value Tolerance	No specific value is required as long as specified min/max range is met when the tolerance is considered.
Cap Placement— Within a Differential Pair	Must be placed at same exact location within the differential pair. Symmetric routing into the caps strongly recommended. Matched line lengths on either side of the caps for each line of the diff pair.
Cap Location— Chip-to-Connector Routing	General Guideline: Place capacitors such that they are *not* located in the center point of a trace route; for example, next to the connector or 1/3 the distance between the connector and the chipset.
Cap Location— Chip-to-Chip Routing	Locate off-center within the interconnect. Example: Placing the caps next to the RX pins of one component is generally better than locating the caps in the midpoint of the interconnect.

Cable Considerations for System Design

While the *PCI Express Base Specification* does not include specific cable requirements for a PCI Express interconnect, it doesn't preclude their use either. In fact, the flexibility of the PCI Express interface actually opens up several options for different implementations of the interconnect. For example, you might use a cable to transmit PCI Express signals from one component to another. The ability to transmit PCI Express signals over a cable can allow for innovative chassis design and usage models.

Currently, the PCI-SIG has not released a formally approved specification about cabling architecture or requirements. In other words, there is currently no such thing as a "PCI Express cable." If you choose or need to use a cable to support your PCI Express implementation, you are on your own in terms of the type of cable and cable headers or connectors that you may use. The absence of a formal standard can make it difficult for your designs to incorporate an external cable interface that can connect to another vendor's PCI Express components.

Using a cable-based interconnect within your system's chassis, however, can have some advantages for your design—for example, when you have to connect together PCI Express components located on separate PCBs within your own system or chassis. If you choose to use a cable-based interconnect, make sure that the selected cable can meet all of the electrical signal quality requirements of the interconnect, such as having low loss and jitter. The same requirement also applies to cable headers or connectors.

With regard to the electrical and timing budget parameters, you should consider the entire cable assembly as part of the host system. With initial speeds of 2.5 GT/s, PCI Express signals require special attention, especially when transmitting over cables. You should properly simulate any cable topology you use, to ensure that it meets all of the PCI Express electrical specifications.

ExpressCard† Internal Cable Interface

Though the PCI-SIG has not released a formal cable specification, the ExpressCard interface from PCMCIA does define an internal cable assembly to be used when connecting PCI Express signals to ExpressCard module interfaces within a given system or chassis. The *ExpressCard Internal Cable Specification* (PCMCIA 2003b) provides specific details and requirements of the cable assembly. From a system design perspective, you need to be aware of the following key points:

■ The cable most likely attaches to a remote daughter card assembly within the chassis. The cable and the entire daughter card assembly are considered a part of the host system's PCI Express electrical and timing budget. You must ensure that any part of your cable interface and daughter card assembly meets all of the electrical and signal quality requirements. For more about daughter cards, see the next section, "Riser and Daughter Card Implementations."

■ The cable does not deliver any of the SMBUS or USB signals associated with ExpressCard nor does it deliver the main 3.3V or 1.5V power rails; 3.3Vaux, however, is transmitted over the cable. You must find other means or cables to deliver these signals and voltages. Power, for example, could be easily supplied directly from the system power supply, but voltage regulators on the daughter card may be required. Table 5.3 lists the pin assignments for the ExpressCard Internal Cable interface.

Table 5.3 ExpressCard† Internal Cable Pin List

Pin No.	Signal	Description
1	------	Not connected
2	------	Not connected
3	RSVD	Reserved for future use
4	OEM Defined	Pins that can be used by an OEM for proprietary
5	OEM Defined	signals. Left unconnected if not used.
6	GND	Ground
7	3.3Vaux	3.3V standby voltage
8	WAKE#	Signal for link reactivation
9	PERST#	PCI Express reset
10	CLKREQ#	Clock control for PCI Express
11	GND	Ground
12	PETp0	PCI Express transmitter differential pair—with
13	PETn0	respect to system board
14	GND	Ground
15	PERp0	PCI Express receiver differential pair—with
16	PERn0	respect to system board
17	GND	Ground
18	REFCLK+	100 MHz, SSC differential reference clock
19	REFCLK-	
20	CPPE#	Clock control for PCI Express

■ Both the main system board and the remote daughter card require a cable header to which the ExpressCard cable assembly can attach. You must observe an appropriate component keep-out region around this header on your PCB, to avoid any interference problems when subsequently trying to attach the cable to it.

To improve the impedance profile of the header interface, remove the PCB ground or reference plane immediately under the contact pads of the PCI Express signals.

Figure 5.10 shows the cable header and recommended PCB dimensions.

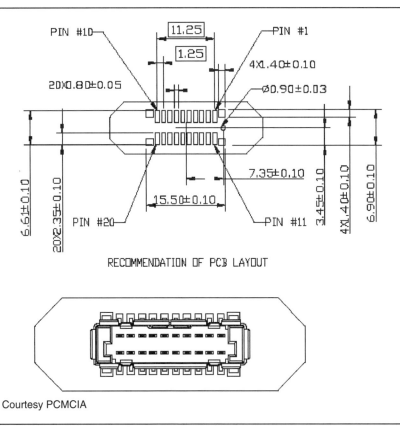

Courtesy PCMCIA

Figure 5.10   ExpressCard[†] Header and Recommended PCB Layout Dimensions

Riser and Daughter Card Implementations

Riser and daughter cards offer several advantages to you as a system designer. They allow you more choice in terms of the placement and location of your PCI Express interfaces. However, you must also account for any riser card or daughter card in the system's electrical and timing budgets. For example, if you intend for your design to interface with a standard add-in card as defined by the CEM Specification, the riser card or daughter card must be included in the host system's loss and jitter budgets, and cannot encroach on the add-in card's budget allowances. The same holds true when interfacing with an ExpressCard Module. Simply put, any riser or daughter card must be considered an extension or part of the host system's interconnect path.

The following section presents two examples of riser cards that exist or could be used with either add-in card or ExpressCard modules. For more information, especially pertaining to ExpressCard designs, refer to the *ExpressCard Implementation Guidelines* (PCMCIA 2003c).

PCI Express† Extension Risers

Extension risers are perhaps the simplest form of riser card to implement. They are completely passive in that they don't contain any additional active devices. The extension risers simply extend all the signals coming through a standard PCI Express connector, including power and auxiliary signals, and route them to an additional connector located some length away on the riser card. Figure 5.11 presents a conceptual illustration of this design.

When the riser card is plugged into a PCI Express connector on the main host system board, the additional connector mounted on the riser offers a perpendicular attachment slot to the plane of the system board, allowing increased form factor implementations. One popular use would be for a low-profile chassis, in which the right-angle mounting of an add-in card into the riser actually reduces the overall vertical space that the add-in card would have consumed had it been placed directly into a connector mounted on the host system PCB.

You need to subtract the impacts of the extension riser and additional connector from the system budget. To accommodate the additional interconnect impacts of the riser extension, ensure that the routing lengths of the PCI Express signals on the main system PCB are shorter than the

maximum allowable lengths typically used. While following routing guidelines similar to those for the system PCB, you should avoid any layer transitions on the riser card routing.

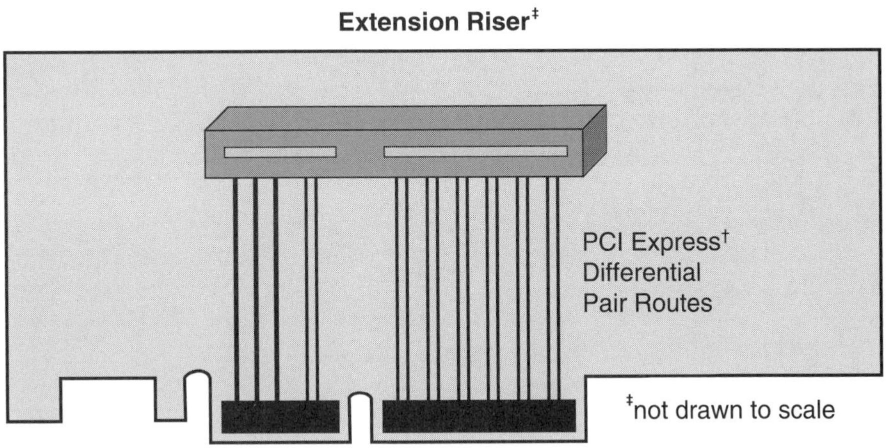

Extension Riser‡

PCI Express†
Differential
Pair Routes

‡not drawn to scale

Figure 5.11   Extension Riser Card Design

Any power rails should also be routed as planes or as very wide
traces—at least 100-mils wide—to reduce DC droop on the supplies. You
might need to make additional power supply provisions if the riser card is
especially large, or if the voltage supplies to the PCI Express connector on
the main system board are especially tight or at the edge of their tolerance
range. For more details, see "Power Delivery," later in this chapter.

You might also use a variation of the extension riser to mount an ExpressCard module interface, especially in a desktop system. The riser could
plug into a x1 PCI Express connector on the host system. Non-PCI Express
signals, such as USB signals needed for an ExpressCard module, could be
sent over a cable assembly to the riser card, as shown in Figure 5.12.

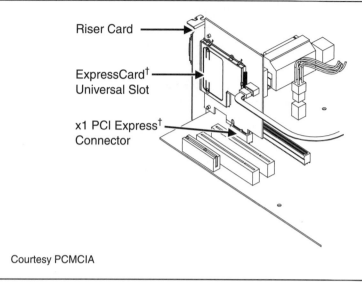

Riser Card

ExpressCard†
Universal Slot

x1 PCI Express†
Connector

Courtesy PCMCIA

Figure 5.12   Extension Riser for an ExpressCard† Module Plugging into the Host
System PCB

For the ExpressCard riser, you would follow the same routing guide-lines discussed previously for the add-in card riser PCI Express signals. Additionally, because ExpressCard voltage requirements are slightly more stringent than the add-in card requirements, you might need to make additional power supply provisions if you don't have sufficient headroom for voltage supply tolerances from the PCI Express connector on the main system board. For more details, see the "Power Delivery" section of this chapter.

Daughter Cards for ExpressCard† Modules

As a variation of the extension riser, you can define a separate "daughter card" PCB on which the ExpressCard module interface resides. You can then place the daughter card in any convenient location within your system's chassis, far removed from the motherboard or host PCB. You connect the PCI Express signals needed for the ExpressCard module through the ExpressCard Internal Cable, as discussed earlier in this chapter. Figure 5.13 presents a conceptual illustration of a daughter card topology design.

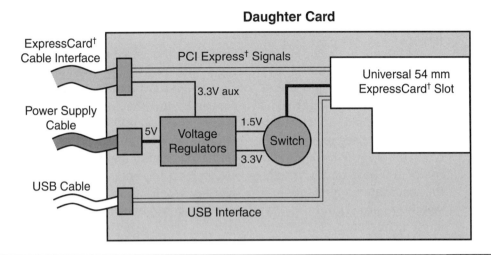

Figure 5.13   Topology of a Daughter Card for an ExpressCard[†] Module Interface

Because the ExpressCard Internal Cable only delivers PCI Express signals, you must supply the USB signals through a separate cable. You would also need to supply the 3.3V and 1.5V power rails through a separate cable. Most likely, you would want to supply power through the 5V output of the main supply, and then use voltage regulators on the daughter card to regulate the power down to the 3.3V and 1.5V levels required with a power switch located on the daughter card as well. Minimizing routing lengths and using very wide trace widths on the power signals helps to limit DC droop.

Because the entire ExpressCard module interface is mounted on the daughter card, you must ensure that all voltage tolerance requirements are met, just as they would need to be if the ExpressCard module interface were mounted on the main system PCB. For additional guidelines about system power delivery, see "Power Delivery" later in this chapter.

Since daughter cards are considered a part of the host system's electrical budget, you should ensure that discontinuities on the link are minimized. For example, no vias should be used for the PCI Express trace routing on the daughter card. Additionally, the trace length for the PCI Express signals should also be minimized, with a maximum recommended routing length of no more than 1.75 inches (PCMCIA 2004). Do not put AC coupling capacitors on the daughter card; instead, place them on the main system PCB for the host system's TX pairs—AC coupling capacitors are already located on the ExpressCard module for the module's TX pairs.

Although a daughter card offers you the flexibility of placement within the system chassis, an existing 3.5-inch drive bay provides straightforward placement and access for an ExpressCard external to the chassis. If you choose this approach, you must ensure that the dimensions are sized appropriately. The daughter card itself would likely need to be mounted in a separate housing assembly for attachment within the drive bay. To help provide a good path to chassis ground for the daughter card, use plated pads on the daughter card's mounting holes. This ensures that the pads are connected to the chassis when used for mounting the daughter card within the drive bay or drive bay housing per your design implementation.

Other System Design Considerations: Power Delivery, Thermal and Acoustical Management, and EMI

A successful PCI Express System design involves many different components in addition to those previously mentioned. As is common throughout engineering, some cross-discipline knowledge is required. As a successful system designer, you must not only consider specific link electrical and routing issues, but you must also be aware of some of the broader impacts of your design to the system. This holistic approach forces you to consider such areas as power delivery, thermal and acoustical management, as well as EMI mitigation.

Power Delivery

By ensuring a clean power source to the PCI Express components in your design, you can help increase performance and reliability. The following general guidelines can help to ensure good power delivery on your system design.

High-Frequency Decoupling

Use high-frequency caps for decoupling of VCC pins on PCI Express interfaces. Typically, values of 0.1uF to 0.01uF are sufficient for this purpose. High-frequency decoupling helps prevent excessive noise on the power supply or ground signals, which could compromise performance.

Bulk Decoupling

You should also use bulk decoupling capacitors, with values ranging from 10uF to hundreds of microfarads on each power supply rail used by your PCI Express components, depending on the anticipated demand of the components. Bulk decoupling helps to meet the instantaneous current demands of the components. Locate these caps in close proximity to the devices they are intended to benefit.

Short, Wide Traces

You should not have any additional trace length between the capacitors and the vias used to attach them to the power or ground planes. Any time you need to use trace routes instead of full planes for power delivery, make the traces as wide as possible, that is ≥100 mils, and for as short a distance as feasible. In other words, take care not to have your power supply trace routes meander around your board. The underlying goal is to minimize loop inductance and DC droop on the power supplies.

Limiting DC droop can be done by properly routing the power supply signals. The resistance of power supply traces depends on the thickness and width of the traces, the length of the trace route, and the tolerances or minimum voltage levels at both the power supply and the destination interface.

Equation 5.1 allows you to calculate the resistance of the trace route for typical copper-plated microstrip traces (PCI-SIG 2003a).

Equation 5.1   Calculating DC Resistance of a Microstrip Trace Route

$$\text{Resistance } (\Omega/\text{inch}) = \sim (0.65866 \times 10^{-6}) / (W * T)$$

where,

 W is the trace width (in inches)

 T is the trace thickness (in inches)

Assuming a trace width of 100 mils (0.1 inches) and a nominal plated 0.5-ounce copper trace thickness of 2 mils (0.002 inches), the predicted resistance would be ~3.3 mΩ per inch. With this resistance, given a minimum allowable DC droop of 54 mΩ on your 12V interface, you could route a 100-mil trace up to 16 inches in length and be just under your limit.

Equation 5.2 yields the maximum allowable impedance that limits the DC voltage droop of a given power supply rail (PCI-SIG 2003a). You need to know the voltage supply and requirement tolerances, along with any additional impedances in the path, such as the resistance of the power pins. For example, if you were routing the 3.3V supply to a x16 connector, assuming that the resistance of each pin of the connector was ~40 mΩ with a total of three 3.3V pins, you would have approximately 31 mΩ of allowable DC resistance for your 3.3V power supply trace route to the connector. The minimum voltage supply output in this case would be 3.135V (3.3V minus 5 percent) and the input requirement would be 3.003V (3.3V minus 9 percent) with a supply current of 3mA. You can then balance this requirement with the trace length and width tradeoffs described in Equation 5.1.

Equation 5.2   Calculating Allowable Impedance of Power Supply Rails

$$Zpwr\ (m\Omega) \leq [(Vps - Vdest)\ /\ Imax] - Zpin\_total$$

where:

$Zpwr$ = total allowable impedance (in mΩ) of power supply rail routing

Vps = voltage supply minimum output

$Vdest$ = minimum voltage supply requirement at the destination

$Imax$ = maximum supply current

$Zpin$ = total impedance (in mΩ) of power pins—either device or connector

---

In addition to the general guidelines for system power delivery, the following guidelines and requirements are applicable when designing a system that interfaces with an add-in card based on the PCI Express CEM specification or with an Express Card module interface. For guidelines about the power delivery on the add-in cards or Express Card modules themselves, refer to Chapter 7, "Add-in Cards and ExpressCard Modules."

Add-in Card System Power Delivery Requirements

The PCI Express Electromechanical Specification allows for up to 75W of power to be consumed by the x16 connector add-in card from the 12V, 3.3V and 3.3Vaux power rails. Table 5.4 lists the power supply rail requirements for the connector interfaces (PCI-SIG 2004b).

Table 5.4   Power Supply Rail Requirements from *PCI Express CEM Specification*

Power Rail	x1 Connector	x4/x8 Connector	x16 Connector
+3.3V			
Voltage Tolerance	± 9% (max)	± 9% (max)	± 9% (max)
Supply Current	3.0 A (max)	3.0 A (max)	3.0 A (max)
Capacitive Load	1000 μF (max)	1000 μF (max)	1000 μF (max)
+12V			
Voltage Tolerance	± 8%	± 8%	± 8%
Supply Current	0.5 A	2.1 A (max)	5.5 A (max)
Capacitive Load	300 μF (max)	1000 μF (max)	2000 μF (max)
+3.3Vaux			
Voltage Tolerance	± 9% (max)	± 9% (max)	± 9% (max)
Supply Current			
Wakeup Enabled	375 mA (max)	375 mA (max)	375 mA (max)
Non-wakeup Enabled	20 mA (max)	20 mA (max)	20 mA (max)
Capacitive Load	150 μF (max)	150 μF (max)	150 μF (max)

The maximum power demand of 75W is most likely to come from a graphics card. To meet the high power demands of graphics cards for desktop systems, you will likely need additional +12V capability beyond that currently supplied by a standard 2x10 pin ATX power supply connection. You can supply the additional power by using a 2x12 pin power supply connector, as specified in the latest *ATX12V Power Supply Design Guide* (Intel 2004). The extra capacity on the 2x12 connector allows for additional +12V, +5V, and +3.3V pins as well as one more ground pin. Keep in mind that while a 2x10 power supply cable fits into a 2x12 header, even though the latch mechanism would be misaligned, a 2x12 cable does not fit into a 2x10 header.

The tolerances in the *PCI Express CEM Specification* for the voltage interfaces at the add-in card connectors are especially tight: ±9 percent for the 3.3V / 3.3Vaux rails and ±8 percent for the 12V rail. Because a typical ATX power supply already has an output tolerance of ±5 percent for both the 12V and 3.3V rails, you must take care when routing these supply lines, so as not to exceed the minimum voltage levels allowed at the add-in card connector interfaces. In order to minimize DC voltage droop when routing the power rails, you must either use entire planes to deliver these voltages or carefully follow the guidelines for trace thickness, width, and length, as described earlier in this section.

ExpressCard⁺ Power Delivery Requirements

Many of the guidelines for add-in card power delivery also apply to ExpressCard power delivery in your system designs. In addition, the following general guidelines and requirements apply specifically to ExpressCard power delivery.

- You must supply clean voltage supplies on the 3.3V, 3.3Vaux, and 1.5V interfaces. The ExpressCard does not use the 12V supply rail that an add-in card might use.

- Any power switch resistance, found especially on mobile and daughter card designs, should be minimized.

- Voltage regulators for ExpressCard interfaces should be placed as close as possible to the ExpressCard module to limit voltage droop.

- Trace resistance should be less than 10mΩ (PCMCIA 2003c).

For specific requirements on ExpressCard module interfaces, refer to the *ExpressCard Implementation Guidelines* (PCMCIA 2003c).

Thermal and Acoustical Management

Thermal and acoustical management issues are strongly related to the power delivery requirements and demands of your design. The more power required, especially in a confined space or area as with an add-in card interface or an ExpressCard module, the more important the thermal and acoustical issues become. Acoustical management itself is actually a direct offspring of thermal management, in that it is mainly concerned with limiting the noise or chatter associated with thermal cooling fans attached to heat sinks. The following system-level guidelines and requirements apply to thermal and acoustical management of add-in card and ExpressCard module interfaces.

Add-in Card Thermal and Acoustical System Recommendations

System thermal management and implementation techniques are most effective when used in concert with the recommendations in Chapter 7, "Add-in Cards and ExpressCard Modules." Here is a brief summary of key guidelines:

■ Make sure that your chassis design supports a good source of cool air for your x16 connectors, which are likely to be populated with high-performance graphics cards. One popular approach is to place cool air vents near the top edge of the chassis where the top of the add-in card is located.

■ When using a pressurized chassis design, consider direct ducting of cool air.

System integrators can implement other effective and less intrusive techniques for thermal management, too. These techniques might include population of add-in card slots with specific profile or sized cards to improve airflow, or leaving certain slots unpopulated altogether.

Acoustical management typically affects add-in card design more than system design, since the primary sources of noise are heat sink fans on graphics cards. By enabling a good system thermal design, however, you can help reduce the need for higher speed fans on the add-in card, thereby reducing overall system noise generation as well.

ExpressCard[t] Thermal and Acoustical System Recommendations

ExpressCard module interfaces don't require a lot of extra work on the part of the host system designer. However, the host system does need to help minimize the ambient temperature in the vicinity of the ExpressCard module interface and not do anything to contribute to a higher than anticipated thermal profile at the ExpressCard module interface.

EMI Mitigation

Electromagnetic interference (EMI) mitigation becomes a concern whenever you are designing a system with high-speed interconnects such as PCI Express. Limiting the effects of EMI in your system saves you time and debug efforts during the regulatory testing phase of your design. What's more, it helps to ensure that your robust design is more likely to meet the electrical budget and signal quality requirements of your PCI Express interface. To limit the effects of EMI, properly route the differential signals in your PCI Express topologies by following the guidelines provided for routing high-speed traces and clocks signals. For details, see "System-level Floor-planning," earlier in this chapter, and Chapter 6, "PCB Design." Additionally, enabling SSC as discussed earlier in the "System Reference Clock" section of this chapter also helps to reduce EMI impacts. Scrambling, an additional feature of the specification discussed in Chapter 1, can also help to mitigate EMI in your design.

Due to the unique nature of an ExpressCard interface, EMI is also a particular concern for systems that integrate ExpressCard modules. The following guidelines and requirements are especially pertinent to system designs that support ExpressCard implementations:

■ ExpressCard *slots* should have some type of metal enclosure to limit EMI effects. The slot cover should be efficiently tied into the system and chassis ground through a low resistance path. This can be done by the use of grounding fingers on the sides of the slot, or by some other means (PCMCIA 2003c).

■ All ExpressCard host systems must also provide a means for grounding the ExpressCard *module*—for example, by providing contact points on the slot enclosure or on the guide rails within the enclosure.

Chapter 6

Printed Circuit Board Design Considerations

...As we know, there are known knowns...we also know there are known unknowns...But there are also unknown unknowns—the ones we don't know we don't know.

—Donald Rumsfeld

Printed circuit boards (PCBs) using Fire Resistant #4 (FR-4) material constitute one of the most prevalent mediums for electrical interconnects. Despite their widespread use, however, fundamental characteristics of the PCB are often overlooked or misunderstood.

To build a successful PCI Express[†] interconnect, you must address certain PCB design considerations. For example, you must decide which layers of the PCB to route the signals on, determine how wide and how long to make the traces, and understand the impact of your routing choices on the product's performance to electrical specifications. You must also understand the physical properties and limitations of the materials that make up the PCB and influence its performance.

PCB Stackup Configurations and Tradeoffs

Each printed circuit board is composed of various materials arranged in a defined manner. The ordering and combination of these materials is often referred to as the PCB *stackup*. For PCI Express interconnects, you can use a wide variety of stackups. For any given design, you must consider such stackup-related factors as overall cost, routing density, power delivery, signal integrity requirements, and reference plane requirements.

Desktop and mobile system implementations are often more cost-constrained than server-type platforms and tend to generally use four-layer stackups, since more layers typically cost more money. For server or workstation system implementations, multi-layer stackups of 6, 8, or even 10 layers are prevalent. Add-in card stackups may vary as to layer count as well, though four-layer and six-layer implementations are typically found among high volume designs intended for desktop and workstation systems.

When defining the layer count in a stackup, the number of stated layers typically refers to the number of copper layers present. For example, a four-layer stackup would have a total of four signal/reference layers.

General Effects of a PCB Stackup on Electrical Performance

The type of stackup, and the properties of the materials used in creating that stackup, directly contribute to the overall loss and jitter characteristics of the PCI Express interconnect.

■ Four-layer based stackups generally utilize *microstrip* routing—traces routed on the outer layers—with power delivery planes occupying the inner layers.

■ Multi-layer designs, such as those with six or more layers, primarily use *stripline* routing—traces routed on the inner layers—as well as microstrip routing for interconnect traces.

Whether you use stripline or microstrip routing, the stackup has an inherent effect on your electrical performance.

■ Microstrip differential traces inherently display greater impedance variations than stripline traces, impacting jitter and loss.

■ Microstrip traces are more susceptible to certain kinds of crosstalk than stripline traces; this can potentially result in more interconnect jitter.

■ Thicker microstrip copper traces demonstrate less skin effect loss, while thinner traces demonstrate more skin effect loss.

■ Stripline traces are generally more susceptible than microstrip traces to discontinuities such as via stubs.

■ Plating of copper traces with non-copper materials such as tin and nickel increases the relative loss as compared with a pure copper trace of the same thickness.

- In general, wider traces demonstrate less loss.

- Thicker dielectrics demonstrate less loss. Dielectric make-up or construction, including fiber weave density and resin-to-glass ratio, also impacts loss.

Four-layer Stackups: Microstrip Trace Designs

Figure 6.1 presents an example of a four-layer printed circuit board stackup using microstrip trace routing. This four-layer stackup assumes a nominal overall board thickness of 0.062 inches, which is typical for most system boards. In fact, the *PCI Express Card Electromechanical (CEM) Specification* (PCI-SIG 2004b) actually requires a 0.062-inch thickness for PCI Express add-in cards. Although Figure 6.1 lists trends in manufacturing variances, these tolerances are only guidelines and should not be used as precise boundaries.

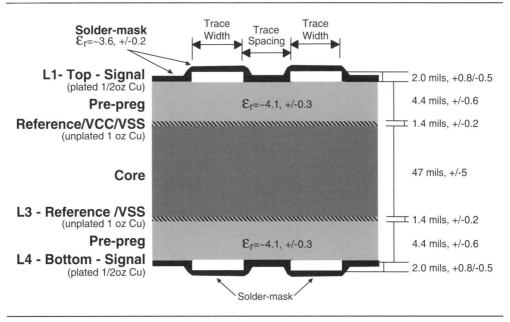

Figure 6.1   Example Stackup of a Four-layer Printed Circuit Board

Several types of pre-preg, or laminate, material may be used for the dielectric located between layers L1/L2 and layers L3/L4. One of the most common implementations is to use a single sheet of 2116 material for the dielectric. This laminate typically produces the nominal thickness and dielectric constant described in Figure 6.1. To form the "core" of the PCB, several sheets of 7628 are commonly used. This type of laminate is quite thick and is typically used for rigid or semi-rigid stackups, thus making it ideal for the center of the PCB.

PCB manufacturers use the number 2116 to identify a particular type of pre-preg or laminate with a given thickness and resin-to-glass ratio. Thinner dielectrics are also available, and can include 1080 and 1500 laminates. Extremely low-loss dielectrics such as Rogers† and Nelco† are also permitted, but typically are cost-prohibitive and are not required for most PCI Express designs.

By understanding several key aspects of the four-layer stackup, you can make better tradeoffs and decisions when you implement your PCI Express design and layout.

■ As mentioned in Chapter 5, components, including AC coupling caps, are typically limited to single-sided placement on the top layer of the board. This requirement is due to increased manufacturing costs associated with double-sided placement for High Volume Manufacturing (HVM) environments.

The location of AC coupling caps on the top layer actually works to your advantage for PCI Express signals. Because all Transmit (TX) pairs must have an AC coupling capacitor, you can simply keep all your TX pairs on the top layer of the motherboard, thus avoiding the use of unnecessary vias.

■ Four-layer stackups generally limit the design to just one power (VCC) reference plane and one ground (VSS) reference plane. The PCI Express specification does not require these two reference planes to be in the locations shown in Figure 6.1. Depending on other system design requirements, you might want to interchange them. Regardless of how you arrange the initial VSS and VCC plane layers, you should follow the reference plane guidelines presented later in this chapter.

■ Signals routed as microstrip traces on layers L1 and L4 are subject to impacts from spacing, solder-mask, plating, etching, and dielectric fiberglass weave. These impacts can greatly affect PCI Express performance.

Plating and etching have a greater negative impact on the impedance tolerance for differential pair signals than they do for signals consisting of a single trace. The differential impedance for microstrip traces is significantly influenced by both the height and shape of the traces that make up a differential pair. Since PCI Express signals utilize differential pair routing, you need to pay more attention to the impedance targets on these signals than with other single-ended signal designs.

Over-etching during the PCB fabrication process causes traces to become narrower than originally specified. Under-etching results in traces being wider than originally specified. Both over-etching and under-etching can affect the differential impedance of your PCI Express signals.

Figure 6.2 shows an example of how etching and plating can influence the shape of a signal trace.

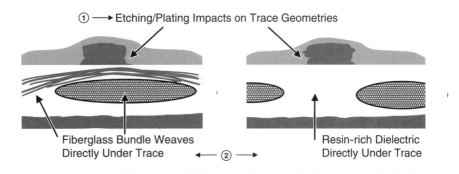

Figure 6.2   Detailed Cross-Sections of Microstrip Traces

As shown in Figure 6.2, the alignment of the two traces of a differential pair over the fiberglass bundles and/or resin-rich areas—called resin troughs—in the PCB dielectric can vary, thus affecting the resulting differential impedance. Such a scenario can contribute to an increase in the amount of common mode voltage found on the differential pair. The *PCI Express Base Specification* (PCI-SIG 2004a) limits common mode voltage, so it is important to find ways to reduce it.

Thinner dielectrics, such as 1080, typically have less dense glass weave patterns, which can further aggravate the common mode effects. For guidelines that can help to minimize interconnect induced common mode voltage, refer to "High-Speed Trace Routing," later in this chapter.

Solder-mask variation also impacts the impedance of differential microstrip traces because the solder-mask application to the PCB is generally not uniform. For example, a thin layer of solder-mask—about 0.5 mils—usually exists immediately above the copper traces, while a thicker layer is present next to and immediately between the pairs of the differential traces. This thicker layer of solder-mask can be almost equal to the thickness of the traces themselves. Figure 6.3 shows an example of what the solder-mask variation may look like. The good news, however, is that the solder-mask does not have as significant an impact on the impedance of PCI Express signals as is found with plating and etching variations.

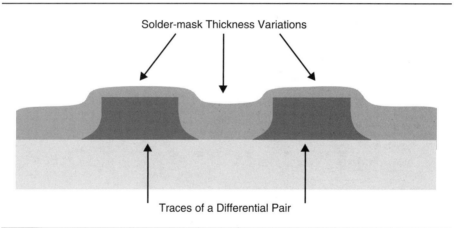

Figure 6.3 Solder-mask Thickness Variations on Microstrip Traces

Note Stackups accommodating stripline routing, such as those with six or more layers, could produce a better differential impedance tolerance than microstrip designs due in part to the absence of solder-mask and plating effects. Impacts due to etching variations are also somewhat more limited. However, fiberglass bundle weave impacts could actually have more impact on striplines than microstrip traces.

■ HVM PCB technology restricts the minimum trace widths that can be used for a design as well as the minimum spacing or air gap that lies between the various traces. These restrictions mean that the "ideal" geometry for your PCI Express design might not be practical to implement. Before you begin your design, contact your PCB vendor(s) to verify their restrictions so that you can avoid any issues or cost adders once fabrication begins.

For specific trace width and spacing targets for PCI Express differential pairs, see "Differential Pairs: Impedance and Routing," later in this chapter.

Multi-layer Stackups: Stripline Trace Designs

As opposed to four-layer designs, multi-layer designs with 6, 8, or 10 or more layers can use internal layers to route PCI Express signal traces as striplines as well as routing microstrip traces on the outer layers. Figure 6.4 shows an example of a ten-layer stackup.

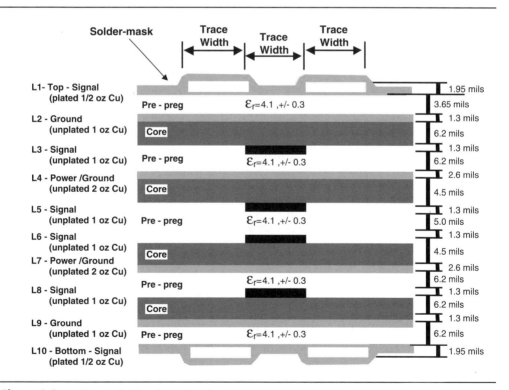

Figure 6.4   Example Ten-layer Stackup

Internal layer signals can be routed as either symmetric or nonsymmetric striplines. In a symmetric stripline signal, the same thickness of dielectric material separates it from the two nearest reference planes above and below the trace. A nonsymmetric stripline signal has a thicker amount of dielectric above it and the nearest reference plane, for example, than below it. Figure 6.5 illustrates both types of stripline implementations.

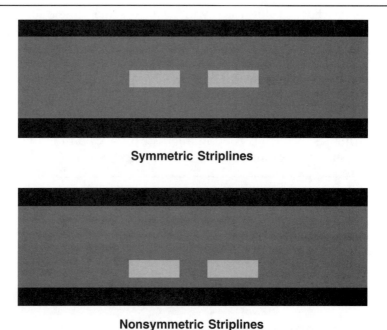

Symmetric Striplines

Nonsymmetric Striplines

Figure 6.5   Symmetric and Nonsymmetric Stripline Routing

Servers, workstations, and even some mobile and communication platforms often require the high layer counts of multi-layer boards in order to fit more traces and components in a constrained area—and can afford the price premium for the additional layers. While such an implementation can incrementally increase the cost and complexity of a design, it can also allow for greater flexibility. Multi-layer stripline designs have some inherent advantages:

■ Additional plane layers become available for power delivery and reference planes. For example, you might now be able to keep all of your external microstrip traces referenced to a continuous ground plane by placing the VSS layers adjacent to your external layers and locating your VCC plane(s) on one or more of the additional internal layers you have added.

■ Because stripline traces are surrounded by a fairly homogenous dielectric medium, they are less susceptible to crosstalk than microstrip traces. Microstrip traces, on the other hand, are surrounded by an FR-4 dielectric below, and a combination of solder-mask and air above. The nearly homogenous medium surrounding stripline traces eliminates almost all effects of far-end crosstalk (FEXT) on the system, significantly improving the performance of your PCI Express differential pairs.

■ Stripline traces also exhibit a better differential impedance tolerance than microstrip traces, due to the absence of solder-mask and plating. Impacts due to etching variations are also somewhat more limited.

■ A multi-layer stackup design also offers the possibility of increased routing density while reducing the overall board size. By keeping the PCB size the same as a four-layer board, additional routing channels are available when additional internal signal layers are added. Having multiple layers available for signal routing can also allow for greater isolation between adjacent PCI Express traces, helping to reduce crosstalk and improve signal integrity.

Simply adding additional layers to a four-layer design does not solve all of your design problems. Using multi-layer stackups with stripline routing does have some disadvantages:

■ *Increased cost.* Simply put, the more layers you have, the more money the PCB vendor will charge you per board. As such, always try to utilize the minimum number of layers that will still give you adequate performance.

■ *Increased design complexity.* Since external layer microstrip traces and internal layer stripline traces have different reference planes and dielectric properties associated with them, you must now manage different trace width and spacing requirements for your PCI Express differential pairs: one set for the microstrip traces and one set for the stripline traces.

■ *Susceptibility to via stubs.* Stripline traces are inherently more susceptible than microstrip traces to stubs from plated through-hole (PTH) vias. Whereas microstrip traces can attach to each end of a via from one layer to another, a stripline trace often intersects a via at a midpoint, thus leaving at times a rather large stub on the trace, as shown in Figure 6.6. Stubs from vias can create discontinuities, negatively affecting the signal integrity of your PCI Express signals.

You can eliminate stubs from PTH vias on stripline traces by using blind and/or buried vias in your design. These types of vias only connect specific adjacent layers of the PCB and do not traverse the entire cross-section of the board as do PTH vias. However, PCB vendors usually charge a price premium for boards with blind and buried vias.

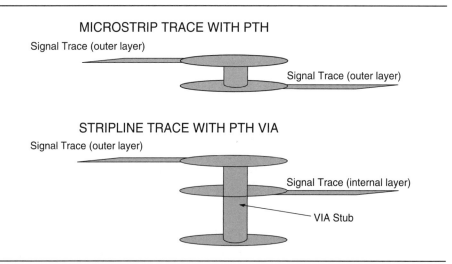

Figure 6.6   Via Stubs on Stripline Traces; No Stubs on Microstrip Traces

Other aspects of multi-layer stackups are similar to four-layer stackups. Although the nominal thickness for some multi-layer boards usually tends to be the same as four-layer boards, that is, 0.062 inches, other multi-layer board designs can actually be quite a bit thicker, 0.090 inches or more. The outer dielectric and microstrip trace routing layers for a multi-layer design can even be made to look just like a four-layer stackup by utilizing the same type of dielectric and copper thickness for both designs. Of course, the microstrip traces on the multi-layer stackup would then be susceptible to the impacts described previously for four-layer boards.

High-Speed Trace Routing

This section provides general guidelines for the PCB trace-related aspects of the PCI Express interconnect. To ensure proper performance and compliance with the loss and jitter budgets of the overall PCI Express interface, you should simulate all interconnect paths.

Differential Pairs: Impedance and Routing

The *PCI Express Base Specification* doesn't explicitly require a specific impedance in order for a PCB to be in compliance with the specification. It simply requires that the PCB meet the loss and jitter budgets of the PCI Express interface. Even so, an impedance target is an important metric that can help you properly manage the layout and fabrication of your design. Additionally, it is important to create some basic routing rules that can be used during CAD layout in order to help ensure that the loss and jitter budgets are indeed being met. The following recommendations have been found to be both helpful and practical during the course of several PCI Express designs.

- An overall impedance of 100 Ω ±20 percent is desirable. Impedance values falling within this range have been found to be adequate for most PCI Express designs. The ±20 percent range must also include the PCB manufacturing tolerances.

Note | A PCI Express system is typically dominated by the overall loss characteristics of the interconnect, not just the impedance of the differential traces themselves. While both impedance and system loss are important, maintaining a *precise* 100 Ω impedance value for the differential pairs is not necessarily required.

- Three main contributors can affect differential trace impedance: spacing within the differential pair, coupling to an adjacent reference plane, and the thickness of the traces within the pair.

  For example, at high frequencies, edge-coupled traces inherently force the current concentration to the extreme inner edge of the trace, closest to the neighboring signal of the differential pair. The thicker the traces are that make up the differential pair, the more coupling they exhibit with each other. Since the differential impedance of the two traces is tied directly to the amount of coupling within the pair, the thickness of the traces dramatically impacts the differential impedance they will produce.

Each contributor should be carefully managed. You can do this by working with your PCB fabrication vendor to maintain the physical geometries specified in Figure 6.1 for four-layer stackups or Figure 6.4 for multi-layer stackups. Also follow the trace spacing recommendations in "Differential Pairs: Width and Spacing," later in this chapter.

Do not assume that just because the PCI Express microstrip signals are differential pairs, they won't couple to the reference plane immediately below them. Although designed as differential pairs, they still exhibit a fair amount of coupling to the adjacent reference plane, which is typically only separated from the traces by a dielectric thickness of a few mils or less. This coupling to the reference plane has a large role in determining the differential impedance of the two traces.

■ Coupling of the differential signals or relative close physical spacing within the differential pair, and increased spacing to neighboring differential pairs and other signals, helps to minimize harmful crosstalk impacts and EMI effects. For specific requirements, see "Differential Pairs: Width and Spacing," later in this chapter.

■ Where possible, trace routes of long distances should be routed at an off-angle to the X-Y axis of the PCB layer in order to distribute the effects of fiberglass bundle weaves and resin-rich areas of the dielectric.

Current data from several test boards suggests that at least a 5-degree offset works well in most situations. Most designs actually do this by default already, since PCI Express components are usually not located directly across from one another; the traces tend to meander around the board, thus providing a natural offset, before they reach their final destination. By ensuring that long trace routing lengths are truly implemented at an off angle, you can help eliminate the common mode effects that can be caused by the different propagation delays of signals traveling over fiberglass bundles versus those traveling over resin troughs. Figure 6.7 illustrates fiberglass weave patterns in the dielectric and some associated routing recommendations.

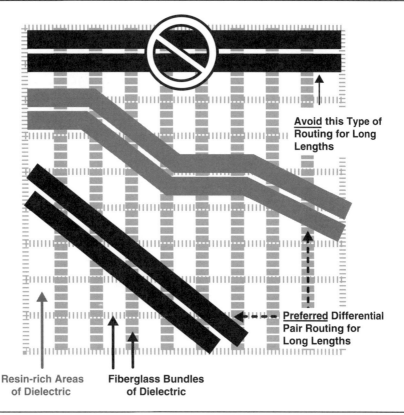

Avoid this Type of
Routing for Long
Lengths

Preferred Differential
Pair Routing for
Long Lengths

Resin-rich Areas
of Dielectric

Fiberglass Bundles
of Dielectric

Figure 6.7 Top View of a PCB Illustrating Fiberglass Weave Patterns in the Dielectric

Differential Pairs: Width and Spacing

Given a particular PCB stackup, the impedance for PCI Express differential traces is determined by the width and spacing requirements you establish. Signal integrity performance is also impacted by whether or not you use an appropriate air gap spacing from your differential pairs to adjacent traces. By heeding the following width and spacing guidelines for PCI Express differential pair traces, you can help to ensure that your interconnect loss and jitter budgets are met. These recommendations are based on the stackups discussed earlier. Some exceptions to these guidelines are allowed in the breakout regions of the PCB; for details, see "Breakout Areas," later in this chapter.

■ As shown in Figure 6.8, all edge-coupled microstrip traces of a differential pair should be 5-mils wide, with a 7-mil air gap spacing between the traces of the pair. This routing implementation can also be referred to as 5-on-7 or 5/7/5 routing.

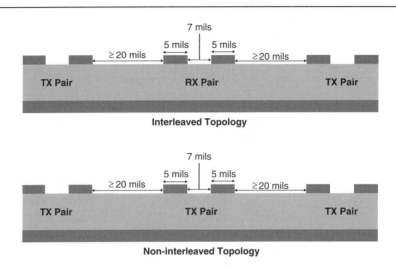

Figure 6.8   Microstrip Trace Width and Spacing Recommendations

Based on simulation results and several test board implementations at Intel, the 5/7/5 routing for microstrip differential pairs was found to be the best compromise between impedance targets, loss impacts, crosstalk immunity, and routing flexibility, even though this geometry actually tends to produce nominal impedance slightly below 100 Ω.

■ All edge-coupled stripline differential traces should use 5/5/5 routing, as shown in Figure 6.9.

Note | If you use thicker or thinner dielectrics than those shown in Figure 6.1 and Figure 6.4, you must adjust the trace width and spacing requirements listed here!

■ To help reduce negative crosstalk effects, maintain a 20-mil edge-to-edge air gap between traces of adjacent pairs. To reduce the effects of near-end crosstalk (NEXT), route all differential pairs in a non-interleaved fashion.

While interleaved routing for microstrip traces can theoretically help eliminate far-end crosstalk (FEXT), simulations have shown that PCI Express signals can be far more susceptible to NEXT than FEXT. If you are using an interleaved routing topology, make sure that you space the interleaved PCI Express differential pairs *at least* as far apart as you would on a non-interleaved topology; for example, 20 mils at minimum.

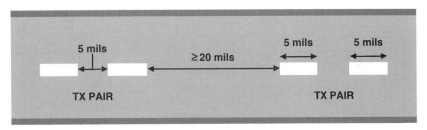

Stripline Cross-section

Figure 6.9   Stripline Trace and Width Recommendations

■ Spacing to all non-PCI Express signals should also be at least 20 mils. If non-PCI Express signals have significantly higher voltage levels and/or edge rates than the PCI Express signals, increase this spacing to at least 30 mils in order to avoid harmful coupling issues.

Note | If other interfaces on your PCB also utilize 5-mil wide traces, you might want to use a unique trace width of 4.9 mils for the PCI Express trace routes, leaving an air gap separation of 7.1 mils with a pair. In this way, the PCB fab vendor can calibrate their etching on these traces around a specific impedance target, independent of the other 5-mil traces on your board.

■ Any uncoupled sections, such as a trace within a differential pair that exceeds the intra-pair spacing rule of 7 mils, can be routed as a 7-mil wide trace—rather than 5 mils—when the distance of the violation in air gap spacing is roughly 100 mils or more. Widening these isolated sections of trace allows them to maintain their differential impedance across the uncoupled region. For an example of this scenario, see Figure 6.10.

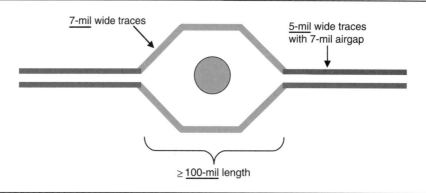

Figure 6.10   Trace Width Variation Guidelines

■ Whenever possible, maintain lateral routing symmetry between the two signals of a differential pair. Figure 6.11 shows the preferred symmetrical routing layout.

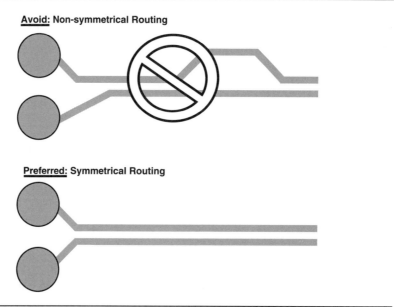

Figure 6.11   Example of Symmetrical and Non-symmetrical Lateral Routing

Differential Pair Routing Lengths

Trace lengths directly impact the loss and jitter budgets of the interconnect. The following general recommendations apply to trace-length routing for multi-width PCI Express links on a four-layer microstrip board, such as x4, x8, x16, and so on. The distances listed include any trace lengths located in the breakout regions of the respective components.

■ Trace routing lengths from chip to chip usually can be routed up to about 15 inches, while still comfortably meeting all the electrical requirements of the PCI Express specification.

This guideline assumes that one wirebond package and one flip-chip package are attached to each end of the interconnect.

■ Trace routing lengths from a chipset pin to a connector pin usually can be routed up to about 12 inches. Following this guideline will help you to comply with the electrical specifications as set forth in the *PCI Express Card Electromechanical Specification* (PCI-SIG 2004b).

This guideline assumes that a flip-chip package and a PTH connector are attached to each end of the interconnect.

■ Differential pairs on an add-in card, connecting the edgefinger pad to the chipset pin, can be routed up to about 3.5 inches in length.

This guideline assumes that a flip-chip package and an edgefinger pad are attached to each end of the interconnect on the add-in card.

Note | These guidelines apply to multi-width PCI Express interconnects where crosstalk from adjacent PCI Express signals may interact with each other. For x1 links and topologies, however, simulations have shown that longer trace lengths may be achievable while still meeting all of the electrical specifications.

Impacts and Tradeoffs with Trace Lengths

Based on inherent physical properties of the PCB differential pairs, PCB traces can introduce as much as 0.25 dB to 0.35 dB of loss, and 1 ps or more of jitter, per inch per differential pair. By understanding these effects of trace length on loss and jitter budgets, you can make informed tradeoffs in your PCI Express design.

If you use shorter lengths in your topologies than those recommended in the previous section, you can make tradeoffs against other restrictions placed on the interconnect. For example, if you can shorten your trace length by a few inches, you may be able to increase the number of vias used on your differential pairs. Similarly, if you need to reduce the pair-to-pair spacing guideline due to a particularly dense routing area of the PCB, you can shorten your trace length by a few inches and allocate the extra budget toward a likely increase in crosstalk.

Other factors, such as vias, data patterns, edge rates, impedance discontinuities, and crosstalk, also contribute to system loss and jitter. After making any tradeoffs with regard to trace lengths, it is always wise to simulate the new topology in order to properly ensure compliance with the overall loss and jitter budgets of the system.

Length Matching—When and Where?

As mentioned in Chapter 5, PCI Express serial differential signals are exempt from many of the stringent length matching requirements of other interconnect architectures, such as source-synchronous or common clock-based designs. As such, there are only a few requirements for length matching with regards to PCI Express.

- Length matching from one differential pair to another is generally not required due to the large pair-to-pair skew allowed at a PCI Express receiving component. However, to reduce possible latency effects at certain components, you might want to match differential pairs within a few inches of each other. You may also be required to minimize length mismatches for the lanes or traces that route to add-in card connectors. Refer to Note 1 in Table 5.1 of Chapter 5 for more information.

- It is important to length match both nets within a given differential pair. Each net should be length matched such that no more than a 5-mil delta exists between the lengths of the two signals.

  While this guideline is not required by the specification, it helps you to ensure optimal signal integrity performance on your PCI Express differential pairs.

- When measuring the overall length of a given net in a differential pair, use the pad or pin edge-to-edge distance rather than the total trace etch present. Most CAD tools count any trace etch located with a pad as part of the overall length of the net being measured, even though such sections of trace are electrically part of the pad itself. However, if the amount of etch routing into every pad or pin is identical, you can use the total etch measurement. Figure 6.12 presents examples of trace etch located within a pad area.

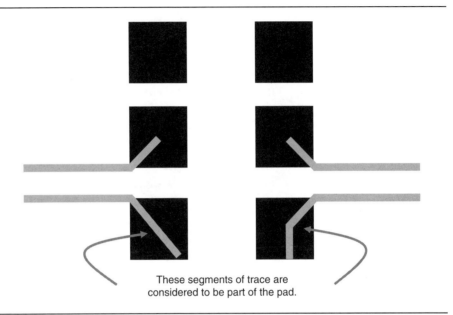

These segments of trace are considered to be part of the pad.

Figure 6.12   Examples of Etch Located Within a Pad of a Component

■ Length matching within a differential pair should occur on a segment-by-segment basis, as opposed to length matching across the total distance of the overall route.

Segments can include the route between two via transitions, between the pin of the component and the AC capacitor pad, or between the capacitor pad and the connector pin or edgefinger.

Whenever possible, length matching should occur at the immediate point of mismatch or discontinuity.

When trying to match lengths between nets of a differential pair, avoid "tight bends." For details, see "Bends," later in this chapter.

Reference Planes

Even though PCI Express traces are routed as coupled differential pairs, the reference plane for microstrip differential pairs still has a large amount of coupling. The following guidelines apply to reference planes.

■ Traces should avoid routing near or across discontinuities in the reference plane, such as splits and other voids. See "Breakout Areas" later in this chapter for some allowances with respect to this guideline.

Good reference planes help to minimize any AC common mode voltage found on the differential pair, as well as benefiting signal quality and reducing EMI impacts.

■ When routing near the edge and parallel to a reference plane, traces should maintain at least a 20-mil air gap to the edge of the plane. This recommendation can be relaxed when routing around minor voids around pins or vias.

■ As stated in the *PCI Express Card Electromechanical Specification* (PCI-SIG 2004b), PCI Express traces on the add-in card must reference the ground plane.

■ Wherever possible, PCI Express traces on your system board should reference the main ground (GND) plane in your board stackup. An alternative is to implement GND islands on the power (PWR) reference plane. These islands should be tied to the main GND plane with stitching vias within 100 mils of the point of signal launch/transition and at non-uniform intervals of no more than 0.5 inches along the edge of the GND island/plane. Possible points of signal launch include the signal pins of the chipset, connector pins, and at via or layer transitions and edgefingers. Up to four differential pairs can share one stitching via, so long as they are within the 100-mil distance requirement. Where possible, provide placement of additional stitching vias.

Stitching vias serve only to connect the upper and lower reference planes together and to help provide adequate signal return paths; they do not attach to your differential traces.

Note   GND pins on a chipset package or other component can be used to fulfill the GND via stitching recommendations.

Figure 6.13 shows example placements of stitching vias with a GND island.

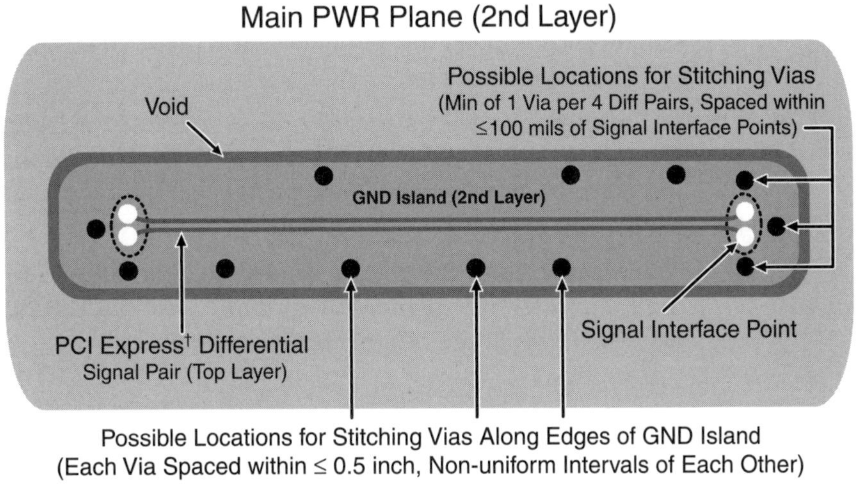

Figure 6.13   Example of PCB with Differential Pair on Top Layer and GND Island on Second Layer (PWR Plane) with Potential Stitching Vias

■ If the differential pairs cannot be GND-referenced on your system board, you can allow the pairs to reference the PWR plane, provided that stitching caps are used when traces switch layers and transition from GND to PWR plane referencing or vice versa.

Ideally, you should place stitching caps within 100 mils of the point where the differential pair transitions reference planes.

A minimum of one stitching cap can be shared by up to four differential pairs. This capacitor is most effective when each pair is within the 100-mil guideline. As the distance increases, its effect is less dominant.

Stitching cap values of 0.1 μF are sufficient.

You must use stitching vias when traces change layers but continue to reference the PWR plane. The same stitching via guidelines listed for GND plane islands also apply to PWR plane stitching vias.

If your design has any non-GND-referenced PCI Express traces on the system board, they will be transitioning reference planes when they cross the connector boundary, since all add-in card differential pairs must be GND-referenced. You should place stitching caps near the connector for these traces, according to the guidelines listed here.

■ Differential pair traces that do not experience a layer transition should not reference both PWR and GND planes along the routing path. In other words, only a single reference plane should be used along the entire routing path.

Additionally, both traces of a differential pair should remain over the same reference plane. For example, one net should not reference GND while the other references PWR.

Bends

Arbitrarily increasing the length of a trace by adding additional bends is known as *serpentine routing*. While serpentine routing is not required to match lengths from one PCI Express differential pair to another, bends or turns are still likely to be encountered while routing a PCI Express interconnect. For example, a coupled differential pair cannot always route in a straight line. Often, the pair must change course, thus requiring some type of bend or turn. In addition, a single trace of the differential pair might require some type of bend or turn as it routes into a component's pin or pad. In any case, you should avoid "tight bends," which can substantially impact the loss and jitter budgets of your system.

Figure 6.14 illustrates several "do's and don'ts" for tight bends. These scenarios are applicable to both coupled differential pairs and uncoupled sections of trace. Additionally, separate guidelines for coupled and uncoupled sections of PCI Express traces are also provided.

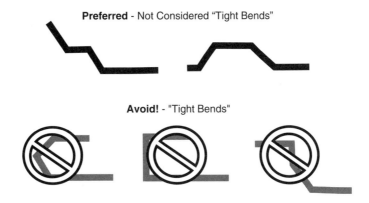

Figure 6.14   Acceptable Bends and Unacceptable "Tight Bends"

The following guidelines apply to *coupled* sections of a PCI Express differential pair.

■ Keep bends to a minimum for coupled differential pairs. Bends can introduce common mode noise into your system, which can affect the signal integrity and EMI effects of the differential pairs.

■ When using bends, follow these prioritized guidelines to avoid creating tight bends. Figure 6.15 illustrates these points.

1. All angles (α) between traces should be $\geq$ 135 degrees; in other words, each section of trace is routed at an angle of at most 45 degrees. There should be no 90-degree bends or turns!

2. The "inner air gap" (A) of a bend on a coupled differential pair should be greater than or equal to the minimum pair-to-pair spacing. Recall that 20 mils is the pair-to-pair spacing recommendation for microstrip traces; for details, refer to "Differential Pairs: Width and Spacing," earlier in this chapter.

3. Segments (B) and (C) should have a length of $\geq$ 1.5x the width of the trace. The trace length is measured with respect to the middle of the trace/bend vertex.

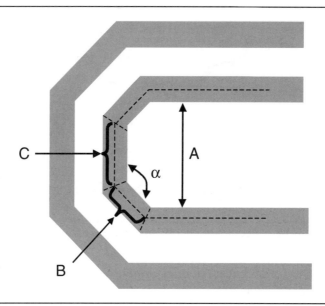

Figure 6.15   Bend Diagram for Coupled Differential Pairs

- Wherever possible, the number of left and right bends should be matched as closely as possible.

  Alternating left and right turns helps to minimize length skew differences between each signal of the differential pair.

The following guidelines apply to *uncoupled* sections of a differential pair that route into a component's pin or pad:

- The uncoupled section of trace routing into a pin or pad should be ≤ 45 mils when multiple bends are used—for example, when length matching the differential pair. Figure 6.16 demonstrates the preferred routing.

  The 45-mil length measurement is made with respect to the middle of the trace/bend vertex from the start of the uncoupled section to the edge of the pin or pad.

  When trace lengths are closely matched, the preferred method of routing is a symmetrical route without multiple bends. In this case, the uncoupled length should be minimized.

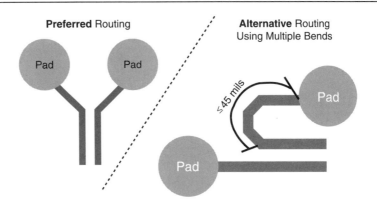

Figure 6.16 Routing/Bend Diagrams for Uncoupled Traces into Component Pins/Pads

■ When using multiple bends, follow these prioritized guidelines to avoid "tight bends." Figure 6.17 illustrates these points.

  1. All angles (α) between traces should be $\geq$ 135 degrees; therefore, traces at 45 degrees are allowed. There should be no 90-degree bends or turns.

  2. The minimum "air gap" (A) of a bend should be greater than or equal to three times the width of the trace.

  3. Segments (B) and (C) should have a length of $\geq$ 1.5x the width of the trace—the length being measured with respect to the middle of the trace/bend vertex.

  4. Segment (D) should be minimized as much as possible.

The direct concerns addressed by rules 3 and 4 are generally alleviated when following rules 1 and 2 and the 45-mil maximum length guideline mentioned previously. Therefore, rules 2 and 3 don't necessarily need to be verified during CAD for each and every net, but instead are provided here for completeness.

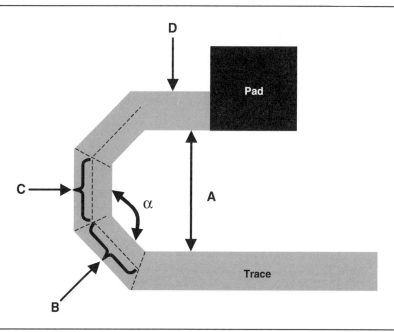

Figure 6.17 Bend Diagram for Uncoupled Section of a Differential Pair

Breakout Areas

Each PCI Express interface contains a "breakout sections" or section of the topology where traces are trying to escape the immediate vicinity of a component or connector. The most crucial areas for PCI Express designs tend to be with regards to a chipset pin or ball field.

By adhering to the following general guidelines, you can achieve a practical breakout strategy while maintaining the signal integrity of your PCI Express signals. These guidelines do not give specific pinout recommendations for various interfaces, such as x1, x2, x16, etc.

◼ If you have the luxury of influencing the design, or ballout, of a chipset you will be using, you should ensure that all the PCI Express signals are to be broken out, or grouped, as differential pairs.

Wherever feasible, use side-by-side breakout routing, to maximize the differential routing while minimizing discontinuities and trace length skew. Figure 6.18 illustrates side-by-side routing, along with other breakout styles.

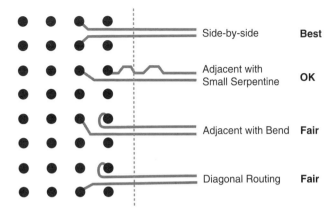

Figure 6.18   Breakout Styles

■ Wherever needed, length matching in a chipset breakout area or connector pin field should occur as close as possible to the signal pins without introducing any "tight bends." Otherwise, length matching should occur within the immediate segment. Refer to the example in Figure 6.19.

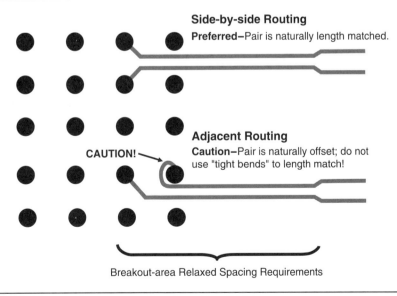

Figure 6.19   Package Pinout/Breakout Possibilities

Small, serpentine bends can also be used on a single net within a differential pair in order to length match it to the other net within the pair. This technique is especially effective in the breakout regions of a PCB. Figure 6.20 shows how to use small serpentines to match length in a breakout area.

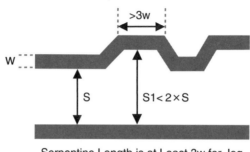

Serpentine Length is at Least 3w for Jog

Figure 6.20   Serpentine Bends in a Breakout Region.

It is sometimes possible, or even necessary, to make exceptions to the general trace routing guidelines to allow for the increased signal density in a component's pinfield. To ensure that your PCI Express traces maintain adequate signal quality in these regions, follow these guidelines:

■ Breakout areas are allowed at the chipset pins, the connector pins, and/or at the add-in card edgefingers.

■ A 250-mil breakout distance is allowed, wherein the trace routing geometry allowances can be reduced to a 5/5/5 layout (width/spacing /width), with a minimum 7-mil air gap to other signals. Wherever possible, use an air gap spacing that exceeds the 7-mil minimum.

■ To ensure that the variances do not negatively impact the crosstalk margin or the jitter and loss budgets, you should simulate deviations to the 250-mil breakout-area guideline.

The small sections of trace used to attach a chipset pin to a via—for example, traces that are less than 25 mils—do not necessarily require any special reference plane considerations. See Figure 6.21 for an example.

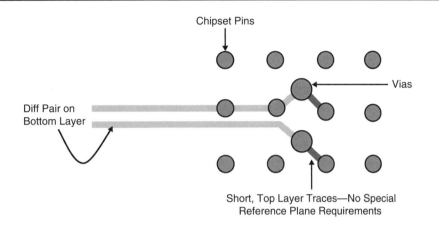

Figure 6.21   Breakout-Area Traces

When routing in a breakout area, via anti-pads may present disconti-nuities in the reference planes. When possible, avoid routing your differ-ential pairs over these areas. However, if you cannot avoid this scenario, minimize the amount of the trace that is over a void—such as a via anti-pad—both in terms of the length and the percentage of the width of the trace. At worst, no more than half of the trace width should be over the via anti-pad at any given time. Figure 6.22 presents an example of trace routing over an anti-pad.

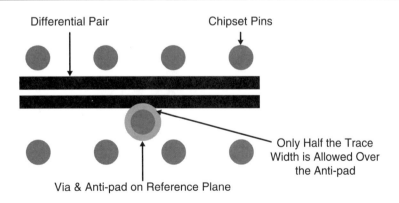

Figure 6.22   Trace Routing Over an Anti-Pad Void

Via Usage and Placement

Vias are often a CAD designer's best friend, allowing for signals to criss-cross layers in their journey across a printed circuit board. However, for high-speed interfaces such as PCI Express differential interconnects, via use should be more limited. Vias have the potential to adversely affect the overall loss and jitter budgets and can limit the maximum achievable routing length.

The following guidelines apply to via usage:

- Vias should have a pad size of 25 mils or less and a finished hole size of 14 mils or less.

- A standard anti-pad size of 35 mils is acceptable.

- Signal vias should have pads on unused internal layers removed.

- Vias should always be placed as a pair; they should be at the same relative location and placed in a symmetrical fashion along the differential pair. Figure 6.23 illustrates the preferred placement.

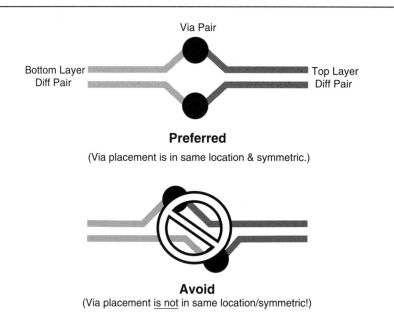

Figure 6.23   Placing Vias as a Pair

- When a differential pair transitions reference planes through the use of vias, follow the guidelines in the "Reference Planes" section of this chapter.

- No more than four via pairs should be used for each TX differential pair of a system board/add-in card topology.

  One via pair is allowed at the breakout section of a chipset to transition layers and/or adjacent to the edgefinger of the add-in card PCB.

  Two pairs of vias are allowed to transition layers and may be used to accommodate placement of the AC coupling capacitors. As noted, it is best to route TX signals that require AC coupling caps on the same layer as the caps themselves, in order to avoid via usage.

  Always treat the plated through-holes (PTHs) of the PCI Express add-in card connector pins as a via pair.

- A maximum of two via pairs are permitted on each Receive (RX) differential pair of a system board/add-in card topology.

  One of the via pairs may be located at the breakout section of a chipset to transition layers and/or adjacent to the edgefinger of the add-in card PCB. The other via pair is used up by the add-in card connector.

These guidelines allow for a maximum of six via pairs for the entire interconnect path when considering both the RX and TX signals respectively on the add-in card and the system board. Therefore, a maximum of six via pairs may also be used for chip-to-chip topologies.

As with the trace length recommendations, tradeoffs in the number of via pairs are permitted, so long as the loss and jitter budgets are still met across the entire interconnect. For example, you could choose to sacrifice overall trace length in order to allow an extra via pair to be present in the interconnect path.

Data gathered on some of Intel's test boards has shown that in some corner cases, each via pair could potentially contribute upwards of 0.25 dB of loss. Also, as discussed earlier in this chapter in the section "Differential Pair Routing Lengths," each inch of trace is anticipated to contribute approximately 0.25 dB to 0.35 dB to the overall loss budget. By subtracting one or two inches of trace from the recommended maximum trace lengths, there may be enough margins for an additional via pair to be present in the system.

Of course, this is a simplistic approach; the location of the via pair, among other things, can play a role in exactly how much of an impact the vias have on the loss and jitter budgets. For this reason, even if you make tradeoffs by reducing the trace length of the PCI Express signals, you should simulate any topologies that use more vias than those described in the guidelines. Such simulations can help you determine the true impact of the vias on the system loss and jitter budgets.

Chapter 7

Add-in Cards and ExpressCard[†] Modules

Live on the edge, but don't fall off.

—Anonymous

Both add-in card and ExpressCard[†] topologies allow system designers to create new and exciting opportunities for the use of PCI Express[†] technology. In many instances, the interconnect design requirements for add-in cards and ExpressCard modules simply require you to extend or borrow from the system-level guidelines presented elsewhere in this book.

This chapter addresses additional design criteria that are specific to add-in cards and ExpressCard modules. In addition to the information presented here, you should understand the system-level design implications for supporting an ExpressCard or add-in card slot, as discussed in Chapter 5, "Successful System Layout Design."

Note that while ExpressCard modules are defined to include both Universal Serial Bus (USB) and PCI Express interconnects, this chapter discusses only the PCI Express aspects of the interconnect.

Form Factor Requirements

Both add-in cards and ExpressCard modules have form factor and mechanical provisions that help to ensure a broad range of compatibility. As a card or module designer, understanding these requirements can help you to achieve optimum interconnect performance for your PCI Express signals. As a system designer, understanding the card and module form factor specification will help you have a fully compatible and functional system.

Exact mechanical specifications and chassis or container details are beyond the scope of this chapter and book. As always, you should obtain all necessary mechanical and chassis requirements from the appropriate specifications.

Add-in Card Form Factors

The *PCI Express Card Electromechanical (CEM) Specification* (PCI-SIG 2004b) defines three types of add-in card form factors for several different link widths:

- *Standard height, full-length.* This form factor is the most prevalent, especially among higher bandwidth systems and cards, and is supported for x1, x4, x8, or x16 link widths.

- *Standard height, half-length.* This form factor is only allowed for x1 link width cards. This form factor may appeal to system designers who want to accommodate a PCI Express add-in card but do not have a lot of space in which to do so. This form factor can be combined with the standard height, full-length form factor within a system.

- *Low-profile height, half-length.* This form factor allows a space- or volume-constrained system chassis to accommodate reduced-height PCI Express add-in cards. This form factor may be more difficult to accommodate due to the inherent space constraints; however, this choice allows your design to be compatible with the greatest number of system chassis.

Table 7.1 lists the height and length requirements for the three add-in card form factors. You are required to accommodate the maximum length for whatever form factor you decide to support. You do not have to design your add-in card to the maximum length, however; in fact, you can design the add-in card to any practical length you choose, up to and including the maximum lengths listed in the table. The maximum height and length are measured from the top to the bottom of the card, and the front to the back, respectively, as shown in Figure 7.1.

For additional mechanical dimensions and specific manufacturing requirements, refer to the *PCI Express CEM Specification* (PCI-SIG 2004b).

Table 7.1   Maximum Length and Height Restriction for Add-in Card Form Factors

Form Factor Type	Link Widths Accommodated	Maximum Height	Maximum Length *
Standard height, full length	x1, x4, x8, or x16	115.15 mm (4.376 inches)	312.00 mm (12.283 inches)
Standard height, half length	x1	115.15 mm (4.376 inches)	167.65 mm (6.600 inches)
Low-profile height, half length	x1, x4, x8, or x16	68.90 mm (2.731 inches)	167.65 mm (6.600 inches)

* Many systems do not actually support the true maximum length listed here, even though the system may advertise "full-length" support. To ensure that your full-length add-in cards have the widest range of interoperability among various systems, the *PCI Express CEM Specification* recommends a more common length of 241.30 mm (9.5 inches) for full-length cards (PCI-SIG 2004b).

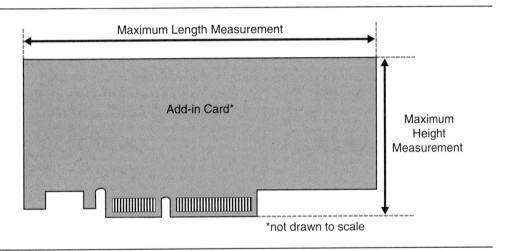

Figure 7.1   Maximum Height and Length Measurements for Add-in Cards

Add-in Card Interoperability

The *PCI Express CEM Specification* (PCI-SIG 2004b) defines an interoperability matrix between add-in cards and connector slots across a variety of link widths. Table 7.2 lists these interoperability definitions.

Table 7.2   Add-in Card and Connector Size Interoperability Matrix.

	x1 Connector	x4 Connector	x8 Connector	x16 Connector
x1 Card	REQUIRED	REQUIRED	REQUIRED	REQUIRED
x4 Card	NO	REQUIRED	ALLOWED	ALLOWED
x8 Card	NO	NO	REQUIRED	ALLOWED
x16 Card	NO	NO	NO	REQUIRED

In Table 7.2, the word "REQUIRED" means that both the system board and add-in card, including their respective PCI Express silicon components, must support this scenario of interoperability. The word "ALLOWED" means that the scenario is not required, but is allowed if and only if it is supported by both the add-in card and system board silicon.

Additionally, the *PCI Express CEM Specification* defines the following scenarios:

■ *Down-plugging*—plugging a larger link width card into a connector slot of smaller link width. This scenario is not allowed, and is physically prevented by the keyed nature of the connector and add-in card edgefingers, as represented by the unshaded region in Table 7.2.

■ *Up-plugging*—plugging a smaller link width card into a connector slot having a larger link width. This scenario is allowed, and is represented by the shaded region in Table 7.2.

To be compliant with the *PCI Express CEM Specification*, PCI Express components on a system board must support up-plugging of at least a x1 width. While it is optional for a system board to offer up-plugging support for all four lanes of a x4 width add-in card plugged into a x16 connector, it is required that the system board support the single, x1 lane of the x4 add-in card. All silicon used either for add-in cards or for system board connector interfaces must always be able to support a x1 link width as the lowest common denominator.

■ *Down-shifting*—plugging a card into a connector slot that is not fully routed for all lanes of the connector. Down-shifting is generally not allowed, except for the following scenario.

A system designer might choose to route only the first four lanes to a x8 connector, in essence demoting the x8 connector to a x4 connector. If an add-in card of a x8 link width is subsequently plugged into the connector, it operates as a x4 link width card, if and only if the x8 silicon component on the add-in allows for its x8 link to become demoted to a x4 width link. Add-in card silicon is not required to support this interoperability; however, if your add-in card does support this feature, it will have a higher degree of compatibility across various system boards. To ensure that your system is compatible with the broadest range of add-in cards, be cautious in employing the down-shifting technique.

> **Note** Despite the flexibility offered by the *PCI Express CEM Specification*, connector sizes offered by most system board manufacturers, especially in the desktop arena, are either x1 size for general purpose I/O or x16 size, likely targeted for high performance graphics. Unless you know of a specific demand for a x4 or x8 width add-in card, it is unlikely that many systems will be compatible with your add-in card design.

ExpressCard† Form Factors and Interoperability

The *ExpressCard Standard* (PCMCIA 2003c) defines two basic mechanical form factors, with a variation allowed for each one. Regardless of the module's physical dimension, the link width supported by each form factor is set by definition to x1. As such, the interoperability of ExpressCard modules is limited only by the mechanical interface, as opposed to the link width scenarios encountered with add-in cards.

As shown in Figure 7.2, the ExpressCard standard defines two module types:

■ ExpressCard/34 modules have a defined width of 34 mm. The standard length module is defined as 75 mm long. The PCI Express link width supported is fixed at x1.

■ ExpressCard/54 modules have a defined width of 54 mm. The standard length module is defined as 75 mm long. The PCI Express link width supported is fixed at x1. This larger module size allows you to accommodate designs that require increased volume and thermal dissipation capacity.

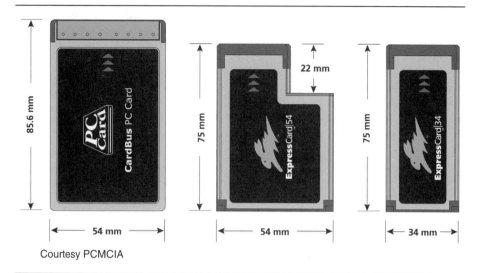

Courtesy PCMCIA

Figure 7.2   ExpressCard†/54 and ExpressCard†/34 Modules, Compared With a CardBus† PC Card

System or host designs that accept ExpressCard modules are not re-quired to support both module sizes, and may often only support one or the other. The physical aspects of the module bays or slots and of the modules themselves, however, allows for some amount of interoperabil-ity. For example, the 54 mm slot is actually defined as a "universal" slot, meaning that it can accommodate either an ExpressCard/34 or an Ex-pressCard/54 module. ExpressCard/34 slots, however, by definition can-not accommodate ExpressCard/54 modules.

Figure 7.3 illustrates the interoperability between ExpressCard mod-ules and the host system with both a 34 mm and 54 mm universal slot. The ability to plug an ExpressCard/34 module into either a 34 mm or 54 mm slot means that your 34 mm module design will be compatible with the largest variety of host systems.

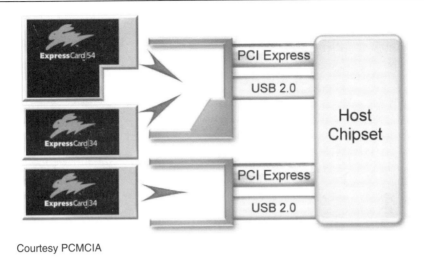

Courtesy PCMCIA

Figure 7.3 Interoperability of ExpressCard† Modules and Slots

The standard module length of 75 mm means that when the ExpressCard is inserted into the host system slot, the module does not stick out or extend beyond the plane of the host system chassis. However, the ExpressCard standard also allows for "extended modules" that, by nature, protrude beyond the chassis plane. They may also increase in nominal height, since the modules are no longer restricted by the slot or bay enclosure on the host system. The additional length and height allowed by extended modules enables you to place larger components and/or external interfaces onto your ExpressCard modules than would otherwise be possible. The following requirements and guidelines are designed to help you achieve a robust extended module ExpressCard design (PCMCIA 2003c).

■ Extended modules must maintain their normal height until they are at least 80 mm long, after which they may increase in height, up to a recommended total height of 18 mm.

The 5 mm buffer—80 mm minus the 75 mm standard length—ensures that the added height of the extended module does not interfere with the host system chassis or slot mechanism. Figure 7.4 illustrates this buffer requirement.

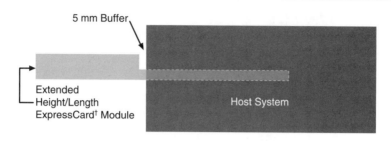

5 mm Buffer

Extended
Height/Length
ExpressCard† Module

Host System

Figure 7.4   Side View of a Host System Mated with an Extended ExpressCard†
Module

While the ExpressCard standard does not specifically preclude extended module heights greater than 18 mm, keeping the module heights below this level allows the modules plenty of clearance on most stacked or riser card-based slots. Note, however, that if a module were more than 18 mm high, it could likely be plugged into the top riser slot so that it wouldn't interfere with any other slots. Figure 7.5 shows an illustration of how stacked ExpressCard Risers might be implemented.

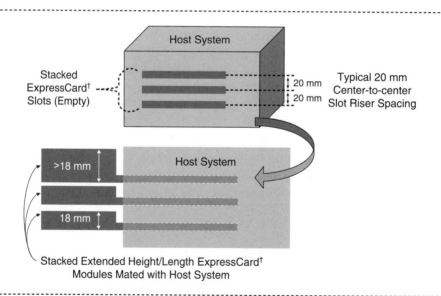

Host System

Stacked
ExpressCard†
Slots (Empty)

20 mm
20 mm

Typical 20 mm
Center-to-center
Slot Riser Spacing

>18 mm   Host System

18 mm

Stacked Extended Height/Length ExpressCard†
Modules Mated with Host System

Figure 7.5   A Stacked ExpressCard† Riser Host System

■ In theory, extended modules can increase to any length. However, you have some practical limits. The *ExpressCard Implementation Guidelines* (PCMCIA 2003c) recommend that extensions not exceed 25 mm, allowing for a total length of 100 mm, due to the risk of increased strain on the guide rail and other components of the host system.

■ Extended modules are limited to a width less than or equal to the defined standard module dimensions—34 mm or 54 mm, respectively, for ExpressCard/34 or ExpressCard/54 modules—along the entire length of the module extension.

So long as the maximum width dimension is not exceeded, the extended portions of the modules do not need to maintain a uniform height, length, or width throughout the entire area of the module extension. The ends of the modules might be rounded, for example, or only the last portion of the module might increase in height, while the width might vary in the middle. Figure 7.6 shows an example of these extended module variations.

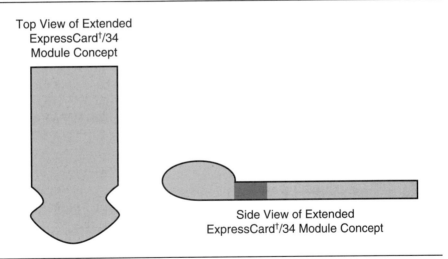

Top View of Extended
ExpressCard†/34
Module Concept

Side View of Extended
ExpressCard†/34 Module Concept

Figure 7.6   Extended Module Height, Width, and Length Variations

For additional mechanical dimensions and specific manufacturing requirements concerning ExpressCard Modules, refer to the *ExpressCard Implementation Guidelines* (PCMCIA 2003c) and the *ExpressCard Standard* (PCMCIA 2003a).

Connectors

Both ExpressCard Modules and add-in cards have specific requirements with respect to the connectors they mate with or attach to. As you understand the functionality of these connector interfaces and the associated design considerations, you will be better positioned to achieve a robust add-in card or ExpressCard module design. Since the connector itself is always located on the main host system, it is also important for system designers to become familiar with the connectors and their associated layout impacts.

Add-in Card Connectors

The *PCI Express CEM Specification* defines a standard connector interface for use with add-in cards. To support up-plugging—the ability to plug a smaller link width card into a larger connector slot—the connectors and add-in cards are keyed, as shown in Figure 7.7. The connectors are sometimes referred to as either an edgefinger connector or a vertical edgefinger connector. Table 7.3 presents the pinout of the connector, and is reproduced from the *PCI Express CEM Specification*. For specific mechanical and performance specifications regarding the connector, refer to the *PCI Express CEM Specification* (PCI-SIG 2004b).

The CEM connector as currently defined only supports widths of x1, x4, x8, and x16 even though the PCI Express base specification supports additional link widths. As mentioned previously, the two most common connectors available, especially for desktop systems, are the x1 and x16 connector.

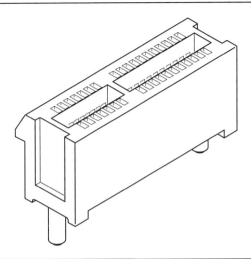

Figure 7.7   Example of a PCI Express† Vertical Edgefinger Connector

Table 7.3   Pinout of the PCI Express† CEM Edgefinger Connector

Pin#	Side B		Side A	
	Name	Description	Name	Description
1	+12V	12 V power	PRSNT1#	Hot-Plug presence detect
2	+12V	12 V power	+12V	12 V power
3	+12V	12 V power	+12V	12 V power
4	GND	Ground	GND	Ground
5	SMCLK	SMBus (System Management Bus) clock	JTAG2	TCK (Test Clock), clock input for JTAG interface
6	SMDAT	SMBus (System Management Bus) data	JTAG3	TDI (Test Data Input)
7	GND	Ground	JTAG4	TDO (Test Data Output)
8	+3.3V	3.3 V power	JTAG5	TMS (Test Mode Select)
9	JTAG1	TRST# (Test Reset) resets the JTAG interface	+3.3V	3.3 V power
10	3.3Vaux	3.3 V auxiliary power	+3.3V	3.3 V power
11	WAKE#	Signal for Link reactivation	PERST#	Fundamental reset

Table 7.3   Pinout of the PCI Express† CEM Edgefinger Connector *(continued)*

Pin#	Side B		Side A	
	Name	**Description**	**Name**	**Description**
Mechanical key				
12	RSVD	Reserved	GND	Ground
13	GND	Ground	REFCLK	Reference clock
14	PETp0	Transmitter differential pair, Lane 0	REFCLK	(differential pair)
15	PETn0		GND	Ground
16	GND	Ground	PERp0	Receiver differential pair, Lane 0
17	PRSNT2	Hot-Plug presence detect	PERn0	
18	GND	Ground	GND	Ground
End of the x1 connector				
19	PETp1	Transmitter differential pair, Lane 1	RSVD	
20	PETn1		GND	Ground
21	GND	Ground	PERp1	Receiver differential pair, Lane 1
22	GND	Ground	PERn1	
23	PETp2	Transmitter differential pair, Lane 2	GND	Ground
24	PETn2		GND	Ground
25	GND	Ground	PERp2	Receiver differential pair, Lane 2
26	GND	Ground	PERn2	
27	PETp3	Transmitter differential pair, Lane 3	GND	Ground
28	PETn3		GND	Ground
29	GND	Ground	PERp3	Receiver differential pair, Lane 3
30	RSVD	Reserved	PERn3	
31	PRSNT2	Hot-Plug presence detect	GND	Ground
32	GND	Ground	RSVD	Reserved
End of the x4 connector				
33	PETp4	Transmitter differential pair, Lane 4	RSVD	Reserved
34	PETn4		GND	Ground
35	GND	Ground	PERp4	Receiver differential pair, Lane 4
36	GND	Ground	PERn4	
37	PETp5	Transmitter differential pair, Lane 5	GND	Ground
38	PETn5		GND	Ground
39	GND	Ground	PERp5	Receiver differential pair, Lane 5
40	GND	Ground	PERn5	

Table 7.3   Pinout of the PCI Express† CEM Edgefinger Connector *(continued)*

Pin#	Side B		Side A	
	Name	Description	Name	Description
41	PETp6	Transmitter differential pair, Lane 6	GND	Ground
42	PETn6		GND	Ground
43	GND	Ground	PERp6	Receiver differential pair, Lane 6
44	GND	Ground	PERn6	
45	PETp7	Transmitter differential pair, Lane 7	GND	Ground
46	PETn7		GND	Ground
47	GND	Ground	PERp7	Receiver differential pair, Lane 7
48	PRSNT2	Hot-Plug presence detect	PERn7	
49	GND	Ground	GND	Ground
End of the x8 connector				
50	PETp8	Transmitter differential pair, Lane 8	RSVD	Reserved
51	PETn8		GND	Ground
52	GND	Ground	PERp8	Receiver differential pair, Lane 8
53	GND	Ground	PERn8	
54	PETp9	Transmitter differential pair, Lane 9	GND	Ground
55	PETn9		GND	Ground
56	GND	Ground	PERp9	Receiver differential pair, Lane 9
57	GND	Ground	PERn9	
58	PETp10	Transmitter differential pair, Lane 10	GND	Ground
59	PETn10		GND	Ground
60	GND	Ground	PERp10	Receiver differential pair, Lane 10
61	GND	Ground	PERn10	
62	PETp11	Transmitter differential pair, Lane 11	GND	Ground
63	PETn11		GND	Ground
64	GND	Ground	PERp11	Receiver differential pair, Lane 11
65	GND	Ground	PERn11	
66	PETp12	Transmitter differential pair, Lane 12	GND	Ground
67	PETn12		GND	Ground
68	GND	Ground	PERp12	Receiver differential pair, Lane 12
69	GND	Ground	PERn12	
70	PETp13	Transmitter differential pair, Lane 13	GND	Ground
71	PETn13		GND	Ground

Table 7.3   Pinout of the PCI Express† CEM Edgefinger Connector *(continued)*

Pin#	Side B		Side A	
	Name	Description	Name	Description
72	GND	Ground	PERp13	Receiver differential pair, Lane 13
73	GND	Ground	PERn13	
74	PETp14	Transmitter differential pair, Lane 14	GND	Ground
75	PETn14		GND	Ground
76	GND	Ground	PERp14	Receiver differential pair, Lane 14
77	GND	Ground	PERn14	
78	PETp15	Transmitter differential pair, Lane 15	GND	Ground
79	PETn15		GND	Ground
80	GND	Ground	PERp15	Receiver differential pair, Lane 15
81	PRSNT2	Hot-Plug presence detect	PERn15	
82	RSVD	Reserved	GND	Ground
	End of the x16 connector			

Source: PCI Express CEM Specification

In Table 7.3, the connector pinout names are defined with respect to the system board:

■ PETp(x) and PETn(x) pins—the transmitter differential pair of the connector—are connected to the Transmit (TX) differential pair on the system board and to the Receive (RX) differential pair on the add-in card.

■ PERp(x) and PERn(x) pins are connected to the RX differential pair on the system board and to the TX differential pair on the add-in card.

For through-hole connectors, the most popular implementation, the pins of a differential pair are offset from each other. Because the PCB trace on the system card should directly account for this mismatch between the pins, your add-in card design does not need to account for this mismatch. The add-in card design must simply length match your PCI Express differential pairs, using the PCB design guidelines in Chapter 6 of this book.

To manage the connector crosstalk, adjacent differential pairs on the connector are separated by two ground pins. These ground pins should directly tie to the ground plane on the system board. Additionally, the add-in card edgefingers that mate with these ground pins should also tie to the ground plane of the add-in card as close to the edgefingers as is allowed by your PCB vendor's manufacturing constraints.

ExpressCard[†] Connectors

As with add-in cards, a standard connector, physically located on the host system, is defined for use with ExpressCard modules. An ExpressCard module is different from an edgefinger add-in card, however, in that it uses a combination connector approach. Instead of having an edgefinger like an add-in card, the ExpressCard module includes a mating connector that mates with the host system connector interface. Figure 7.8 presents an example drawing of this connector. Table 7.4 provides the corresponding pinout diagram. The *ExpressCard Standard* (PCMCIA 2003a) contains the mechanical and performance requirements for this surface mount connector.

Host System Connector on Left, Module Interface on Right

Courtesy PCMCIA

Figure 7.8   ExpressCard[†] Connector/Mating Interface

Table 7.4   ExpressCard[†] 26-Pin Connector Pinout

| Pin No. | Signal | I/O | Interface Type(s) on card | | | Host | Notes |
			PCI Express	USB	Both		
26	GND		R	R	R	R	
25	PETp0	I	R	NC	R	R	4
24	PETn0	I	R	NC	R	R	4
23	GND		R	R	R	R	
22	PERp0	O	R	NC	R	R	5
21	PERn0	O	R	NC	R	R	5
20	GND		R	R	R	R	
19	REFCLK+	I	R	NC	R	R	
18	REFCLK-	I	R	NC	R	R	

Table 7.4   ExpressCard† 26-Pin Connector Pinout *(continued)*

Pin No.	Signal	I/O	Interface Type(s) on card			Host	Notes
			PCI Express	USB	Both		
17	CPPE#	O	R	NC	R	R	3
16	CLKREQ#	O	R	NC	R	Opt	2
15	+3.3V		R	R	R	R	
14	+3.3V		R	R	R	R	
13	PERST#	I	R	NC	R	R	
12	+3.3Vaux		Opt	Opt	Opt	R	
11	WAKE#	O	Opt	NC	Opt	Opt	2
10	+1.5V		Opt	Opt	Opt	R	
9	+1.5V		Opt	Opt	Opt	R	
8	SMBDATA	I/O	Opt	Opt	Opt	Opt	
7	SMBCLK	I/O	NC	NC	NC	Opt	
6	RESERVED		NC	NC	NC	NC	1
5	RESERVED		NC	NC	NC	NC	1
4	CPUSB#	O	NC	R	R	R	3
3	USBD+	I/O	NC	R	R	R	
2	USBD-	I/O	NC	R	R	R	
1	GND		R	R	R	R	

I = signal is input to the card

O = signal is output from the card

R = signal is required

Opt = signal is optional

NC = signal is not to be connected

Notes:

1. Reserved for future use by the card interface. Leave these pins unconnected.

2. If implemented, a host pull-up resistor ($\pm$ 5 K Ω) tied to no higher than +3.3Vaux is required on this pin. For more information regarding pull-up resistor values, refer to the *ExpressCard Implementation Guidelines* (PCMCIA 2003c).

3. A host pull-up resistor of 100 K Ω to 200 K Ω is required on these pins.

4. Connect PETp0 and PETn0 to the Transmit (TX) differential pair on the host and to the Receive (RX) differential pair on the ExpressCard module.

5. Connect PERp0 and PERn0 to the Receive (RX) differential pair on the host and to the Transmit (TX) differential pair on the ExpressCard module.

The following are criteria and recommendations that you should be aware of when implementing designs with ExpressCard connectors:

- The ExpressCard connector only allows for a single x1 PCI Express lane to be connected to the ExpressCard Module.

- The pinout names of the connector are defined with respect to the system board just as they are with the PCI Express add-in card connectors.

- All ground pins of the connector on the host system and mating interfaces on the ExpressCard module should be connected to the ground plane.

- To help improve the impedance profile of the ExpressCard module interface, remove the ground or reference plane immediately under the solder pads of pins of the interface.

Edgefinger and PCB Design

PCI Express add-in cards and ExpressCard modules require you to observe specific design guidelines in order to achieve a robust interconnect with minimal impact to the loss and jitter budgets of the overall system. By conforming to the following guidelines, you can minimize signal integrity discontinuities in your design, thereby allowing you to achieve optimal performance.

Edgefinger and Mating Interface Design Guidelines

The edgefingers of an add-in card are designed to interact with the properties of the connector pins in order to produce an acceptable impedance target and ensure a robust signaling path. A similar relationship exists for the ExpressCard module mating interface.

The following guidelines and considerations apply to the edgefinger design for an add-in card and to the ExpressCard mating interface. For actual mechanical dimension requirements, refer to the *PCI Express CEM Specification* (PCI-SIG 2004b) and the *ExpressCard Standard* (PCMCIA 2003a).

Add-in Card Edgefingers

Simulations and lab validation have shown that removing the reference planes underneath the edgefingers or pins of an add-in card improves the interconnect path of the connector mating interface.

Figure 7.9 presents an example of how you might remove the reference planes.

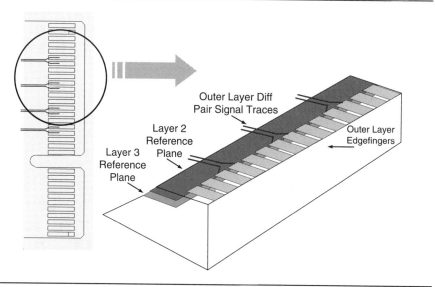

Figure 7.9   Example of PCI Express† Reference Plane Voids for a x4 PCI
Express Edgefinger Interface

Follow these guidelines when removing the reference planes under add-in card edgefingers.

- Remove the reference planes on the inner layers, immediately underneath the gold edgefinger areas on the outer layers of the PCB.

- Remove the planes along *the entire length* of the edgefinger component that contains PCI Express differential pair signal traces.

- Restrict the removal of the reference planes to the actual area of the edgefingers only; do not extend the removal out to the trace routing area.

- For PCI Express signals, remove the entire ground and power planes under the entire edgefinger. This applies to both top and bottom layer edgefingers.

- For ExpressCard mating interfaces, remove the reference planes directly beneath the solder pads of the mating connector for the PCI Express pins.

- During the PCB manufacturing process, remove any plating bars for the gold fingers.

The *PCI Express CEM Specification* requires you to ensure that the PRSNT#1 edgefinger pad is physically connected, by means of a trace on the add-in card, to the PRSNT#2 pin located farthest from it. Doing this on the add-in card allows the system board to implement presence detect and hot-plug support.

The edgefingers for these PRSNT1# and PRSNT2# pins are also required to be shorter than the other pins in order to facilitate a "last mate/first break" scenario when the system design employs optional hot-plug support.

PCB Design Guidelines for Add-in Cards and ExpressCard† Modules

To be fully compliant with the *PCI Express CEM Specification* and *ExpressCard Standard*, and to be compatible with host systems that your add-in card and ExpressCard designs would plug into, you need to follow certain PCB layout guidelines. Many of the techniques discussed in Chapter 5, "System Layout Design," and Chapter 6, "Printed Circuit Board Design," can be applied to your add-in card design as well. These techniques include areas such as impedance targets and trace dimensions, bend guidelines, reference planes, and AC coupling. Additional guidelines for the add-in card and ExpressCard modules are as follows:

■ Since the specification dictates that AC coupling capacitors are associated with the transmit pairs of a design, AC coupling capacitors must be located on the card for each of the TX pairs originating from the component located on the add-in card or ExpressCard module. For more details on AC coupling capacitor requirements, refer to Chapter 5, "System Layout Design."

■ Table 7.5 lists guidelines or restrictions that apply specifically to the add-in card. The guidelines in the table assume that the add-in card is designed with microstrip routing on the four-layer example stackup discussed in Chapter 6, "Printed Circuit Board Design."

■ Table 7.6 provides similar guidelines for ExpressCard Modules based on the same stackup assumptions as mentioned for Table 7.5.

These guidelines provided in these two tables are based on system-level simulations and test vehicle validation. You can adapt the guidelines for stripline routing with multi-layer stackups; to do so, adjust the trace width and spacing parameters so that you can obtain the proper impedance target.

Table 7.5   Add-in Card PCB Design Guidelines

Parameter	Add-in Card—Main Routes	Special "Breakout-Area" Rules
Diff. Impedance Target	~100 Ω ±20% (~60 Ω Single-Ended ±15%)	N/A
Trace Width	5 mils	7 mils if un-coupled length ≥ 100 mils
Diff Pair (within pair) Air Gap	7 mils	5-mil air gap OK
Pair-to-Pair Air Gap Spacing	≥ 20 mils	7-mil air gap OK
Trace Length Restrictions	Maximum of 3.5 inches	"Breakout-Area" length ≤ 250 mils (considered part of total length allotment in left column)
Length Matching Within a Pair	Max 5 mil delta per segment	N/A
Length Matching Pair-to-Pair	No requirements between TX and RX pairs[1]	N/A
Reference Plane	GND Plane Best (actually required by CEM specification)	GND islands on VCC layer must be tied to GND in breakout area
Splits/Voids	No routing over splits No routing over voids	No more than half of the trace width should be over via anti-pad
Via Usage (6 total, entire path)	4 vias max per TX trace 2 vias max per RX trace	OK to place one of the allocated vias in the breakout area
Bends	Match left and right turn bends where possible No 90-degree or "tight" bends	Avoid "tight bends" when routing in breakout areas

Note: While the *PCI Express Base Specification* allows for an enormous skew tolerance of 20 ns between lanes, the *PCI Express CEM Specification* places a maximum limit on the amount of lane-to-lane skew allowable on add-in card traces. For example, skew is limited from one TX differential pair to another TX differential pair. The maximum skew value of 0.35 ns translates roughly into about 2–3 inches of maximum trace length mismatch across all lanes on an add-in card (PCI-SIG 2004b).

Table 7.6 ExpressCard† PCB Design Guidelines

Parameter	Add-in Card-Main Routes	Special "Breakout-Area" Rules
Diff. Impedance Target	~100 Ω±20% (~60 Ω Single-Ended ±15%)	N/A
Trace Width	5 mils	7 mils if un-coupled length ≥ 100 mils
Diff Pair (within pair) Air Gap	7 mils	5-mil air gap OK
Pair-to-Pair Air Gap Spacing	≥ 20 mils	7-mil air gap OK
Trace Length Restrictions	Maximum of 1.75 inches	"Breakout-Area" length ≤ 250 mils (considered part of total length allotment in left column)
Length Matching Within a Pair	Max 5 mil delta per segment	N/A
Length Matching Pair-to-Pair	No requirements between TX and RX pairs	N/A
Reference Plane	GND Plane Best	GND islands on VCC layer must be tied to GND in breakout area
Splits/Voids	No routing over splits No routing over voids	No more than half of the trace width should be over via anti-pad
Via Usage on Module	No vias per TX trace (AC caps on same side as the connector) Maximum of one via per RX trace	OK to place the one RX via in the breakout area
Bends	Match left and right turn bends where possible No 90-degree or "tight" bends	Avoid "tight bends" when routing in breakout areas

Reference Clock Considerations and Requirements

As with most PCI Express components, the devices on most add-in cards and ExpressCard modules need a frequency reference clock to be provided to them. Both the *PCI Express CEM Specification* and the *ExpressCard Standard* require that the system board supply the interfaces with a 100 MHz differential reference clock that can optionally support spread spectrum clocking (SSC). While the *PCI Express CEM Specification* explicitly states that the add-in card actually doesn't need to use the reference clock supplied to it, most devices do indeed require its use in order to meet the ppm data rate requirements of the *PCI Express Base Specification* (PCI-SIG 2004a). This is especially true when SSC is enabled on the reference clock, since it is very difficult to track the SSC modulated data without having a frequency reference employing the same modulation on the receiving end. What does this mean to you as a module or add-in card designer? To be safe, you should always route the 100-MHz reference clock to the device on the add-in card or ExpressCard module.

In routing the differential reference clock to the PCI Express components on your design, follow the design layout guidelines in Table 7.5 and Table 7.6. The maximum trace length routing guidelines for the reference clocks is the same as stated in the two tables: up to 3.5 inches for add-in cards and up to 1.75 inches for ExpressCard modules. Like the high-speed PCI Express signal pairs, each reference clock is a differential, point-to-point connection and is not daisy-chained to multiple devices. Also, you should not supply any additional termination schemes for the clock on the add-in card or ExpressCard module; this is the responsibility of the host system.

Cable Considerations

PCI Express interconnects allow for a multitude of topology variations due to their point-to-point, serial differential signaling. One such variation involves the use of a short cable interconnect over which the PCI Express signals are transmitted from a host system to receiving device. Proprietary systems can utilize a cable interface in any way that you wish, so long as all the electrical and timing requirements of the *PCI Express Base Specification* (PCI-SIG 2004a) are met. However, a cable topology is specifically defined only for ExpressCard modules; no such specification is defined for add-in cards. For details and requirements of the cable assembly and pinout for ExpressCard designs, refer to the *ExpressCard Internal Cable Specifications* (PCMCIA 2003b).

The cable assembly has no effect on your module design. In fact, the cable assemblies for ExpressCard designs are actually considered part of the host system, and do not detract from the module electrical and timing budgets. In almost all instances, the cable assembly actually attaches to a daughter card on which the ExpressCard module mates with the standard ExpressCard connector. As a system designer, you should ensure that your electrical and timing budget allotments accommodate the additional impact imposed by the cable assembly.

Additional Design Considerations for Power Delivery, Thermal/Acoustical Management, and EMI

Just as a successful system design must consider related disciplines in order to ensure that the overall design is robust, add-in cards and ExpressCard modules must also be responsible for their own power delivery, thermal and acoustical considerations, and EMI impacts. Both the host system and the add-in modules must adequately design for these considerations together, however; a breakdown on either end would compromise the effectiveness of the other, regardless of how well it was designed. For further details of these design considerations, beyond those included in this chapter, refer to the *PCI Express Graphics Card Electromechanical Design Guideline for Mainstream Desktop Systems* (PCI-SIG 2003) and to the *ExpressCard Implementation Guidelines* (PCMCIA 2003c).

Add-in Card Power Delivery Guidelines

The *PCI Express CEM Specification* allows for up to 75 Watts (W) of power dissipation on a x16 add-in card. The current is drawn directly, in varying amounts, from all three voltage rails supplied by the host system connector interface: 12V, 3.3V, and 3.3Vaux.

Table 7.7 illustrates the maximum allowable power dissipation limits for each add-in card form factor (PCI-SIG 2004b). Each form factor has different restrictions. Depending on the anticipated power needs of your design, you may be precluded from using a low-profile or smaller link width add-in card design.

Table 7.7   Maximum Allowable Power Dissipation Limits for Add-in Cards

Maximum Power Dissipation Limits	x1 Link Width		x4/x8 Link Width	x16 Link Width	
Standard Height Cards	10 W*	25 W	25 W	25 W*	75 W*
Low-Profile Cards	10 W		10 W	25 W	

*Note: Standard Height x1 add-in cards are limited to 10W max power unless they are full-length cards and are configured as high power devices after power-up. They may then draw a maximum of 25 W. Similar conditions apply to x16 width add-in cards, though they may draw 25W initially and then up to 75 W after configuration as a high power device.

Of course, the ability of the add-in card and system chassis to adequately dissipate the amount of energy listed in the table is also extremely important in determining the maximum power consumption. The *PCI Express CEM Specification* assumes that you, as the add-in card designer, as well as the system designer, properly design for the listed amounts of power to be dissipated. For more information, see "Thermal Design," later in this chapter.

Though not explicitly defined in the *PCI Express CEM Specification*, it is possible for add-in card designs to consume more than 75 W of power, such as with ultra high performance graphics cards. Such card designs require an external voltage supply in addition to that supplied through the edgefinger connector. Of course, higher power consumption also requires improved thermal dissipation abilities by the card and system chassis, which often impose the maximum limit on power consumption.

Note   The system board is not required to sequence the connector power supply rails in any given order. If your add-in card design requires specific voltage rail power sequencing, you must provide your own power sequencing circuit directly on the add-in card.

While each add-in card design is different in terms of the decoupling requirements it needs to ensure a clean power network, the following minimum guidelines are generally applicable. Several of these guidelines appear in the *PCI Express CEM Specification* (PCI-SIG 2004b).

■ The add-in card should average 0.01 µF per VCC pin for all devices on the add-in card.

■ The trace length between a decoupling capacitor and the power supply or ground via should be less then 0.2 inches (5.08 mm), and should be a minimum of 0.02 inches (0.508 mm) in width to help ensure a minimal inductive loop and DC power droop.

■ A bulk decoupling capacitor greater than 10 µF is recommended at the add-in card edgefinger for each of the three power supply rails: 3.3V, 3.3Vaux, and 12V.

■ A bulk decoupling capacitor greater than 10 µF is recommended on each power supply rail used within the actual silicon device on the add-in card. This bulk decoupling capacitor should be located in close proximity to the add-in card device it is intended to benefit.

■ Whenever possible, use power planes on the add-in card to deliver the 3.3V and 12V supplies. Very wide, outer layer plane floods may also be used for power delivery, especially for 3.3Vaux power.

ExpressCard[†] Power Delivery Guidelines

As with add-in cards, but to a much greater extent, the power consumption of ExpressCard modules is limited not just by the available supply current from the power supply rails, but also by the ability of your module and the host system mating interface to properly dissipate the power.

ExpressCard modules are supplied with power from two main power rails: 1.5V and 3.3V. Additional power is supplied through the standby power on 3.3Vaux. Unlike add-in cards, ExpressCard modules do not have a 12V power rail. Though the majority of the effort to provide a clean power supply to the ExpressCard module actually rests with the host system designer, you should also follow the following basic guidelines to ensure a good power delivery network on your module:

■ High-frequency decoupling capacitors located on the module for the PCI Express device's VCC pins (0.01 µF).

■ Use of power planes to deliver the main power rails to the components. You can also use wide traces or outer layer floods for 3.3Vaux power.

The following additional power delivery information is taken directly from the *ExpressCard Implementation Guidelines* (PCMCIA 2003c):

> System designers are required to provide voltages of 1.35V min for the 1.5V rail and 3.0V min for the 3.3V and 3.3Vaux rails, measured at the module connector solder pad. But meeting those minimum voltage requirements is challenging, considering the losses due to the PCB traces, power switch, and ExpressCard connector, …[and] the voltage regulator tolerances. As a result, the system may not be designed with any margin for the minimum voltages. Hence, it is strongly recommended that module designers make their best efforts to design … ExpressCard modules that can tolerate … voltages smaller than the … [minimum voltages] specified by the ExpressCard Standard. Module designers should also be aware that the current drawn by a module is not only limited by the current limit specified in the ExpressCard Standard, but also by the thermal power constraints [of a module]. For example, the ExpressCard Standard allows a 1.0A max average current for the 3.3V rail; but this does not mean that the module can dissipate 3.3 W of thermal power. In fact, the standard length 54 mm module allows only 2.1 W max power dissipation [and 1.3W max power for the ExpressCard/34 module]. It is the module designers' responsibility to manage the current level to meet both electrical and thermal requirements.

Add-in Card Thermal and Acoustic Management

Add-in cards, along with the host system chassis, have an important responsibility in the area of thermal and acoustic management. As mentioned earlier, the maximum power consumption of each add-in card hinges greatly on the card's ability to dissipate the thermal power appropriately in conjunction with the system chassis.

Thermal requirements become especially important for cards, such as graphics cards, that consume high amounts of power in the 60–75W range. Such high power designs almost assuredly require the combined use of a heat sink and heat sink fan. In your design, consider the following points:

- Use an appropriately sized fan to maintain an airflow of at least 4CFM (PCI-SIG 2003a).

- Use a fan heat sink shroud to properly direct fan exhaust away from the fan intake. Figure 7.10 provides two examples of recommended exhaust directions based on anticipated cool air sources in a system. To take full advantage of a 75W design, you should anticipate the location of the cool air source from the system chassis that contains your card.

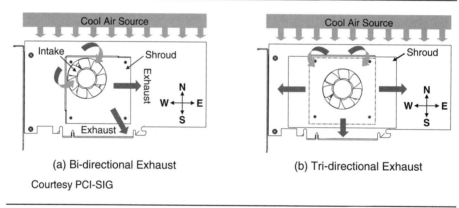

(a) Bi-directional Exhaust (b) Tri-directional Exhaust

Courtesy PCI-SIG

Figure 7.10 Examples of Recommended Bi-Directional and Tri-Directional Exhaust

A simple method to increase the separation of the fan intake air source from the fan exhaust might include moving the fan off-center toward the non-exhaust side of the heat sink and closer to the cool air source. You could then use a thin shroud design to guide the airflow more efficiently to the heat sink fins for increased cooling. Alternatively, consider using an extended shroud that protrudes beyond the heat sink base in order to increase the separation distance of the fan intake to the fan's exhaust. Figure 7.11 shows examples of shroud usage, both good and bad.

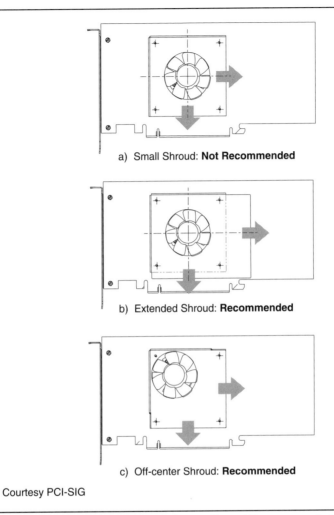

a) Small Shroud: **Not Recommended**

b) Extended Shroud: **Recommended**

c) Off-center Shroud: **Recommended**

Courtesy PCI-SIG

Figure 7.11   Examples of Heat Sink Fan Shroud Recommendations

Acoustic Design

Good acoustic design requires that a good thermal design is in place. If the thermal design is sufficient, you can use lower fan speeds—and thus have quieter fans—for your add-in card design. On the other hand, relying on higher fan speeds to compensate for a poor thermal design only serves to exacerbate the noise levels for your add-in card. The following guidelines are recommended to help you achieve a good acoustic design (PCI-SIG 2003a):

■ Use a fan speed control mechanism to alter the fan speed based on the temperature. Two possible designs include a thermistor control and a diode-controlled implementation.

The thermistor on the fan is used to measure the air temperature at the fan intake or inlet. The fan speed is then adjusted based on the detected temperature.

A thermal diode-based design offers a more advanced speed control approach. Associated control circuitry on the add-in card then adjusts the speed of the fan based on the measured temperatures.

■ Use the largest fan size possible, based on your card's space constraints. Larger fans produce less noise for the amount of airflow delivered.

■ Use continuous fan speed controls. Discrete fan speed setting can actually amplify the perceived noise due to the distinct sounds produced as the speed is switched.

■ Remove obstructions near the fan. Obstructions to airflow can create noise.

ExpressCard† Thermal and Acoustic Management

Due to the size constraints of ExpressCard modules, you cannot use fans and large heat sinks to manage temperatures as you would on add-in card designs. For ExpressCard modules, good thermal design requires simply that you limit the consumption of the devices on the module itself, and that you construct the module of materials that dissipate heat most effectively.

Another difference between add-in cards and ExpressCard modules is the factor of human interaction. Since ExpressCard modules are inserted and removed by hand, they must not be too hot to the touch. Depending on whether or not your module is constrained by the power consumption of internal components or the ergonomics of the casing temperature, you can optimize your module with the choice of either a metal or a plastic housing with a low thermal conductivity.

EMI Considerations for Add-in Cards and Modules

As with any electronics design, certain regulatory requirements limit the amount of emissions allowed. While add-in cards and modules differ widely in terms of form factor and size, the same basic design practices can be used to limit the EMI impacts. By adhering to the principles discussed in this book for high-speed signal routing, you can mitigate many EMI effects. Additionally, you should observe the following guidelines for your add-in card and ExpressCard module designs:

- Place noisy components away from I/O interfaces such as connectors, cables, and edges of the module or add-in card.

- Place devices that require large amounts of current close to their power source where possible, without violating the previous guideline.

- Reduce the number of layer transitions for high-speed signals, especially repetitive pattern signals such as clock traces.

- Utilize inner layer stripline routing where available to help contain the emissions of noisy signals.

- Enable spread spectrum clocking on your designs.

- Ensure that proper decoupling is used. Keep decoupling close to I/O pins. Filter capacitors can also be used on non-grounded nets as appropriate.

- Feed power to high-speed devices through a ferrite bead. Ensure that the I/O filter capacitor is placed between the ferrite or inductor and the I/O connector.

The following EMI considerations are specific to ExpressCard module enclosure design:

- Use the module enclosure to contain emissions of internal module components and to shield the module from external interference.

  The module enclosure should have no openings over the entire surface of the module, so that it can act as an electrical shield. Where seams are present, such as where the top and bottom of the enclosure may meet, ensure that the seams are sealed.

- When inserted into a host, the module enclosure/shield should electrically contact the host system chassis.

Chapter 8

Validating the Design

Never assume anything works right the first time.
If you can't validate it, assume it's broken.

—Anonymous

Just as successful PCI Express[†] interconnect design requires careful attention to detail, so too does validating the design. For example, consider the act of measuring the vertical opening of an eye diagram using an oscilloscope. This measurement may seem relatively straightforward, but consider the following:

- Because the voltage swings in PCI Express technology are less than half those of conventional low-voltage CMOS technology used in DDR memory systems, for example, measurement errors introduced by the oscilloscope's noise floor and vertical system can become a significant percentage of the total measurement.

- Using two single-ended probes to make differential measurements adds further error.

- Likewise, the finite bandwidth of the measurement equipment itself distorts an eye diagram, and in extreme cases, renders a measurement result worthless.

- If that is not enough, at gigahertz speeds even the best low capacitance probes load the link and distort the measurement.

- Finally, you must also be aware of how measurements taken *in system* relate to measurements taken into a compliance test load, and how to prove specification compliance.

Fortunately, with a basic understanding of measurement methodology, you can minimize these errors and account for those that do occur. This chapter focuses on the limitations of the test equipment and the related measurement methodologies, and discusses how to account for these limitations as well as the measurements needed to prove specification compliance.

Real-Time Versus Equivalent-Time Sampling Scopes

Traditionally, measurements of jitter and related characteristics of high-speed serial busses have been done with a very high-bandwidth equivalent-time sampling scope set to an infinite persistence display. However, the way that the *PCI Express Base Specfication* (PCI-SIG 2004a) specifies jitter lends itself to an alternate method of measuring jitter using a real-time sampling scope and data post-processing. Before getting into details about ways to measure jitter and the use of the eye diagram, you might find it helpful to understand the difference between real-time and equivalent-time sampling scopes, and why an equivalent-time scope overstates jitter relative to the way the base specification specifies jitter.

Real-Time Sampling Scopes

Digital oscilloscopes sample and store an incoming analog signal in one of two basic ways: real-time sampling or equivalent-time sampling. As the name implies, a real-time sampling scope samples the incoming analog signal in *real time*; upon triggering, the scope takes multiple samples of the incoming waveform, with each sample separated by a time interval of 1/sample rate. Each sample is digitized and stored in the scope's memory, in order, then made available for later processing. Figure 8.1 illustrates how each sample is plotted on a display, forming a picture of the sampled waveform.

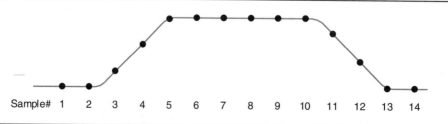

Figure 8.1   Real-Time Sampling Scope Sampling Points

The primary advantage of a real-time sampling scope is that it can capture non-repetitive waveforms or single-shot events. Another advantage is the ability to observe sequential and short-term events, particularly cycle-to-cycle jitter. However, the sampling nature of this type of scope imposes an upper limit on the frequency of the waveform that the scope can faithfully capture. To avoid aliasing, the sampling frequency must exceed two times the maximum scope bandwidth, that is, the sample frequency must be greater than twice the maximum frequency present in the signal. This proportion is called the *Nyquist Criteria*.

As shown later in this chapter, the bandwidth of the real-time scope must exceed the maximum frequency of interest of the input signal, and for PCI Express waveforms this equates to a scope bandwidth of 6 GHz. For a 6-GHz oscilloscope, a minimum sample rate greater than 12 giga-samples per second (Gsa/sec) is required in order to have enough sample points to uniquely reconstruct the waveform via sinX/X interpolation. Of course, more sampling points allow greater resolution of waveform detail, and are in fact required if a simple linear interpolation is used to reconstruct the waveform. Most real-time scopes offer sampling rates of up to 20 Gsa/sec, and in practice you should use the highest sample rate available.

Equivalent-Time Sampling Scopes

Unlike a real-time sampling oscilloscope, an equivalent-time sampling scope samples the waveform once per trigger event. The scope is triggered multiple times; by varying the delay between the trigger event and sample, a composite picture of the waveform is built up and displayed on the scope's display. The delay between the scope trigger and waveform sample can be varied randomly or by introducing a very small delta between consecutive trigger/sample pairs. The display is built up using a composite of all the samples, as shown in Figure 8.2.

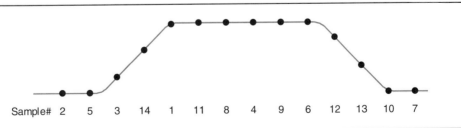

Sample# 2   5   3   14   1   11   8   4   9   6   12   13   10   7

Figure 8.2   Equivalent-Time Scope Sampling

Equivalent-time sampling scopes are suitable only for capturing repetitive signals. The benefit is that the useful bandwidth of the scope is not limited by sample rate or aliasing. However, because an equivalent-time sampling scope creates the eye diagram from many unrelated waveform samples over a relatively extended period of time, the resultant eye diagram tends to overstate the peak jitter. The displayed eye contains jitter from low-frequency coupling, clock drift, and other such behavior that the receiver can easily track.[1]

So which type of scope is suitable for validating PCI Express? The base specification states that jitter and voltage measurements must be made over a minimum period of "any consecutive 250 UI" (unit intervals). Only the real-time scope has the ability to sample the incoming waveform such that it captures a record of consecutive unit intervals. In addition, only a real-time scope has the ability to save the waveform in memory for later post-processing which, as shown in Chapter 9, is a requirement for generating the eye diagram. Therefore, to validate compliance to specification, you must use a real-time scope.

While you can use an equivalent-time sampling scope to capture an eye diagram, the resultant eye diagram would overstate the actual jitter seen by the receiver and might well exceed the overall jitter budget, especially if spread spectrum clocking (SSC) is used on the motherboard clock.

Minimum Bandwidth Requirements

What is the minimum scope bandwidth needed to accurately measure an eye diagram? The answer depends on several factors, including whether one wants to measure the eye at the transmitter or receiver. However, the biggest factor is the rise and fall time of the signal being measured.

The finite bandwidth of a scope tends to distort the eye by increasing the rise time and fall time of the transitions that make up the walls of the eye. The effect is to "close the eye" in a manner similar to that shown in Figure 8.3.

---

[1] Obviously, this statement does not apply if the sampling scope has a clock data recovery module attached, or is otherwise recovering a clock from the incoming data. In these cases, the scope is effectively tracking low-frequency drift in the data just as a receiver would.

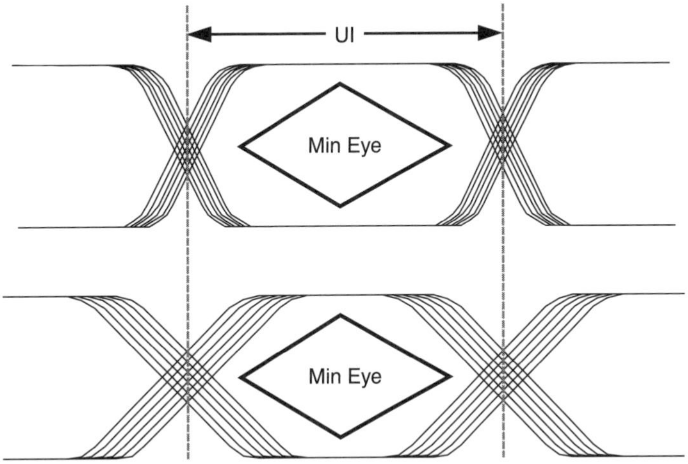

Figure 8.3   Eye Closure Due to Increased Rise and Fall Times

In the top drawing in Figure 8.3, the signal rise and fall times are about 25 percent of the total unit interval. The bottom drawing illustrates how the eye opening changes when the rise and fall times are increased to 50 percent of the unit interval. As shown, the bottom eye diagram has much less space between the diamond shape that delimits the minimum eye and the inner eye wall.

So how much does the finite bandwidth of an oscilloscope degrade the rise time? You can use Equation 8.1 to calculate the measured rise time of a signal.

Equation 8.1   Rise Time Measurement

$$T_{RISE\_MEASURED} = \sqrt{T_{RISE\_SIGNAL}^2 + T_{RISE\_EQUIPMENT}^2}$$

where:

$T_{RISE\_MEASURED}$ = the apparent rise time of the signal

T_{RISE_SIGNAL} = the actual rise time of the signal

$T_{RISE\_EQUIPMENT}$ = the rise time of the measurement equipment

From Equation 8.1, it is apparent that if the rise time of the measurement equipment approaches that of the signal being measured, then the measured rise time of the signal increases. Figure 8.4 shows the error percentage based on the ratio of signal rise time to measurement equipment rise time.

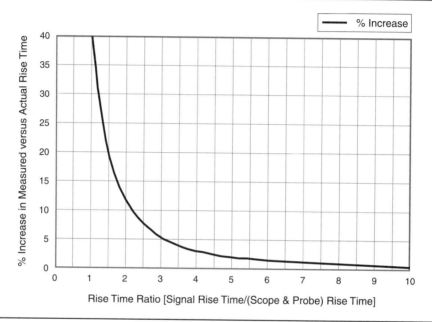

Figure 8.4   Rise Time Measurement Errors Due to Bandwidth Limits

As shown in Figure 8.4, if the rise time ratio—the ratio of signal to scope time—is 1:1, the measurement error is 40 percent. That is, the measured rise time is 40 percent greater than the actual rise time of the signal. For a 2:1 ratio, the error in measuring rise time due to the finite scope plus probe bandwidth drops to 12 percent.

The base specification limits the minimum, or fastest, allowed rise/fall time of a signal at the transmitter pad to 0.125 UI, or 50 ps. In reality, losses in the transmitter's package traces slow the rise/fall time to ~75–100 ps at the transmitter package balls. As a reasonable estimate, to introduce no more than a 12-percent measurement error at the transmitter, the combined rise time of the scope and probe combination should be 75 ps/2 = 37 ps.

Scopes and probes are usually specified in terms of their 3 dB bandwidth (BW_{3dB}). Rise time is related to bandwidth by either Equation 8.2, if 10-percent to 90-percent rise time is desired, or Equation 8.3, if 20 percent to 80-percent rise time is desired.

Equation 8.2   Calculating 10-Percent to 90-Percent Rise Time from 3 dB Bandwidth

$$T_{RISE}(10\% - 90\%) = \frac{0.35}{BW_{3dB}}$$

Equation 8.3   Calculating 20-Percent to 80-Percent Rise Time from 3 dB Bandwidth

$$T_{RISE}(20\% - 80\%) = \frac{0.22}{BW_{3dB}}$$

Both equations assume that the scope and probe system together have a frequency roll-off that approximates a single-pole, low-pass filter.[2] Given that assumption, Equation 8.4 presents the minimum required bandwidth of the scope and probe system to limit the rise time measurement error to 12 percent.

---

[2] While the single-pole response assumption may hold for older oscilloscopes, the very high-bandwidth real-time oscilloscopes suitable for PCI Express validation tend to use built-in digital signal processing (DSP) algorithms to create a "brick wall" type frequency response. In this case, the numerator of the rise time equation would be something other than 0.35 or 0.22. Because the exact value varies with the characteristics of the filter algorithms response, check with your oscilloscope vendor before trying to convert an oscilloscope's bandwidth specification into its rise time performance.

| **Equation 8.4** | Minimum 3dB Bandwidth for Measuring PCI Express† Signal Rise Times |

$$BW_{3dB} = \frac{0.22}{37ps} = 5.9GHz$$

Equation 8.4 is only an estimate of the minimum required bandwidth, and is based only on the idea of limiting errors in eye diagrams due to rise time limitation. As a check, engineers at Intel conducted an extensive study in which they compared the eye diagram generated from raw simulation waveforms with an eye diagram generated by simulation waveforms that had been run through a filter that represented a typical high-speed scope and probe combination. The study concluded that to minimize timing error, the scope and probe combination had to pass at a minimum all frequencies up to the second harmonic of the PCI Express fundamental frequency of 1.25 GHz. To reduce voltage error, at an absolute minimum, all frequencies up to the fourth harmonic must be passed. This result translates into a measurement system bandwidth of 5 GHz. As a practical minimum, the bandwidth of the measurement system should be 6 GHz. Because most of the harmonic energy of a PCI Express signal is contained in the rising and falling edges, you could assume that measurement error is determined by the rise time of the signal and by the scope's ability to respond to this edge without significant slowing or distortion.

Because board interconnect is not perfectly lossless, signals propagating along the interconnect will have high frequencies attenuated, which results in a degradation of that signal's rise time. For example, measurements taken at the end of a 10-inch long, 5-mil wide trace over FR-4 reveal that a 50-ps rise time edge can be degraded by 100 ps or more. Because of this, a measurement made at the end of the interconnect—that is, at the receiver—tends to be more accurate than a measurement made at the transmitter. Fortunately, the signal at the receiver is the one most important for validation and compliance.

Effects of Probe Capacitance

When selecting a scope and probe combination, you should also consider the effect of the probe's input capacitance on the circuit being probed. When dealing with gigahertz frequencies, even a very small amount of input capacitance can significantly affect the circuit. As an example, consider a scope probe with a 1.5 pF input capacitance placed across the termination impedance of a PCI Express channel. Assuming a 1.25-GHz fundamental frequency (2.5-GHz data rate), the impedance of the capacitor can be approximated as shown in Equation 8.5.

Equation 8.5   Scope Probe Impedance

$$\mathrm{Xc} = \frac{1}{(2 \times \pi \times 1.25\mathrm{GHz} \times 1.5\mathrm{pF})} = 84.8\Omega$$

If this impedance is placed in parallel with a 100 Ω differential termination, the magnitude of the complex termination impedance of the channel is reduced to 46 Ω at 1.25 GHz, less than half of its DC value. This reduction in impedance can drastically affect the channel's *return loss* because the amount of energy returned to the transmitter from impedance mismatches at the load. In reality, both the package and scope input impedance are complex magnitude and phase quantities, and they interact. To fully account for the effects of scope probe capacitance, you would need to perform circuit level simulations that include the effects of transmission line loss.

Simulating the Effects of Bandwidth Limits and Probe Loading

As mentioned previously, the only way to fully account for the effects of bandwidth-limited scopes and probe loading is to perform system-level simulations that include the scope and probe. In general, these simulations vary the same system parameters as the ones used to determine the design space: interconnect length, impedance and loss, transmitter edge rate, and so on. The difference is the addition of an electrical model of the probe. The scope probe model should model the bandwidth and gain of the measurement system from the probe tip to the output of the oscilloscope's receiver circuitry, as well as the probe's impedance versus frequency. Most likely, you would need to obtain such a model from your scope manufacturer.

You should perform these simulations over a range of scope input capacitance values. You should also vary the probe distance from the package, as the physical distance from the package pin or ball affects interaction with the scope probe. When doing the simulation, compare the waveforms at the receiver with the waveforms at the output of the probe model. The metrics for comparison should be eye height at the center of the waveform and differences in maximum jitter.

Don't forget to include the effects of scope landing pad structures. For more information on scope and probing structures, see Chapter 9, "Measurement Techniques."

Scope Noise Floor and Gain Errors

The previous sections have focused on measurement inaccuracies caused by scope bandwidth limit and probe loading issues. However, the ultimate limiter of accuracy and precision in PCI Express measurement is the oscilloscope's noise floor and gain accuracy.

The noise floor (NF) of an oscilloscope represents the amount of random noise present in the analog front end of the scope. This noise is present even in the absence of an external signal, and determines the fundamental lower limit of measurement resolution. The noise that makes up the noise floor consists mostly of the random thermal noise present in the semiconductor, and is proportional to the bandwidth of the scope—in other words, the higher the bandwidth of the particular scope, the higher the noise floor. The noise is Gaussian in nature and its value is usually expressed in μV or mV rms. Consult the oscilloscope maker to determine the factor used to convert the rms value to a peak-to-peak (NF_{p-p}) value.

Other major sources of measurement inaccuracy include DC gain and offset errors and errors due to the sampling scope's D/A conversion.

- DC gain errors (GA) represent the inaccuracies in the scope's Volts/Div gain setting, and are usually specified as a percentage of the deflection from the vertical centerline of the scope display.

- Offset errors (OA) are introduced when the user adds an offset to the input signal or uses the scope's "position" knob to adjust a signal so that it can be displayed on the scope screen.

- Integral non-linearity (INL) errors represent deviations from the straight line DC transfer function. These errors represent the effective resolution of the sampling scope's D/A converter.

Adding all these errors together, we arrive at Equation 8.6, which represents the measurement bounds for a typical scope's measurement error.

Equation 8.6	Measurement Accuracy Bounds Due to Scope Measurement Errors

$$measurement\_bound = measurement \pm (GA + OA + INL + NFpeak)$$

Obviously, the specific values to use for gain error, offset error, integral non-linear error, and noise floor are dependent on the make and model of the oscilloscope. However, it is possible to make a couple of general observations:

- When measuring the vertical opening of an eye diagram, use the smallest practical Volts/Div setting such that the waveform fills the vertical dimension of the display without clipping. In this way, errors due to noise floor and INL are minimized.

- Do not apply position offset or adjustment offset to the waveform. In this way, OA errors are eliminated. Given that PCI Express signals are DC-coupled at the receiver, this should not be a problem for measurements made at the receiver.

You can measure and/or calibrate noise floor and other errors out of a measurement. For details about how to do this, refer to Chapter 9.

Differential versus Single-ended Probing

All other things being equal, you should measure eye diagrams using a single differential probe rather than two single-ended probes. The reason has to do with the scope noise floor. As described in the "Transmitter Eye Diagram" section later in this chapter, creating an eye diagram using two single-ended probes involves subtracting the waveform measured by one probe from the waveform measured by the other. Because the random noise on the corresponding scope channels are not correlated, the noise floor from *each* channel must be added as uncertainty to the final result, thus doubling the measurement uncertainty. Another way to state this is that the noise floor of a measurement involving the combination of two scope channels is twice that of a single channel measurement. Differential probes also tend to have lower input capacitance and higher common mode rejection ratio—that is, more noise immunity—than single-ended probes.

You can use differential probes in a single-ended configuration to take common mode measurements by attaching the D+ or D– lead to ground.

Understanding the AC and DC Specifications

Before discussing how to measure the AC and DC specifications, it is helpful to understand the difference between validating the performance of a component "in system" and validating "compliance to specification." To prove specification compliance, the measurements dealing with the transmitter and receiver eye diagrams, as well as measurements of the AC and DC common mode voltages, must be done using the compliance load as specified in the base specification. In addition, these measurements usually are made directly at the package pins of the transmitter or, in the case of receiver measurement, at the compliance load itself. In practice, the receiver or driver in an actual system does not comply with the compliance load called out by the specification, and surface mount packages do not allow direct access to the pins of the package.

However, this does not mean that useful measurements cannot be made. A measurement of the eye at the receiver pins is valid in that it does reveal what the receiver "sees." Assuming that a receiver package meets the return loss and DC impedance specifications, the measured eye is representative of the receiver eye under compliance load conditions.

Measuring the transmitter eye is generally less useful because the eye is distorted by reflections from the DC blocking capacitor vias and other discontinuities. Of course, transmitter eye measurements can reveal functional defects, such as the lack of de-emphasis, or gross waveform problems.

True compliance measurements are needed when a system is exhibiting errors and the cause cannot be obviously determined. In such cases, the system must be decomposed into its constituent components of receiver, interconnect, and transmitter. To begin, the receiver package is removed from the board, a compliance load soldered into place, and a measurement of the receiver eye is taken. If the receiver eye meets specification, the fault is assumed to be with the receiver silicon. On the other hand, if the eye does not meet specification, a further decomposition is required. The transmitter pins are isolated from the interconnect, a compliance load is attached, and a measurement is taken. If the transmitter eye meets spec, the fault must lie with the interconnect.

Understanding the Tx and Rx Eye Diagrams

Accurate eye diagram measurements are crucial to validation of a PCI Express system's electrical performance. The next few sections provide detailed explanation of the key parameters associated with eye diagrams, beginning with a discussion of the unit interval.

The Unit Interval

As discussed in Chapter 1, the base specification states that the unit interval (UI)—the high or low time of an individual bit—must be 400 ps ±120 fs. Determining the transmitter UI by measuring the time interval between the crossing points of a single data cell is almost impossible. The normal edge-to-edge variation due to jitter is much greater than 120 fs. Instead, UI is measured by calculating an average UI over a large number of cycles. To estimate how many cycles are required to average out errors due to jitter on the first and last edge, assuming no spread system clocking (SSC), consider that the first and last edges used in the measurement can be offset from their "ideal" position by a maximum of 0.15 UI, or 60 ps. The total interval error due to jitter is 120 ps. By taking the interval measurement over 20,000 unit intervals, as an example, the error in the first and last edge due to jitter would contribute a maximum of 6 fs of error to the UI calculation. Over 250 UI, a 6 fs error in the UI accumulates to less than 1 percent error in the position of the 250th edge.

If the transmitter clock employs SSC, it becomes more difficult to determine the number of cycles over which to average UI. A compromise must be reached between the error due to edge jitter and the error introduced by the SSC itself. The software used for compliance testing calculates an average value of UI over 3,500 UI, where 3,500 UI is 1.4 μs.[3] This amount of time equates to approximately 1/20 of the time it takes the unit interval to vary over its maximum range.

---

[3] In actuality, the compliance software employs an algorithm for calculating the UI from the data that is much more robust to jitter than a simple edge-to-edge averaging. Refer to Chapter 9 for more details.

Transmitter Eye Diagram

Figure 8.5 represents an eye diagram at the transmitter. If this eye diagram were placed over a scope display and centered in the UI, no part of the displayed waveform should be inside the triangle defined by $V_{TX\_DIFF\_P-P}$ and T_{TX_EYE}.

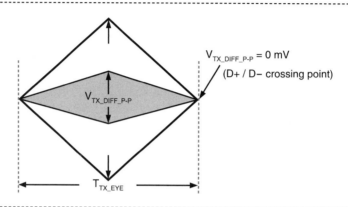

Figure 8.5   Eye Diagram at the Transmitter

According to the base specification, T_{TX_EYE} must be a minimum of 0.75[4] UI, as measured between the D+ / D– crossing point. Assuming a nominal UI of 400 ps, the minimum width of T_{TX_EYE} would be 280 ps. A minimum T_{TX_EYE} must be maintained over any 250 consecutive transmitter UIs. The PCI Express specification states that the differential peak-to-peak voltage ($V_{TX\_DIFF\_P-P}$) for a transition bit is between 800 mV and 1200 mV.[5] $V_{TX\_DIFF\_P-P}$ is defined as $2 * |(V_{D+} - V_{D-})|$. This value is twice the value of the transmitter differential peak voltage V_{DIFF_PEAK}, which is defined as $|(V_{D+} - V_{D-})|$ or 400 mV to 600 mV.

When measuring differential voltage, a differential probe placed between D+ and D– measures the differential peak-to-peak value, while two single-ended probes placed from D+ to ground and D– to ground, respectively, measure the differential peak value. To properly measure $V_{TX\_DIFF\_P-P}$ using two single-ended probes, use the math function on the scope to

---

[4] Per version 1.1 of the base specification, the Tx eye is measured with a "clean" reference clock. Refer to the latest base specification for more details.

[5] For both transition and de-emphasized bits, the maximum $V_{TX\_DIFF\_P-P}$ value must not be exceeded anywhere within the UI. On the other hand, the minimum $V_{TX\_DIFF\_P-P}$ value applies only at the center of the eye.

subtract the two scope channels, then display the result.[6] Note that algebraically subtracting two signals results in the same range of values as calculating the absolute value of the difference between two signals and then doubling that absolute value.

In Figure 8.5, the shaded diamond shape represents the eye when the transmitter is sending a de-emphasized data bit. De-emphasis reduces the differential voltage swing by 3.5 dB ±0.5 dB. The differential peak-to-peak voltage of a de-emphasized data bit is between 505 mV (which is 4 dB down from 800 mV) and 850 mV (which is 3 dB down from 1200 mV). When validating de-emphasized voltage levels to specification, the 3.5 dB ±0.5 dB voltage level reduction is measured relative to the nominal voltage level of the immediately preceding transition bit.

When analyzing the transmitter eye, you must analyze the non-de-emphasized transition data and de-emphasized data separately to verify that they conform to their respective eye diagrams. In general, you would perform this discrete analysis by capturing the waveform in oscilloscope memory and then post-processing the waveform to separate transition bits from de-emphasized bits.

To prove specification compliance, T_{TX_EYE} and $V_{TX\_DIFF\_P-P}$ are measured at the pins of the transmitter package while the transmitter is driving the compliance test load. However, in a system environment under practical conditions, it is very difficult to take a meaningful measurement of the transmitter eye, not only because of probing difficulties, but because the transmitter usually is driving several inches of PC traces, not the compliance load. In practice, the transmitter eye in a real system is measured only if you need to isolate a specific system problem. Most measurements are taken at the receiver.

Receiver Eye Diagram

Figure 8.6 is a representative eye diagram at the receiver. If this eye diagram were placed over a scope display, no part of the displayed waveform should be inside the triangle defined by $V_{RX\_DIFFP-P}$ and T_{RX_EYE}. As with the transmitter specifications, receiver specifications are measured at the pins of the device package.

---

[6] As explained in the preceding discussion of "Differential versus Single-Ended Probing," using two single-ended probes results in a measurement containing twice the scope noise floor error. Whenever possible, use a differential probe to make eye diagram measurements.

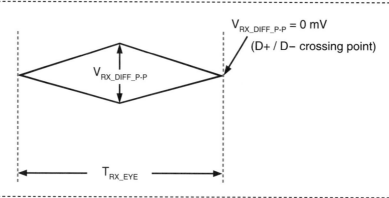

Figure 8.6   Eye Diagram at the Receiver

The minimum horizontal opening at the receiver ($T_{RX\text{-}EYE}$) is specified as 0.4 UI, or 160 ps. The minimum vertical opening ($V_{RX\_DIFF\_P\text{-}P}$) is 175 mV. Given that the minimum transmitter differential peak-to-peak voltage ($V_{TX\_DIFF\_P\text{-}P}$) is 505 mV, which is the minimum voltage for a de-emphasized bit, the transmitter package and interconnect can attenuate the differential peak-to-peak voltage by up to 8.2 dB. Note that if $V_{RX\_DIFF\_P\text{-}P}$ falls below the minimum electrical idle detect threshold ($V_{RX\ IDLE\ DET\ DIFFp\text{-}p}$ min), the receiver assumes that the transmitter is in *electrical idle*. Signals at the receiver that are greater than the minimum electrical idle detect threshold value of 65 mV, but less than the minimum valid vertical eye opening of 175 mV, are considered to be undefined. These eye specifications must be met over any consecutive 250 UI.

As mentioned in the discussion of the transmitter eye diagram, when measuring differential voltage, a differential probe placed between D+ and D– measures the differential peak-to-peak value. However, two single-ended probes placed from D+ to ground and from D– to ground measure the differential peak value, which is half of the min and max values given above. To properly measure $V_{RX\_DIFF\_P\text{-}P}$ using two single-ended probes, use the math function on the scope to subtract the two scope channels and then display the result.

To prove specification compliance, $V_{RX\_DIFF\_P\text{-}P}$ and T_{RX_EYE} must be measured with the receiver replaced by the compliance load. In reality, as long as the receiver is close to the nominal DC impedance specification and meets the return loss specifications, the eye measured at the receiver package pins is a fair approximation to the true compliance eye. Also note that to properly measure the eye at the receiver, the transmitting source must meet the specifications for DC differential TX impedance, transmitter differential return loss, and common mode return loss.

The Eye at the Add-in Card Connector

In addition to the transmitter and receiver eye diagrams specified by the base specification, eye diagrams are defined at the edge of the interface between an add-in card and its connector. The *PCI Express Card Electromechanical (CEM) Specification* (PCI-SIG 2004) specifies these eye diagrams; to measure them, use the same techniques as the transmitter and receiver eye diagrams.

DC Common Mode Voltage

Common mode voltage is defined as the voltage that is "common" to both the D+ and D– outputs. For purposes of the specifications, the DC common mode voltage is calculated as the average voltage on the D+ and D– outputs over a large number of unit intervals, with a minimum of 250 UI. This DC average is calculated as shown in Equation 8.7.

Equation 8.7   Calculating DC Common Mode Voltage

$$V_{CM\text{-}DC} = |V_{D+} + V_{D-}| / 2 \text{ (over 250 UI minimum)}$$

Two specifications deal with DC common mode voltage. The first, $V_{TX\text{-}CM\text{-}DC\text{-}ACTIVE\text{-}IDLE\text{-}DELTA}$, specifies the maximum allowable difference between $V_{CM\text{-}DC}$ during electrical idle and $V_{CM\text{-}DC}$ during active operation, referred to as the "L0" state. You can measure $V_{TX\text{-}CM\text{-}DC\text{-}ACTIVE\text{-}IDLE\text{-}DELTA}$ by first calculating the DC average, as shown in Equation 8.7, from a waveform captured during electrical idle, and then performing the same calculation on a waveform captured during a data transfer. The maximum allowable difference is less than or equal to 100 mV.

The second specification, $V_{TR\text{-}CM\text{-}DC\text{-}LINE\text{-}DELTA}$, is concerned with the difference between the common mode voltages of the individual D+ and D– outputs. This difference may arise because the two outputs do not have the same duty cycles—one output spends more time in the high or low state than the other, or because one output does not swing symmetrically about its common mode voltage. Both these conditions are illustrated in Figure 8.7.

In Figure 8.7, the D– waveform exhibits both duty cycle distortion and nonsymmetric swing around the average voltage of the D+ waveform. The end result is that the crossing point of the two waveforms is not at the 50-percent point, thereby increasing inter-symbol interference (ISI) and jitter at the receiver.

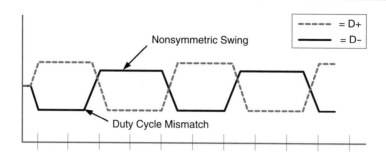

Figure 8.7   Nonsymmetric D+ and D– Waveforms

To measure $V_{TX-CM-DC-LINE-DELTA}$, use a real-time sampling scope to capture the individual D+ and D– waveforms, then post-process the waveform data to calculate the DC average of the individual D+ and D– waveform. The difference between the two should be less than or equal to 25 mV, when measured over a minimum of 250 consecutive transmitter UIs. In practice, a full scope acquisition is recommended. Note that the DC average of a waveform is data dependent, so use a data pattern that has an equal number of ones and zeros—that is, a data pattern that has an overall running disparity of zero.

For strict specification compliance, you should measure both $V_{TX-CM-DC-ACTIVE-IDLE-DELTA}$ and $V_{TR-CM-DC-LINE-DELTA}$ at the transmitter pins, into the standard compliance load. In practice, one would measure these quantities as close to the pins of the transmitter package as practical.

AC Common Mode Voltage

In contrast to the DC common mode voltage specifications, the AC common mode voltage specifications deal with the difference between the DC long-term average of the differential signal and the instantaneous value of the differential signal. Mathematically, this difference can be expressed as shown in Equation 8.8, where V_{CM-DC} is the DC average of the differential signal as calculated in Equation 8.7.

Equation 8.8   Calculating AC Common Mode Voltage

$$V_{CM-AC} = (|V_{D+} + V_{D-}| / 2) - V_{CM-DC}$$

AC common mode voltages can be caused by crosstalk from an adjacent signal, or signals, coupling onto the differential pair. AC common mode voltages also arise when there is a phase shift between the two signals of a differential pair. Figure 8.8 shows an example of this effect.

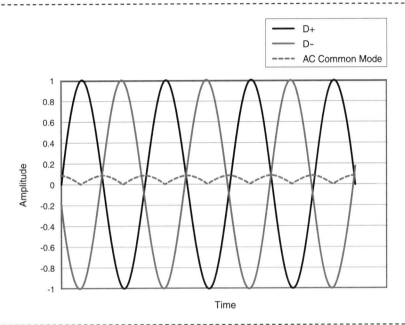

Figure 8.8   AC Common Mode Voltage Due to Phase Shift

Figure 8.8 shows two sine waves of opposite polarity, each with a magnitude of one, plotted on the same axis. One wave was offset from the other by a small amount (10 degrees), and then the difference in amplitude between the two waveforms at each point in time was plotted. The smaller amplitude signal is this difference signal, which represents the AC common mode signal. Be aware that an AC common voltage waveform is periodic within a unit interval, while DC common voltage is a steady state value.

Phase shift can occur when the two traces of a differential pair are not the same length due to differences in routing length, or when both signals of a differential pair do not propagate at the same velocity. This latter condition can be caused by non-homogeneous dielectrics—for example, differences in fiberglass weave density surrounding each circuit board trace.

To measure AC common mode, use a real-time sampling scope to capture the individual D+ and D– waveforms, then post-process the waveform data to calculate the AC common mode signal. AC common mode noise at the transmitter driving the standard test load should be less than 20mV peak, while at the receiver it should be less than 150mV peak. Note that unlike the DC common mode signal, the AC common mode signal is not data dependent.

Rise and Fall Times

The base specification states that the minimum allowable signal rise and fall time at the transmitter package pins into the standard test load is 0.125 UI, or 50 ps. To measure a signal rise time of 50 ps with less than 5 percent error requires a measurement system 3dB bandwidth of approximately 13 GHz. For a complete discussion on the relationship between bandwidth and rise time and how they affect measurement, see "Minimum Bandwidth Requirements," earlier in this chapter.

If the scope does not have adequate bandwidth, the measured rise time is significantly slower than the actual signal rise time. In this case, you would calculate the actual signal rise time from the measured value using Equation 8.9.

Equation 8.9   Actual Signal Rise Time Calculation

$$T_{RISE\_ACTUAL} = \sqrt{T_{RISE\_MEASURED}^2 - T_{RISE\_SYSTEM}^2}$$

where:

T_{RISE_ACTUAL} = the actual rise time of the signal

$T_{RISE\_MEASURED}$ = rise time as measured by the scope

T_{RISE_SYSTEM} = the rise time of the measurement equipment

Note that *all* rise times in Equation 8.9 must be expressed as the same 20-percent to 80-percent or 10-percent to 90-percent quantities. Measured rise and fall times can be observed by triggering a scope on either the rising or falling edge of the signal under test, and then capturing the resulting waveform on the screen. Cursors are positioned at the 20-percent and 80-percent points of the waveform, and the rise or fall time is read directly from the display. In order to get a clean waveform for measurement, it is recommended that the device transmit an alternating 1's and 0's pattern.

In practice, if you use a typical high-bandwidth (>= 40 GHz) equivalent-time scope to make the measurement, the difference between the measured rise time and the calculated actual rise time of the signal under test is small enough that you can use the measured value directly. If a typical real-time sampling scope with a 6 GHz bandwidth is used, then use Equation 8.9 to calculate the actual rise time.

The output rise time or fall time of a PCI Express transmitter can be affected by adjacent output switching activity. Adjacent outputs can be non-switching, for quiescent conditions; switching in the same H→L or L→H direction as the output under test, for *even mode* switching conditions; or switching in the opposite direction of the output under test, for *odd mode* conditions. It is not always clear which condition would produce the fastest or slowest rise time, so rise/fall measurements should be made under all three conditions.

Lane-to-Lane Skew

Thus far, we have concentrated on measuring parameters related to the electrical performance of the link. The lane-to-lane skew parameters, on the other hand, are related more to the logical operation of the transmitter. These parameters require the use of analog test equipment to verify operation.

Transmitter Lane Skew

The base specification states that in a link with multiple lanes, the bytes in a multi-byte data transfer are distributed across each lane. For example, consider a four-byte data transfer over a x4 link, that is, a link with four lanes. Byte zero is transferred on lane zero, byte one on lane one, and so on; the four bytes are transferred in parallel. In order to limit the amount of buffering required at the receiver to re-align the bytes, the base specification limits the amount of skew between any two transmitters on a port to 8 UI maximum, or the $L_{TX-SKEW}$ specification. In other words, the delay between the first lane to start transmitting and the last lane to start transmitting must be 8 UI or less. Figure 8.9 presents an example of lane-to-lane skew.

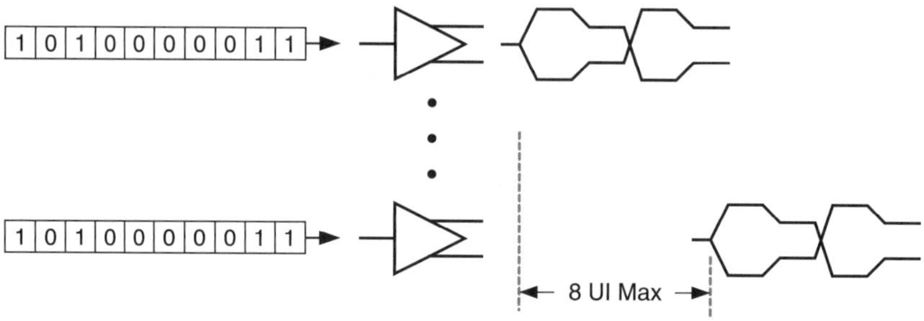

Figure 8.9   Illustration of Transmitter Lane-to-Lane Skew

The lane-to-lane skew specification can be validated by taking advantage of the normal de-skew features of the PCI Express bus protocol. The PCI Express specification states that the COM symbol at the beginning of a training sequence or the skip ordered sets that are periodically injected into the data stream must be transferred simultaneously across all lanes of a multi-lane link. Therefore, the COM symbol or skip ordered set can be used as an oscilloscope trigger either directly or through a logic analyzer. The delay between any two lanes can then be read directly from the screen cursors on the scope.

Lane-to-Lane Skew at the Receiver

In addition to the transmitter lane-to-lane skew, the PCI Express bus specification has a separate specification for the lane-to-lane skew at the receivers ($L_{RX-SKEW}$). A separate specification is required because the bus allows the presence of *bus repeaters.* A bus repeater is used on especially long links to electrically buffer or re-power the data signal as it makes its way from transmitter to the receiver. The specification allows up to two bus repeaters. However, as described in the section on clock tolerance compensation in Chapter 1, a bus repeater may add or subtract a SKP symbol as it receives the data to be retransmitted. Because bus repeaters on a multi-lane link cannot be perfectly synchronized, the data arriving at the final destination of a multi-lane link can be out of sync by up to four SKP symbols. For example, one lane might have two added symbols and another lane might have two fewer symbols.

The maximum value of lane-to-lane skew at the receiver ($L_{RX-SKEW}$) is 20 ns. This includes the skew introduced by the potentially different number of SKP symbols on each lane as well as skew due to the interconnect. In a system with two bus repeaters, the maximum amount of skew due to interconnect can be calculated as shown in Equation 8.10.

Equation 8.10   Maximum Interconnect Skew

Max Interconnect Skew = $L_{RX-SKEW-max}$ – Max SKP Symbol Skew – Max Transmitter Skew

Max Interconnect Skew = 20ns – (4 symbols X 4ns/symbol) – (8 UI X 400 ps/UI) = 800ps

---

In non-bus repeater designs, validating that the receiver's logic can tolerate maximum $L_{RX-SKEW}$ is difficult, and requires the assistance either of a low loss analog delay line capable of accurately reproducing the signal or of a test mode in the transmitter that adds extra delay between lanes.

Common Mode and Differential Impedance

When dealing with busses like PCI Express that transmit data differentially, you need to be aware of two types of impedance:

■ *Differential* impedance is the impedance measured across the D+ and D– traces of a differential pair when one trace is stimulated with a signal and the other with its complement.

■ *Common mode* impedance is the impedance measured from a single D+ or D– trace to a common reference, usually ground, when both traces of the pair are stimulated with the same signal.

To minimize reflections in a differential system, the drivers and receiver must match both the differential and common mode impedances of the interconnect.

In a PCI Express bus system, a receiver's differential impedance is specified to be 100 Ω nominal, while the common mode impedance is specified as 50 Ω nominal. As mentioned previously, these are DC impedance values that usually are implemented as a pair of 50 Ω resistors, one from the D+ terminal to ground and one from the D– terminal to ground. Because they are DC impedance values, you could measure them directly by applying power to the device and then using an ohmmeter to take the appropriate measurement. In practice, the receiver pins must be disconnected from the PC board traces; therefore, this measurement usually is made on the bench or tester using a test fixture that allows direct access to the D+ and D– pins.

The PCI Express specification specifies the differential output impedance of the transmitter when transferring data to be 100 Ω nominal. The transmitter common mode output impedance is specified to be a minimum of 40 Ω. Measuring a transmitter's output impedance in a static test using an ohmmeter is difficult, because the transmitter output impedance can vary depending on its logical state set by bus protocol. In practice, measurement of this value usually requires putting the device into a special test mode.

Measuring the differential and common mode impedances of the PC board traces requires the use of a differential Time Domain Reflectometer (TDR). While a complete tutorial on TDR theory and usage is beyond the scope of this book, suffice it to say that a TDR is, in essence, a very high-bandwidth equivalent-time sampling scope that samples the output of a built-in pulse generator. Figure 8.10 presents a conceptual block diagram of a TDR.

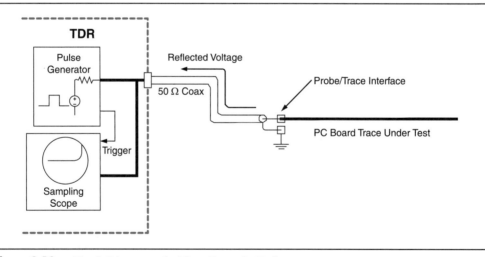

Figure 8.10   Block Diagram of a Time Domain Reflectometer

As shown in Figure 8.10, the pulse generator is connected to the PC board trace under test via a coax cable. The generator launches a very fast (20–30 ps) edge of known amplitude into the trace under test, then after a short delay triggers the sampling scope. The scope samples the voltage reflected from the interface of the probe and PCB trace under test. This reflected voltage is displayed by the TDR as a trace impedance over time.

A differential TDR operates in a very similar manner, except that it launches opposite polarity edges into the traces that make up the differential pair, then displays the reflected voltage from one of the traces. Because the traces are stimulated with opposite polarity signals, the differential impedance is displayed.

The current PCI Express design rules for signal trace width and spacing result in a differential pair that has a common mode impedance of 60 Ω. The 10 Ω nominal difference between the interconnect common mode impedance and the receiver common mode impedance means that any AC common mode voltages present on the interconnect are reflected by the receiver's termination, thus degrading the system noise margin. This explains why it is important to control sources of AC common mode noise.

Understanding Bit Error Rate (BER)

Bit error rate (BER) is a measure of how reliably a system can transmit data without failure. Specifically, BER is a measure of the probability that a data bit will be successfully transferred between a transmitter and receiver. For example, if a system has a BER of 10^{-12}, there is a 1 in 10^{12} chance that any single data bit would be interpreted incorrectly at the receiver. Another way of stating this measurement is that, on average, one out of every 10^{12} bits transferred is received incorrectly.

BER is tied directly to the amount of random jitter (Rj) present in the system. As described previously, random jitter is assumed to have a Gaussian distribution, and one feature of a Gaussian distribution is that the maximum value is unbounded. While a system might be designed so that it is very tolerant to jitter, because of the unbounded nature of the underlying sources of random jitter, the system cannot be made completely error-free. Run the system for long enough—that is, transfer enough data across the link—and at some point a jitter event occurs that is beyond what the receiver can tolerate. Of course, the BER of the link might be so low that bit errors due to jitter are swamped by errors caused by software, power failures, component failures, and so on, but the jitter is still there. A BER specification is a way to acknowledge this fact.

The base specification states that the "UI allocation must meet a maximum BER of 10^{-12} for the (given) Tj." In other words, the system design must allocate the total jitter budget of the transmitter, receiver, and interconnect so that the system not only meets the eye diagrams, but that the random jitter does not cause the system to exceed a maximum BER of 10^{-12}.

Measuring BER

The statistical nature of jitter and BER raises an interesting question: how does one measure BER? At first glance, it may be tempting to simply transfer 10^{12} bits across a link and then count the errors. At a data rate of 2.5 Gbits/sec, 10^{12} bits can be transferred in about 7.5 minutes. If no more than one error was recorded, the link meets the BER specification. However, one test alone is not enough. The link must be run for an extended period to ensure that that one didn't just "get lucky." The questions then become, how long to run the link, and again, given the random nature of the underlying process, what level of confidence is there that the result wasn't due to chance?

A way to view this problem is to consider that each bit is transferred as a binominal or two-state "test." A bit is received either correctly or incorrectly. Statisticians refer to a test of this sort as a *Bernoulli trial*. Furthermore, each test is independent; the success or failure of one data transfer does not depend on the success or failure of any other. Finally, there is a very small chance that any particular bit will fail. Fortunately, these conditions meet the criteria of a *Poisson distribution*. Equation 8.11 presents the formula for calculating the probability of having exactly X number of events occurring, given a system that has an expected value λ of the number of events occurring.

Equation 8.11   Poisson Distribution for Calculating the Probability of an Event

$$P(x, \lambda) = \frac{\lambda^x \cdot e^{-\lambda}}{X!}$$

In Equation 8.11, the expected value λ is the product of the number of trials times the probability of a particular event occurring per trial. In our case, $\lambda = 10^{12}$ bits transferred $* 10^{-12}$ failure/bit $= 1$.

As an example, Equation 8.12 calculates the probability of recording exactly one error in 10^{12} bit transfers for a system that has a BER of 10^{-12}.

Equation 8.12   Example BER Calculation

$$P(x,\lambda) = \frac{1 * e^{-1}}{1!} = e^{-1} = 0.3678$$

In our case, we wish to calculate how many bits to transfer until the likelihood of recording at least one error is very high, assuming the BER is really 10^{-12}. From Equation 8.11, the probability of recording no errors in 10^{12} bits, that is $x = 0$ in the equation, is 0.3678, or approximately 37 trials out of 100. If 2×10^{12} bits are transferred, where λ in the equation equals 2, the probability of recording no errors drops to 0.1353. If λ equals 3, the probability of recording no errors is approximately 0.05. Continuing in this fashion, we find that the probability of transferring a block of 8×10^{12} bits without an error is 0.0003. It takes about 53 minutes at 2.5 Gbits/sec to transfer 8×10^{12} bits, thus we can say with a high degree of confidence that if a link can run at full speed for 53 consecutive minutes without an error, the BER of the link is at most 10^{-12}.

Chapter 9

Measurement Techniques

Thinking that you're doing it right does not count.
If you can't measure it, it's just an opinion.

—Mark Goodridge

An important part of any design process is verifying that the design meets its specifications. To do this, specific observation hooks must be built into the design. Properly designed hooks allow test equipment such as oscilloscopes and logic analyzers to attach to the system without significantly degrading the probed signals. This chapter explains how to select and build proper test hooks into the system as well as how to take the basic electrical measurements of the transmitter and receiver eye.

Stimulus for Data Acquisition

One of the most basic problems in trying to perform electrical validation of PCI Express is determining the optimum data patterns to use for stimulating the interconnect. Ideally, the data patterns will maximize jitter and *inter-symbol interference* (ISI) on an individual lane while at the same time producing maximum crosstalk on adjacent lanes. Furthermore, there is the practical problem of programming a device to generate the pattern(s) in the proper sequence on a continuous basis without running into such bus features as data scrambling or buffer full conditions that limit bus performance.

Fortunately, the authors of the PCI Express specification anticipated this problem and provided a special test state called *compliance measurement mode* (CMM). When a link is in CMM, the transmitters on that link send a repeated data pattern called the *compliance pattern* across the bus. The compliance pattern is a set of data patterns intended to evoke worst-case jitter at the receiver. As the name implies, these patterns are used as the reference pattern when validating the system's compliance to specification. CMM mode and the compliance patterns are fundamental to proving specification compliance.

Compliance Measurement Mode (CMM)

As described in Chapter 1, the transmitters on a link perform a receiver detect sequence on power-up or after a physical reset. If a transmitter detects that its lane is terminated with a nominal 50 Ω to ground, it assumes that there is a receiver at the end of the lane and attempts to establish communication by sending several TS1 or TS2 *ordered sets.*[1] If the transmitting port detects the presence of a receiver, but does not receive a response after sending 32 consecutive TS1 or TS2 ordered sets, the transmitter assumes that the receiver is actually a piece of test equipment and drops into compliance measurement mode (CMM).

While in compliance measurement mode, each port's transmitter continually transmits a four-symbol data pattern. Table 9.1 shows the four symbols and the data pattern that corresponds to each symbol.

Table 9.1   Compliance Measurement Mode (CMM) Data Pattern

Symbol	K28.5-	D21.5	K28.5+	D10.2
Pattern	0011111010	1010101010	1100000101	0101010101

Each lane transmits this four-symbol pattern in a continuously repeating stream. In a multi-lane device, the N*8 (where N=1,2,3...) lane starts out by prefixing and suffixing the four-symbol pattern with two extra K28.5 symbols, also known as delay characters. Once sent, this modified pattern is advanced to the next lane and so on, until all eight lanes in the group have transferred the altered pattern. Table 9.2 shows the result.

---

[1] An ordered set is a data packet that contains specific control and format information. For more about the TS1 and TS2 ordered sets, refer to the base specification.

Table 9.2   CMM Patterns in a Multi-Lane Device

Lane 0	D	D	K28.5-	D21.5	K28.5+	D10.2	D	D	K28.5-	D21.5	K28.5+	D10.2
Lane 1	K28.5-	D21.5	K28.5+	D10.2	K28.5-	D21.5	K28.5+	D10.2	D	D	K28.5-	D21.5
Lane 2	K28.5-	D21.5	K28.5+	D10.2	K28.5-	D21.5	K28.5+	D10.2	K28.5-	D21.5	K28.5+	D10.2
Lane 3	K28.5-	D21.5	K28.5+	D10.2	K28.5-	D21.5	K28.5+	D10.2	K28.5-	D21.5	K28.5+	D10.2
Lane 4	K28.5-	D21.5	K28.5+	D10.2	K28.5-	D21.5	K28.5+	D10.2	K28.5-	D21.5	K28.5+	D10.2
Lane 5	K28.5-	D21.5	K28.5+	D10.2	K28.5-	D21.5	K28.5+	D10.2	K28.5-	D21.5	K28.5+	D10.2
Lane 6	K28.5-	D21.5	K28.5+	D10.2	K28.5-	D21.5	K28.5+	D10.2	K28.5-	D21.5	K28.5+	D10.2
Lane 7	K28.5-	D21.5	K28.5+	D10.2	K28.5-	D21.5	K28.5+	D10.2	K28.5-	D21.5	K28.5+	D10.2
Lane 8	D	D	K28.5-	D21.5	K28.5+	D10.2	D	D	K28.5-	D21.5	K28.5+	D10.2
Lane 9	K28.5-	D21.5	K28.5+	D10.2	K28.5-	D21.5	K28.5+	D10.2	D	D	K28.5-	D21.5

The basic four-symbol pattern alternates between maximum data frequency (alternating ones and zeros) and minimum data frequency (five consecutive ones or zeros). Alternating data frequency tends to maximize any ISI due to frequency-dependent interconnect loss.

As shown in Table 9.2, for most of the time, any two adjacent lanes carry the same data pattern. This means that the low-to-high or high-to-low data transitions occur at the same time on each lane. When two adjacent lanes carry the same exact in-phase data pattern, any crosstalk between the two differential pairs that make up the lanes is called *even mode* crosstalk. When the delay character is introduced, however, the data pattern between two adjacent lanes is shifted so that low-to-high or high-to-low data transitions between adjacent lanes are now out of phase. This creates *odd mode* crosstalk. It is this shift from even mode to odd mode crosstalk that introduces the maximum interconnect jitter.

As mentioned in Chapter 8, jitter and voltage margin measurements are made over 250 UIs. When using the compliance patterns to measure jitter and voltage margins, the 250 UI segment must include the shift from even mode to odd mode crosstalk data patterns. Ideally, the measured 250 UI segment should be centered on the 160 UI odd mode crosstalk-producing pattern, thus recording the transition into and out of this data pattern as well as the jitter produced by each data pattern in turn.

When capturing waveforms in scope memory, the start of the delay pattern depends on which lane number is being measured. The point in time at which the delayed pattern starts, relative to the start of the compliance pattern itself, can be calculated from Equation 9.1.

Equation 9.1   Calculating the Start of the CMM Pattern

$$StartingUI = (N - 1)*8 \text{ (for } N \geq 1)$$

where:

N = the lane number

A port remains in compliance mode until one of its receivers detects an exit from electrical idle.

Loopback

In addition to compliance mode, the base specification requires that all PCI Express devices support a loopback mode. When in loopback mode, a port re-transmits (loops back) the data it receives back to the device that transmitted it. Figure 9.1 illustrates the loopback configuration.

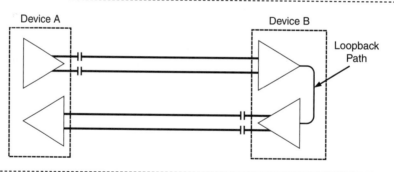

Figure 9.1   Loopback Configuration

In Figure 9.1, Device A is the transmitting device. It initiates the loopback and is considered the *loopback master*. Device B is the receiving device. It receives and retransmits the data and is considered the *loopback slave*. This kind of loopback path is referred to as a *retimed loopback*.[2] The received analog signal is converted into digital '1' or '0' data and entered into the receiving device's data buffers. This data is then looped back to the receiving device's transmitting port for transmission back to the loopback master. The loopback slave must retransmit the same exact data that it received; this includes both SKP symbols and symbols that contain errors.

Just as in normal operation, the loopback slave is required to insert skip ordered sets into the data stream at the prescribed intervals. For details on the use of skip ordered set, refer to the PCI Express Specification.

To put a lane into loopback mode, the loopback master transmits two TS1 ordered sets with the loopback bit set.[3] On receipt of these TS1 ordered sets, the loopback slave transitions into loopback mode. Once both devices are in loopback mode, they remain in loopback until the loopback master transmits an electrical idle order set.[4]

Using Loopback in Electrical Validation of a Link

In its most basic application, loopback mode provides a method for measuring the bit error rate (BER) of a link under actual system conditions. A device is programmed to enter loopback mode, data is sent across the link, and the returned data is checked for errors. Assuming the data transfer rate is known, you can calculate a BER for the entire link. However, some caveats apply when using loopback at this programmatic level. Because of the nature of the PCI Express transaction layer protocol, all data transfers are tagged with information specifying the originating and destination device. Programmatic data transfers while the link is in loopback mode are no different; therefore, the loopback master's transaction logic must be able to handle received data with "illogical" source and destination tags. In general, this means that special test modes to

---

[2] This is to distinguish it from an *analog loopback*, in which a device's transmitters are wired directly to its receivers without an intervening device.

[3] The base specification does not specify how the programmer tells the device to set the loopback bit. Getting into and out of loopback mode is implementation-specific.

[4] The base specification does not specify how the loopback master is to determine when the slave device has processed the loopback command and is in loopback mode. One possible method is to wait for the TS1 ordered set with the loopback command set to be returned, but in general, the detection mechanism is implementation-specific.

recognize and handle loopback data must be built into the device's transaction routing logic. In addition, in the case of a data error, there is no indication if the symbol was received incorrectly by the loopback master or loopback slave.

Loopback mode is especially effective if combined with specific on-die validation hooks that allow you to adjust transmitter and receiver characteristics and to check the returned data at the hardware level. If these hooks are present, you can use the loopback mode to perform both margin analysis and bit error rate (BER) testing. In one possible scenario, you would adjust the loopback master transmitter so that the transmitter eye just meets specification. You would then initiate loopback transfers, and the device acting as the loopback master detects errors (usually 8b/10b symbol errors) on the returned data. This scenario assumes that any errors detected by the loopback master are the result of the loopback slave receiving incorrect data. You can adjust the loopback master transmitter until errors occur (margin testing), or the system can be run long enough to verify BER compliance.

Similarly, you can adjust the receiver on the loopback master device to detect marginal conditions on the loopback slave's transmitter. Errors in the loopback slave transmitter to loopback master receiver path show up as 8b/10b symbol errors or as "failure to achieve lock" type errors, thus distinguishing them from errors in the transmit path.

Oscilloscope Calibration and Probe De-skew

Before beginning any test or data acquisition, the oscilloscope must be warmed and calibrated, and probes must be de-skewed and compensated for gain. Oscilloscope calibration includes two parts: oscilloscope self-calibration (OSC) and DC calibration.

Oscilloscope Self-Calibration (OSC)

Oscilloscope self-calibration is the oscilloscope vendor-specific routine that compensates for the scope's internal gain, offset, and timing path errors caused by temperature changes or local environmental conditions.

Oscilloscope self-calibration is a required part of any scope calibration routine and should be performed first, before DC calibration or probe de-skew. The actual steps for performing OSC are oscilloscope-specific, but they generally occur through the scope's utilities or options menu. When performing a self-calibration, you must disconnect all scope probes or cables attached to the signal inputs. This prevents the oscilloscope's input from picking up stray voltages that might upset the scope's OSC routine.

You should perform OSC every time the scope is powered on. Most oscilloscope vendors recommend that you wait 20 minutes or so after power on for the oscilloscope's internal temperature to stabilize before performing OSC. Likewise, you should perform OSC if there has been a significant change in the surrounding ambient air temperature or humidity.

DC Calibration

DC calibration is performed after SPC and after the probes or cables are connected back to the scope. Essentially, DC calibration allows you to measure and then compensate for the scope's DC gain and offset inaccuracies. Measuring these inaccuracies is critical when, for example, there is very little margin between the inner eye wall of the eye diagram and the triangle associated with the minimum spec eye.

DC calibration is a three-step process:

1. Measure and record the oscilloscope's noise floor.

2. Measure the noise added by the probes and the external DC source used in the DC calibration routine.

3. Measure and record the scope's DC measurement error itself.

Note

> DC calibration does not compensate for errors caused by probe loading and bandwidth limitations. Also, if you change the gain and offset setting—essentially, if the deflection of the measured peak changes—then you must perform DC calibration again.

Measure and record the oscilloscope's noise floor

To measure the uncertainty due to the oscilloscope's noise floor, perform the following procedure:

1. Set the scope to the same vertical scale (Volts/Div setting) and offset position that is used when capturing PCI Express waveforms. If you haven't already done so, remove any scope probes.

2. Set the scope to trigger on voltage level and measurement mode to measure the maximum peak-to-peak voltage.

3. Since the noise floor of the scope is measured with the probes disconnected, set the trigger mode to "Auto."

4. Set the scope to GND coupling. Then adjust the trigger level so that the scope triggers on the internal noise.

5. Run the measurement until 1000 or so measurements have been accumulated. Record the measured peak-to-peak voltage.

Equation 9.2 calculates the measurement uncertainty (MU$_{GND}$) due to the voltage noise floor.

Equation 9.2   Measurement Uncertainty Due to Scope Noise Floor

$$MU_{GND} = V_{MAX\_PK-PK} / 2$$

where:

V_{MAX_PK-PK} = maximum peak-to-peak noise voltage

For example, if the scope measured a maximum peak-to-peak noise voltage of 70mV, the measurement uncertainty (MU$_{GND}$) would be 70mV/2 = 35mV. Because an oscilloscope's noise floor varies dramatically with Volts/Div setting, you should perform this procedure at all Volts/Div settings that will be used for signal capture.

Measure the noise added by the probes and the external DC source

Once you have established the scope's noise floor, the next step is to measure the noise and offset introduced by the scope probes and the external DC source that will be used later for the actual DC calibration. Again, the procedure is fairly straightforward.

1. Set the scope to DC coupling and apply 0V DC from a DC source to the scope, using the same probes that are used when capturing actual PCI Express waveforms.

2. As before, set the scope's Volts/Div and offset settings so that they match the settings used when capturing PCI Express waveforms.

3. Connect a digital voltmeter across the output terminals of the external source to get an accurate measurement of the applied voltage. A four-and-a-half digit meter should provide the required accuracy and precision.

4. Record the peak-to-peak noise the scope measures with the DC source attached, over a measurement sample size of 1,000 or so.

Equation 9.3 calculates the measurement uncertainty with DC source attached (MU$_{DC}$).

Equation 9.3   Measurement Uncertainty With Probes and DC Source Attached

$$MU_{DC} = (V_{MAX\_PK-PK}) - (V_{MAX\_PK-PK}/2) - DC\_Voltage$$

where:

    V_{MAX_PK-PK} = maximum peak-to-peak voltage of the noise

    $DC\_Voltage$ = DC voltage read from the external voltmeter

---

For example, if the scope measured a maximum peak-to-peak voltage of 75mV and a DC voltage of zero volts with the DC source attached, MU$_{DC}$ is calculated as 75mV – (75mV/2) – 0v = 37.5mV.

Measure and Record the Scope's DC Measurement Error Itself

To calculate the noise contributed by the DC source and scope probes alone (DCSN), take the difference of the two noise floors. See Equation 9.4.

Equation 9.4   Noise Floor of the DC Source and Probes

$$DCSN = |MU_{DC} - MU_{GND}|$$

Once you know the DCSN, you can calculate the DC error in a measured waveform. Apply a DC signal to the scope that is equal in magnitude to the voltage along the inner eye wall of the eye diagram as reported by the scope. For example, if the scope reports the waveform along the inner eye to be 826mV in magnitude, apply 826mV DC, as measured by the digital voltmeter, from the DC source to the scope. The intent is to supply a known voltage and observe the actual scope deflection from the vertical center of the scope.

The DC error of the scope is the difference between what the scope reports, the peak value of the DC source, and what the DMM measures, as expressed in Equation 9.5.

Equation 9.5   Calculating DC Error

$$DC\_error = V_{SCOPE} - V_{DMM\_MEASURED}$$

where:

V_{SCOPE} = voltage measured by the scope

$V_{DMM\_MEASURED}$ = voltage measured by the DMM

You can then calculate the actual signal level of the waveform, as shown in Equation 9.6.

Equation 9.6   Calculating the Actual Signal Level

$$Actual\_Signal = Measured\_value - (DC\_error) \pm DCSN$$

where:

$Measured\_value$ = value measured by scope

DC_error = the DC error, as calculated by Equation 9.5

$DCSN$ = DC noise floor, as calculated by Equation 9.4

Bear in mind that DC calibration is purely a function of the deflection of the measurement. As such, you must repeat this calibration if the measurement point (peak) changes. For example, if you performed this operation for a PCI Express signal that had a peak measurement of 1.15V, and then probed another waveform that peaked at 0.7V, you would need to repeat this whole procedure, since the deflection for the latter waveform is greater (at same Volts/Div and offset/position) when compared to the former.

Probe De-skew

Another critical part of scope calibration is probe de-skew. De-skewing the probes is required when taking a measurement that requires using two individual probes—for example, recording an eye diagram using two probes, one on the D+ signal and one on the D− signal of a PCI Express channel. Improperly de-skewed probes add additional AC common mode noise to measurements, as well as distorting eye diagrams by shrinking the apparent horizontal opening of the eye. Probe de-skew is not generally a part of the oscilloscope's automated self calibration routine and must be done separately. You should perform probe de-skew each time a probe is changed, or whenever probes are moved between scope channels.

De-skewing involves adjusting the time delay on one channel of an oscilloscope until both channels have identical delay between the probe tip and sampling input. To do this, you must have a signal source with a rise time fast enough to resolve a 1 or 2 ps delay difference between the probes. While the probe calibration output available on most scopes can be used as a signal source, the edge rate on most calibration outputs is so slow that it is not possible to adjust the scope timebase to be fast enough to resolve a 1 or 2 ps delay. For best accuracy, use a separate signal source such as a high-speed clock generator.

Another common high edge rate signal source is the output of a TDR head. Figure 9.2 shows two 50 Ω coax cables connected to a Tektronix TDR head through a 50 Ω, three-way power splitter designed to accommodate a 3.5mm or SMA connector. The TDR head has a rise time on the order of 20 ps to 30 ps, fast enough to resolve a 1 ps delay. A TDR head makes an especially convenient de-skew signal source for test setups that use coax cables as oscilloscope probes.

The TDR head is used as a signal source for probe de-skew. Notice the 50 Ω power splitter.

Figure 9.2   Tektronix Sampling Scope with TDR Head

For standard active probes, most oscilloscope makers provide a probe de-skew fixture. Figure 9.3 illustrates one such type of fixture.

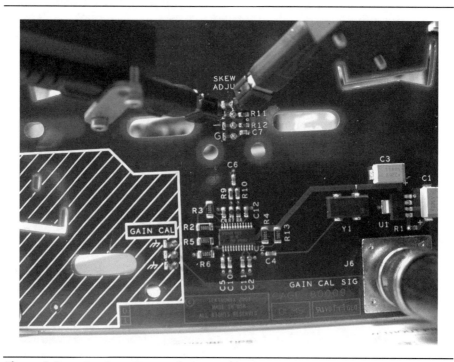

Figure 9.3 De-skew Fixture for Active Probes

When using this type of de-skew fixture, the probe tips must land on the same pad, so as to minimize potential skew induced by the de-skew fixture itself.

When de-skewing, select the oscilloscope's highest interpolation setting. Select the minimum Volts/Div setting such that the entire vertical height of the scope display is filled; this ensures that the entire range of the oscilloscopes analog to digital converter is being used. Most oscilloscopes permit precise alignment to within 1 ps. To offset some of the effects of jitter, it is helpful to use average sample mode during the de-skew process. Finally, remember to return to normal sample mode once the probes are de-skewed.[5]

---

[5] As discussed in the section on post-processing, you must turn off scope data interpolation when taking data for measurement.

Once the de-skewing process is complete, save the channel-to-channel skew relationship in the scope's setup memory; that information may be needed for later user setups and by the software that post-processes the data.

Using Coax Cables as Oscilloscope Probes

Before selecting the channels to be used for the coax cables, be aware that slight impedance mismatches can result in degradation of the measured signal integrity. You should select channels that come as close as possible to the nominal 50 Ω input impedance (at x1 attenuation). You can obtain this information from the oscilloscope's calibration report, available from the manufacturer or calibration labs. It's also critical that cables be low loss over the frequency range of interest—in this case, up to a minimum of 6 GHz. While more helpful in the frequency domain for VNA measurements than in the time domain with oscilloscope measurements, phase matching of the cables is a good starting point for ensuring low skew cables.

Test Platform

A frequently overlooked factor is the physical arrangement of the test platform used to hold the board and oscilloscope probes. Ideally, the test platform should be a solid mounting point for the PCB under test, provide easy access to the back side of the PCB, and provide a solid base with which to attach probe positioners. The positioners should reach all areas of the PCB where signals are to be measured.

■ Place the oscilloscope close to the test platform so as not to place tension on the probe and SMA cables.

■ Since probe points are so small and workspaces are usually confined to a dark corner of the lab, flexible and powerful light sources are highly desirable, making it easier for the technician to place the probes.

Figure 9.4 shows an example test platform.

Note the vertical uprights that secure the PCB and allow for probing from front or back.

Figure 9.4   Sample Test Platform

The example test platform shown in Figure 9.4 was machined from aluminum at a local machine shop. Aluminum uprights are drilled to accommodate sheet aluminum that is further drilled to accommodate the mounting holes of the PCB or device under test. While such well-built and sturdy platforms might be extravagant for casual use, they are ideal for repetitive measurements that last months on end, offering flexibility and strength, and accommodating nearly any size or shape of PCB.

Figure 9.5 shows the same setup, complete with board and scope probes. The authors of this book used a test platform very similar to the one shown in Figure 9.5 to collect data for this book.

High power light source to help see probe points

Probe positioners keep probes steady

Slot for routing power supply and disk drive cables

Test platform includes board under test, power supply, probes and positioners, and light source. Note that test equipment is kept above the workspace well within reach of scope probes.

Figure 9.5   Fully Configured Test Platform

Measurement Acquisition

Once you have calibrated the oscilloscope and performed probe de-skew, you can begin to acquire actual measurements. This section discusses the actual acquisition, from bus stimulation to probing the channel both at the transmitter and at the receiver.

As a reminder, measurements made to validate compliance to specification are taken with the transmitter driving a dedicated compliance test structure. Figure 9.6 shows this test structure, or *compliance load*.

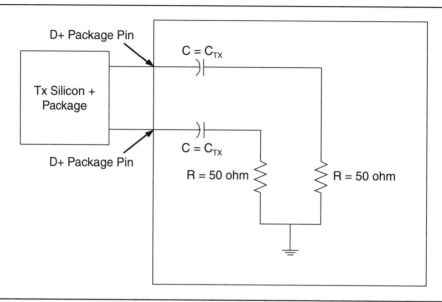

Figure 9.6   PCI Express Compliance Load

In essence, all compliance measurements should be made with the transmitter driving a 50 Ω resistor connected via uncoupled trace to a clean 50 Ω load. The DC blocking capacitors are optional. As defined in the PCI Express specification, you should take compliance measurements within 0.2 inches of the package pin.

For the purposes of measurement, the compliance load can take one of two forms:

■ Differential traces routed directly into the DC blocking caps, then connected to 50 Ω coax cables via SMA connectors. In this scenario, the 50 Ω DC termination of the oscilloscope terminates the bus.

■ Differential traces routed directly into the DC blocking caps, into two 50 Ω non-coupled PC traces terminated by 50 Ω resistors to ground. In this case, the scope probes must be high-impedance differential or single-ended probes.

The PCI Special Interest Group (PCI-SIG) supplies a *compliance base board* (CBB), which implements the required termination and/or SMA connectors. The CBB is available for add-in card vendors to use in validating the compliance of add-in cards. For more information on the compliance base board, visit the PCI-SIG Web site at www.pcisig.com.

The following sections provide a general procedure for acquiring compliance data. For its members, PCI-SIG provides a detailed compliance checklist and measurement procedure.

Data Acquisition at the Transmitter

Table 9.3 lists the PCI Express transmitter measurements relevant to compliance mode analysis that you can obtain with an oscilloscope. For each measurement, Table 9.3 provides the following information:

- The recommended probe configuration for making the measurement: either a single differential probe, or two differential probes configured such that one probe measures the signal on the D+ interconnect while a second probe measures the signal on the D– interconnect.

- The scope acquisition mode: how the data is acquired and stored. Most measurements require the scope to trigger once (single-shot) and store one acquisition's worth of data in the scope memory for subsequent post-processing. For other measurements, the scope is set to continually trigger and display the results on the scope display. Data acquisition begins with the PCI Express ports being put into compliance mode.

- Whether the acquired data is saved in memory for post-processing.

Table 9.3   Transmitter Compliance Mode Measurements

Measurement	Probe Configuration	Scope Acquisition Mode	Post Process	Comments
UI	Differential Probe	Single-shot	Yes	
$V_{TX-DIFF-p-p}$	Differential Probe	Single-shot	Yes	
$T_{TX-DE-Ratio}$	Differential Probe	Single-shot	Yes	
T_{TX-EYE}	Differential Probe	Single-shot	Yes	
$T_{TX-EYE-MEDIAN-to-MAX-JITTER}$	Differential Probe	Single-shot	Yes	
$T_{TX-RISE}$, $T_{TX-FALL}$	Differential Probe	Multiple trigger on data rising edge	No	Use cursors to mark 20/80% level and measure delta time
$V_{TX-CM-ACp}$	Two probes configured for single-ended operation	Single-shot	Yes	Can be measured quickly on the scope or using post-processing software
$V_{TX-CM-DC-LINE-DELTA}$	Differential Probe	Single-shot	Yes	
$L_{TX-SKEW}$	Differential Probe	Single-shot	Yes	Measure skew using cursors or scope's built-in measurement mode

With the exception of the signal rise and fall times, all values in Table 9.3 can be measured with post-processing software. Rise and fall times must be analyzed on the scope using cursors to accurately determine the steady state high and low voltages, and to calculate from there the 20 percent and 80 percent levels.

Due to random variations in noise between data acquisitions, you should take multiple acquisitions and check them to form a session level confidence interval.

To set up for the measurements in Table 9.3, connect the probes to the best characterized channels (or those that show the least skew from the scope's calibration report). While scope settings depend somewhat on the physical characteristics of the system in question, Table 9.4 provides some reasonable default settings.

Table 9.4 Scope Setup for Post-Process Data Acquisition (Except $T_{TX-RISE}/T_{TX-FALL}$)

Trigger Mode	Single-Shot
Horizontal	200 ns/div (disable any scope data point interpolation)
Sample Rate	at least 20 Gsamples/sec (50 ps/point)
Vertical	50 mV/div to 100 mV/div (or fill the ADC with the entire waveform)
Sample Size	200,000 points

As described in the section on "Data Post-Processing and Analysis" later in this chapter, the acquired data is exported to the post-processing software, where it is analyzed for eye diagram violations.

Data Acquisition at the Receiver

Table 9.5 outlines the PCI Express receiver measurements relevant to compliance mode analysis that you can obtain with an oscilloscope. For each measurement, Table 9.5 provides the following information:

■ The recommended probe configuration for making the measurement: either a single differential probe, or two differential probes configured such that one probe measures the signal on the D+ interconnect while a second probe measures the signal on the D- interconnect.

■ The scope acquisition mode: how the data is acquired and stored. For all measurements in Table 9.5, the scope must trigger once (single-shot) and store one acquisition's worth of data in the scope memory for subsequent post-processing. Data acquisition begins with the PCI Express ports being put into compliance mode.

■ Whether the acquired data is saved in memory for post-processing.

Table 9.5   Receiver Compliance Mode Measurements

Measurement	Probe Configuration	Scope Acquisition Mode	Post Process	Comments
UI	Differential Probe	Single-shot	Yes	
$V_{RX-DIFF-p-p}$	Differential Probe	Single-shot	Yes	
T_{RX-EYE}	Differential Probe	Single-shot	Yes	
$T_{RX-EYE-MEDIAN-to-MAX-JITTER}$	Differential Probe	Single-shot	Yes	
$V_{RX-CM-ACp}$	Two differential probes configured for single-ended operation	Single-shot	Yes	Can be measured quickly on the scope or using post-processing software
$L_{TX-SKEW}$	Differential Probe	Single-shot	Yes	Measure skew using cursors or automatic measure

For strict specification compliance, compliance mode measurements at the receiver are measured at the receiver pins, with the receiver package and silicon replaced by 50 Ω resistors. In practice, if the receiver package meets the return loss specification, you can make a reasonably accurate measurement at the receiver pins.

A motherboard manufacturer might also want to measure the eye at the connector on the baseboard. In this case, the proper compliance load is supplied by a *compliance load board* (CLB), which (like the CBB) is available from the PCI-SIG. A CLB is also very handy for plugging into the connector at the end of a channel, thereby placing the transmitter in CMM mode.

To set up for the measurements in Table 9.5, connect the probes to the best characterized channels (or those which show the least skew from the scope's calibration report). While scope setting depends somewhat on the physical characteristics of the system in question, Table 9.4 provides some reasonable default settings.

Data Post-Processing and Analysis

Once you have acquired the data, it must be post-processed. The SIGTEST post-processing software turns the individual data points from the scope's sample memory into an eye diagram which you can compare against the minimum eye template for violations of the specification.

SIGTEST was developed at Intel and executes on a PC under Windows XP. It is available for download from the PCI-SIG Web site. At the time of this writing, SIGTEST accepts data in the form of comma-separated data files (.csv files) exported from Tektronix Model TD6604, Agilent Infiniium 54855A, and LeCroy SDA 6000 series real-time oscilloscopes. The PCI-SIG Web site provides setup files specific to supported oscilloscopes as well as detailed SIGTEST installation and operating instructions.

While a detailed description of the SIGTEST analysis algorithm is beyond the scope of this book, the following general outline explains some of the scope setup requirements.

1. The resolution of the raw data, taken at 50 ps/sample, is increased via interpolation between data points. SIGTEST uses a sin/sinX algorithm.

2. If the PCI Express channel was probed using two single-ended probes (that is, separate D+ and D– waveform data were taken), the data must be combined into one differential waveform. SIGTEST uses the channel-to-channel skew data contained in the header of the exported data file to perform the de-skew (mathematically shift one waveform relative to another). One channel is then subtracted from another to create a single differential waveform.

3. The zero crossings of the entire differential waveform are recorded and stored.

4. At this point the data is in the form required to calculate the maximum jitter outlier and voltage margins.

5. Using a "minimize absolute deviation" algorithm, SIGTEST calculates the UI period over the first 3,500 UIs. This 3,500 UI window is referred to as the *clock recover window*.

6. SIGTEST calculates and stores the *phase jitter*—the difference between the zero crossing predicted by the calculated UI and the actual zero crossing for each waveform zero crossing.

7.   The medium value of the phase jitter for the 250 UIs in the center of the clock recover window jitter is calculated. From that value, SIGTEST calculates the magnitude of the maximum jitter outlier. This number is stored for reference.

8.   Likewise, over the same 250 UIs in the center of the clock recover window, the vertical height of the waveform is measured against the eye mask and the voltage margin is recorded.

9.   SIGTEST then advances the clock recover window starting point by a user-selected increment and repeats steps 4 through 7. The software keeps advancing through new clock recover windows until the entire data set (10,000 UIs or so) has been analyzed.

The output of the SIGTEST software is a Go/NoGo indication of the system's compliance to the PCI Express electrical specification as well as eye diagrams. Many scope manufacturers also incorporate the SIGTEST algorithm in their jitter analysis software packages. In the case of non-compliance, jitter analysis software packages allow you to further analyze the data. One useful test is to do an FFT of the period jitter data, thus revealing the frequency content of the jitter. In many cases, the result points directly to the source of the excessive jitter.

Measuring PCI Express† Version 1.1 Compliance

At the time of this writing, the PCI-SIG is releasing an updated version of the PCI Express specification. Version 1.1 of the specification now specifies an explicit clock recovery function to be used when measuring jitter at the transmitter. The specification also places restriction on the bandwidth of the transmitting device's PLL. In addition, the add-in card specification, *PCI Express Card Electromechanical (CEM) Specification* (PCI-SIG 2004), has been revised to include specifications that limit the maximum allowable jitter of the baseboard reference clock. Finally, new system eye diagrams have been defined for a BER of 10^{-6}. While the full impact of these changes to the compliance and measurement methodologies has yet to be assessed, the basic considerations for bandwidth and proper measurement technique have not changed. Indeed, they remain as important as ever.

Layout Rules for Probes and SMA Connectors

The previous discussions have addressed the mechanics of scope calibration and the setup required to perform the measurement. All this assumes that the scope probe can be successfully attached to the proper measurement point with a high fidelity connection. This section outlines the layout rules for both standard scope probe landing pads as well as SMA type connectors.

Building Good SMA Footprints

Most measurement setups in this chapter assume the use of a high-impedance differential or single-ended scope probe. An alternate method of probing PCI Express signals is to connect a scope directly to the signals under test using SMA connectors. SMA connectors, along with a set of phase matched and low loss coax cables, allow for a potentially very low loss, high-bandwidth connection to the device under test. While not generally applicable to a production board layout, SMA connectors are used extensively on test boards in a component validation environment.

Proper layout of the SMA connector footprint is critical in achieving multi-gigahertz performance. When designing the footprint for an SMA connector, you must follow two general rules:

■ No stubs as the signal transitions from the PCB to the SMA connector. In effect, the signal trace must be routed on the opposite side of the board from the SMA connector, and the center conductor of the SMA should not extend beyond the outside of the board.

■ Minimize any excess capacitance seen by the signal as it travels under the center of the connector body. This means that the PCB's power and ground planes must be voided under the body of the connector.

Figures 9.7 and 9.8 illustrate the recommended footprint for a Rosenberger SMA connector (Rosenberger part number 32K153-400_LV1). This layout is for a standard four-layer, 0.062-inch thick PCB. Figure 9.7 shows a cutaway view of the layout. Figure 9.8 shows the layout as seen from the bottom of the board.

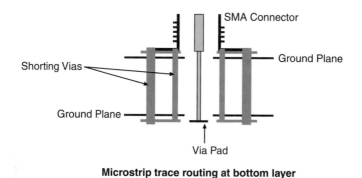

Microstrip trace routing at bottom layer

Figure 9.7   SMA Connector with Shorting Vias and Surface Layer Planes, Cutaway View

In Figure 9.7, note the shorting vias that tie the top surface of the SMA connector housing to the copper area on the bottom side of the board.

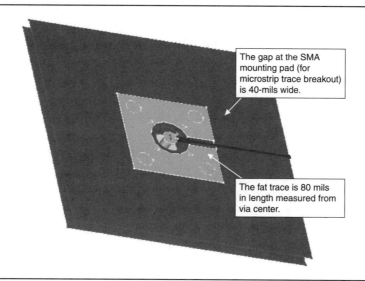

The gap at the SMA mounting pad (for microstrip trace breakout) is 40-mils wide.

The fat trace is 80 mils in length measured from via center.

Figure 9.8   SMA Connector Showing Bottom Side Trace Breakout

As shown in Figure 9.8, both surface layers of the PCB (top and bottom) contain a square pad of copper tied to ground. The signal trace is routed on the backside of the board and connects to the SMA center conductor via a cutout in the bottom side ground fill. The trace is fattened to 20 mils as it approaches the center conductor. Table 9.6 lists the dimensions of the SMA footprint and connector.

Table 9.6 SMA Footprint and Connector Dimensions

Ground Pad Size	375-mils x 375-mils square
Anti-Pad Size	120 mil (diameter) at ground plane, 160 mil (diameter) at top and bottom layer
Inner Four Shorting Vias	15 mils (diameter), (70 mils, 70 mils) away from center
Outer Four Shorting Vias	62 mils (diameter), (125 mils, 125 mils) away from center
Center Conductor	40 mils (drill size)
Via Pad Size	60 mils

Simulation results indicate that this footprint and connector provide greater than –20 dB return loss at 10 GHz. Figure 9.9 shows the simulated TDR response for the footprint.

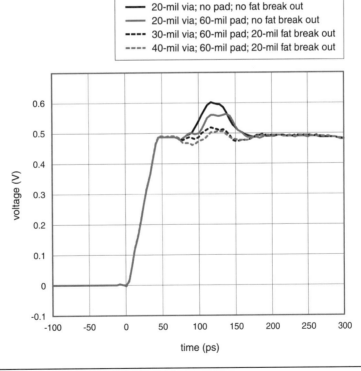

Figure 9.9   TDR Response of SMA Footprint

Figure 9.10 shows the simulated return loss (S11 versus frequency) plot of the connector and footprint. Both of these simulations show the importance of including the 20-mil fat breakout on the incoming signal trace.

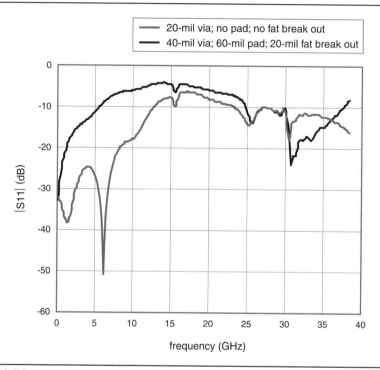

Figure 9.10   Plot of S11 versus Frequency

Probing Points and Layout Rules for Scope Landing Pads

In general, you should perform measurements for PCI Express specifications at the package pins or balls. However, depending on the routing, it may be difficult or impossible to probe right at the package. In general, the closest available probing locations for a differential pair are:

■ For traces routed on the bottom layer, the transition via after the breakout region.

■ For traces routed on the top layer, as the breakout traces emerges from under the package.

For bottom layer traces, the breakout vias provide a handy non-solder-masked area in which to probe, provided that the probe tips can be placed close enough together to fit in that area and a ground via is available. This leads to the first layout rule:

> If at all possible, the board breakout for bottom side traces should follow a consistent signal/signal/ground pattern that matches the pin layout of the intended differential probe(s). Via spacing should match the pin-to-pin spacing of the probe(s), usually in the range of 30 to 50 mils.

For topside traces, the layout should incorporate into the trace 20-mil-wide, non-solder-masked "scope probe landing pads" adjacent to the trace being probed. Figure 9.11 shows an example layout of scope probe landing pad patterns.

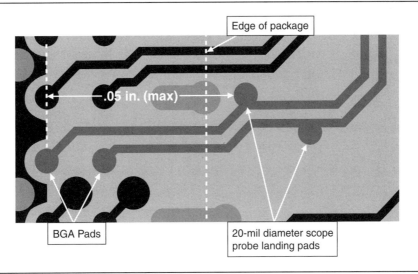

Figure 9.11   Typical Scope Landing Pad Patterns (Topside Traces Shown)

In Figure 9.11, note that the scope landing pads are not placed directly across from one another. This pad offset is required in order to equalize the trace length between the BGA pads and the scope landing pads. Unequal trace length adds skew between the two differential signals at the probe tips; depending on the amount of trace length difference, this skew can be up to 20 ps.

The availability of differential scope probes that work with the 75- to 100-mil scope landing pad offset can vary, depending on the oscilloscope manufacturer. Also, there may not be enough space to add landing pads to adjacent lanes of a multi-lane channel. At a minimum, two lanes need to be probed. One of those lanes should be lane 0.

When adding scope probe landing pads to PCI Express designs, observe the following guidelines:

- Having probe points close in at the receiver is generally more critical than probe points at the transmitter.

- If you have a choice, route receiver lanes on the back side (non-component side) of the PC board. In this way, you can use the breakout vias as scope probing points.

- Keep scope landing pads as close as possible to the package balls. Simulations on typical topologies have shown that topside probe pads must be placed no further than 0.5 inches away from the ball.

- Do not add an extra via that taps a bottom side trace to the top of the board for probing. This action would violate the general layout guideline of no more than two vias per trace.

- In keeping with the general layout guidelines, landing pads must be the same for each trace and should be located at the same physical location along the trace, as measured from the BGA pad. Don't forget to specify that these pads are not solder-masked.

- Include a via or 20-mil pad connected to ground close (within 0.1 inch) of the topside scope landing pads. For exact dimensions, check with the preferred scope probe vendor. These pads are intended for scope probe ground.

References

Adam, Stephen F. 1991. *Microwave Theory and Applications*. Englewood Cliffs, NJ: Prentice-Hall, Inc.

American National Standards Institute / Electronic Industries Alliance (ANSI/EIA). 1999. *I/O Buffer Information Specification (IBIS)*. Arlington, VA: EIA. Portable Document Format.

Ansoft Corporation. 2003. *HFSS Version 9.0 Manual*. Pittsburgh, PA: Ansoft Corporation.

Bansal, Rajeev. 2004. *Handbook of Engineering Electromagnetics*. New York, NY: Marcel Dekker.

Peripheral Component Interconnect Special Interest Group (PCI-SIG). 2003a. *PCI Express Graphics Card Electromechanical Design Guideline for Mainstream Desktop Systems*. Portland, OR: PCI-SIG. Portable Document Format.

————. 2003b. *Mobile Graphics Low-Power Addendum to the PCI Express Base Specification*. Portland, OR: PCI-SIG. Portable Document Format.

————. 2004a. *PCI Express Base Specification 1.0a*. Portland, OR: PCI-SIG. Portable Document Format.

————. 2004b. *PCI Express Card Electromechanical (CEM) Specification*. Portland, OR: PCI-SIG. Portable Document Format.

Personal Computer Memory Card International Association (PCMCIA). 2003a. *ExpressCard Standard 1.0*. San Jose, CA: PCMCIA. Portable Document Format.

————. 2003b. *ExpressCard Internal Cable Specification*. San Jose, CA: PCMCIA. Portable Document Format.

————. 2003c. *ExpressCard Implementation Guidelines*. San Jose, CA: PCMCIA. Portable Document Format.

Ramo, Simon, John R. Whinnery, and Theodore Van Duzer. 1993. *Fields and Waves in Communication Electronics*. New York, NY: John Wiley and Sons.

Index

66 *As the pace of technology introduction increases, it's difficult to keep up. Intel Press has established an impressive portfolio. The breadth of topics is a reflection of both Intel's diversity as well as our commitment to serve a broad technical community.*

I hope you will take advantage of these products to further your technical education. *99*

Patrick Gelsinger
Senior Vice President and Chief Technology Officer
Intel Corporation

**Turn the page to learn about titles
from Intel Press for system developers**

Break Through Performance Limits with PCI Express†

Introduction to PCI Express†

A Hardware and Software Developer's Guide
By Adam Wilen, Justin Schade, and Ron Thornburg
ISBN 0-9702846-9-1

Written by key Intel insiders who have worked to implement Intel's first generation of PCI Express† chipsets and who work directly with customers wanting to take advantage of PCI Express, this introduction to the new I/O technology explains how PCI Express increases computer system performance. The book explains in technical detail how designers can use PCI Express technology to overcome the practical performance limits of existing multi-drop, parallel bus technology. The authors draw from years of leading-edge experience to explain how to apply these new capabilities to a broad range of computing and communications platforms.

Introduction to PCI Express† explains critical technical considerations that both hardware and software developers must understand to take full advatage of PCI Express technology in next-generation systems.

From these key Intel technologists, you learn about:

- Metrics and criteria for developers and product planners to consider in adopting PCI Express

- Applications for desktop, mobile, server, and communications platforms that will benefit significantly from PCI Express technology

- Implications for hardware and software developers of the layered architecture of PCI Express

- Features that make PCI Express different from PCI-X†, and Conventional PCI†

❝ This book helps software and hardware developers get a jump start on their development cycle that can decrease their time to market. ❞

Ajay Kwatra, Engineer Strategist, Dell Computer Corporation

● *Designing High-Speed Interconnect Circuits*
Advanced Signal Integrity Methods for Engineers
By Dennis Miller
ISBN 0-9743649-6-7

Written for practicing engineers, this practical guide provides solid information and effective design techniques for circuits that handle data rates extending into multiple-gigahertz frequencies. Whether you are an electical engineer, board designer, layout engineer, or signal integrity engineer, you can catch up on current issues in the design of printed circuit boards for use in personal computers. This "how-to guide" book provides sample applications of practical rules.

> ❝ *...practical information... do yourself a favor and study these pages.* ❞
>
> Jay Diepenbrock,
> Senior Technical
> Staff Member, IBM

● *The Complete PCI Express† Reference*
Design Insights for Hardware and Software Developers
By Edward Solari and Brad Congdon
ISBN 0-9717861-9-4

The first book to offer detailed interpretations of the PCI Express† specifications, *The Complete PCI Express Reference* was written as a comprehensive resource for hardware and software developers designing PCI Express-based systems. It explains critical technical considerations that developers must understand in detail. Illustrations and cross-references not found in the PCI Express specifications offer unique insight into the benefits and limitations of specific design choices. *The Complete PCI Express Reference* gives developers the basis to know their PCI Express design is correct and complete.

> ❝ *Very comprehensive... a great resource... very clear about the advantages of PCI Express.* ❞
>
> Marc Pyne,
> Program Marketing Manager,
> Texas Instruments

● Serial ATA Storage Architecture and Applications
Designing High-Performance, Low-Cost I/O Solutions
By Knut Grimsrud and Hubbert Smith
ISBN 0-9717861-8-6

Serial ATA, a new hard disk interconnect standard for PCs, laptops, and more is fast becoming a serious contender to Parallel ATA and SCSI. Computer engineers and architects worldwide must answer important questions for their companies: "Why make the change to Serial ATA? What problems does Serial ATA solve for me? How do I transition from parallel ATA to Serial ATA and from SCSI to Serial ATA?" The authors of this essential book, both Intel Serial ATA specialists, have the combined expertise to help you answer these questions. Systems engineers, product architects, and product line managers who want to affect the right decisions for their products undoubtably will benefit from the straight talk offered by these authors. The book delivers reliable information with sufficient technical depth on issues such as Phy signaling and interface status, protocol encoding, programming model, flow control, performance, compatibility with legacy systems, enclosure management, signal routing, hot-plug, presence detection, activity indication, power management, and cable/connector standards.

❝ *This book provides explanations and insights into the underlying technology to help ease design and implementation.* **❞**

Rhonda Gass, Vice President, Storage Systems Development, Dell Computer Corporation

● USB Design by Example
A Practical Guide to Designing I/O Devices
By John Hyde
ISBN 0-9702846-5-9

John Hyde, a 23-year veteran of Intel Corporation and recognized industry expert, goes well beyond all the Universal Serial Bus specification overviews in this unique book, offering the reader the golden opportunity to build unparalleled expertise, knowledge, and skills to design and implement USB I/O devices quickly and reliably. Through a series of fully documented, real-world examples, the author uses his practical customer training experience to take you step by step through the process of creating specific devices. As a complete reference to USB, this book contains design examples to cover most USB classes and provides insights into high-speed USB 2.0 devices.

❝ *We could implement a USB design with this book alone.* **❞**

Chris Gadke, Design Engineer, Tektronix, Inc.

Special Deals, Special Prices!

To ensure you have all the latest books and enjoy aggressively priced discounts, please go to this Web site:

www.intel.com/intelpress/bookbundles.htm

Bundles of our books are available, selected especially to address the needs of the developer. The bundles place important complementary topics at your fingertips, and the price for a bundle is substantially less than buying all the books individually.

About Intel Press

Intel Press is the authoritative source of timely, highly relevant, and innovative books to help software and hardware developers speed up their development process. We collaborate only with leading industry experts to deliver reliable, first-to-market information about the latest technologies, processes, and strategies.

Our products are planned with the help of many people in the developer community and we encourage you to consider becoming a customer advisor. If you would like to help us and gain additional advance insight to the latest technologies, we encourage you to consider the Intel Press Customer Advisor Program. You can **register** here:

www.intel.com/intelpress/register.htm

For information about bulk orders or corporate sales, please send email to
bulkbooksales@intel.com

Other Developer Resources from Intel

At these Web sites you can also find valuable technical information and resources for developers:

developer.intel.com	general information for developers
www.intel.com/IDS	content, tools, training, and the Intel® Early Access Program for software developers
www.intel.com/netcomms	solutions and resources for developers of networking and communications products
www.intel.com/software/products	programming tools to help you develop high-performance applications
www.intel.com/idf	worldwide technical conference, the Intel Developer Forum

INTEL
PRESS

About the Authors

DAVE COLEMAN is a Staff Platform Application Engineer with 19 years of electrical engineering experience. At Intel, he specializes in electrical modeling and simulation of PCI Express[†] platform designs. Dave is the co-author and editor of Intel's *PCI Express Design Guide*, and has contributed articles to *Printed Circuit Design* magazine.

SCOTT GARDINER is a Senior Hardware Engineer at Intel and holds a Master's degree in Electrical Engineering. Since joining Intel in 1997, Scott has made significant contributions to various high-speed interconnect and PCB designs. Involved with PCI Express since its inception, Scott was the lead engineer on one of Intel's first prototype PCI Express boards and a key contributor to Intel's first PCI Express desktop motherboard.

MOHAMMAD KOLBEHDARI is a Senior Staff Hardware Engineer at Intel involved with PCI Express interconnect design and simulation. He developed a 3-D full-wave modeling methodology for high-speed bus and package design used extensively throughout Intel, and he is a co-author of the second-generation *PCI Express Design Guidelines*. Mohammad holds a PhD in Electrical Engineering and is a regular contributor to IEEE professional journals, *COMPEL*, and to the *Journal of the Franklin Institute*.

STEPHEN PETERS leads a group at Intel developing methodologies for validating next generation chip and board-level interfaces for PCI Express. Over the past 15 years, Stephen has designed high-speed bus interfaces and solved signal integrity issues. From 2001 through 2003, he served as chair of the I/O Buffer Information Specification (IBIS) Open Forum and continues to be a major contributor to the IBIS specification.